Sovereign st₍
or political comm

MANCHESTER
UNIVERSITY PRESS

Sovereign states or political communities?

Civil society and contemporary politics

Darrow Schecter

Manchester University Press
Manchester and New York

distributed exclusively in the USA by St. Martin's Press

The right of Darrow Schecter to be identified as the author of this work has been asserted by him in accordance with the Copyright, Designs and Patents Act 1988.

Published by Manchester University Press
Oxford Road, Manchester M13 9NR, UK
and Room 400, 175 Fifth Avenue, New York, NY 10010, USA
www.manchesteruniversitypress.co.uk

Distributed exclusively in the USA by
Palgrave, 175 Fifth Avenue, New York NY 10010, USA

Distributed exclusively in Canada by
UBC Press, University of British Columbia, 2029 West Mall,
Vancouver, BC, Canada V6T 1Z2

British Library Cataloguing-in-Publication Data
A catalogue record for this book is available from the British Library

Library of Congress Cataloging-in-Publication Data
A catalog record for this book is available from the Library of Congress

ISBN 978 0 7190 8286 3 *paperback*

First published by Manchester University Press 2000

First digital paperback edition published 2011

Printed by Lightning Source

For Chris Thornhill

Contents

Acknowledgements   ix

Introduction   1

1 Civil society and the origins of modern political theory   25

2 Violence and the state   49

3 The public sphere   78

4 Community as politics   112

5 Civil society and recognition   141

   Conclusion   176

   Select bibliography   188

   Index   199

Acknowledgements

This book is the result of a course on civil society taught with Neil Stammers for the first time in 1994 on the MA in Social and Political Thought at the University of Sussex. I would like to first thank Neil and all of the students who participated in those seminars, without whose help the book would have retained its original form as a series of intuitions in the IDS bar and the Battle of Trafalgar pub. A number of students on the MA at Sussex have been adept in waking me from my dogmatic slumbers: Arianna Bove, Jorge del Rio Fernandez, Crystal Ecohawk, Eric Empson, Michael Mangroo, Nina Schultz, John Varty and Gudrun Young.

The following people have helped me see why and understand how good thinking almost always has a critical and utopian dimension: Fernand Avila, Bitti Bauck, Martin Blobel, Nick Bogiazides, Costantino Ciervo, Paolo Dasgupta, Mick Dunford, Dan Fausey, Chris Fox, Jeremy Lester, Volker Lorek, Ben Loveluck, Mick McKinley, Catherine McVarish, John O'Neill, William Outhwaite, Panos Papadopoulos, Davide Però, Steve Robinson, Mand Ryaïra, Jarret Schecter, Imke Schmincke, Mick Underhill, and Martin Zeiske.

Three particularly brillant teaching experiences have been an important source of inspiration. Thanks to all of the students on the Sussex 1997–98 and 1998–99 MA in Social and Political Thought, and all of the participants in the 1998–99 MEM Social and Political Thought seminar.

A very generous grant from the Nuffield Foundation's *Social Science Small Grants Scheme* enabled me to go on sabbatical in the autumn of 1997. Pippa Kenyon and Nicola Viinikka at Manchester University Press made the final rewriting of the book much easier than it would have been with another publisher; I'd like to thank them both here for their patience and support.

Special thanks go to Céline Surprenant, who read and commented on an early draft, and to Drew Milne, for the splinter in my eye which has indeed been a great magnifying glass.

To my absolute astonishment and delight, I have had the privileged experience that it is possible to see other individuals as the basis of rather than the barrier to one's own freedom. The intellectual and emotional impact of Diana Göbel and Chris Thornhill on me in recent years has been too important to merely acknowledge, and too profound to describe. I'll simply say that the best ideas and impulses in this book are theirs.

Introduction

Since the imposition of martial law in Poland in December 1981 and the subsequent rise to international fame of the Solidarity movement in the same country, there has been a tremendous interest in both the explanatory and the possible transformatory potential of civil society. It was and continues to be argued in both the East and the West that the network of Polish workers, students, intellectuals and their associated institutions of trade union, press, radio, church and reading groups constituted civil society as an autonomous socio-political space against the state.[1] In the wake of the events leading up to and following the 1989 revolutions there has been a steady flow of books, articles and conferences on the subject of civil society and this shows no sign of abating. In the introduction to the 1990 German edition of his *Structural Transformation of the Public Sphere* (1962), Jürgen Habermas maintained that the focus of his thesis would be referred to today as the 'rediscovery of civil society'.[2] Academics, journalists, politicians

[1] Z.A. Pelcynski, 'Solidarity and the Rebirth of Civil Society', in John Keane (ed.), *Civil Society and the State: New European Perspectives*, London: Verso, 1988, pp. 371–2.

[2] Jürgen Habermas, *Strukturwandel der Öffentlichkeit (Structural Transformation of the Public Sphere,* first published in 1962 by Luchterhand), Frankfurt: Suhrkamp, 1990, p. 45. Habermas retains this emphasis on civil society in his last major work, *Faktizität und Geltung: Beiträge zur Diskurstheorie des Rechts und des demokratischen Rechtstaats (Between Facts and Norms).* Frankfurt: Suhrkamp, 1992. Here Habermas insists on the continuing normative and analytical relevance of the state/civil sociey distinction. Thus he argues for example that the rule of law alone will not suffice to guarantee that a society is governed democratically. He states that the decisive difference between the liberal model and his version of democratic discursive will formation is that in the latter, civil society plays the crucial role in securing free

and activists across Western Europe, the United States, Africa, Latin and South America began comparing the events in Eastern Europe with the post-1968 flourishing of the feminist, peace, ecological, gay rights, indigenous people's rights, and other New Social Movements (NSMs) in their own countries. They announced that civil society had been rediscovered in Eastern Europe, and that the symptoms of this renaissance had also been detected in their own countries. Thus from the dissident movements in Eastern Europe to the Zapatista revolution in Mexico to the revival of Naples and other European cities, it has been argued that civil society will be the key site of political struggle and political change in the twenty-first century. *Sovereign States or Political Communities?* undertakes to evaluate this claim by exploring the modes of political action in civil society. The thesis defended in this book is that there are three main categories of political action with which one might develop a theoretical overview of NSMs and other comparatively recent forms of opposition and resistance. While allowing for the specificity of each context, it will be suggested that NSMs and related opposition movements such as those in Eastern Europe can be theoretically understood as attempts to create a public sphere, to build community and to enact a praxis of political recognition. Later on in the Introduction and throughout this book it will become clear why these categories of political action stand out amongst other possible frameworks of analysis. It will also become clear that beyond their usage in this book as a theoretical frame of reference for analysing various forms of political action in civil society, the terms public sphere, community and recognition also indicate possible approaches to enacting politics in ways which go beyond the boundaries of class and identity politics, to embrace politics as a truly universal category of human action distinct from questions of interest, power, and technical reform.

In a great deal of contemporary usage, civil society is extremely complex and difficult to locate precisely. This makes a useful theoretical discussion of the term difficult. By way of introduction, however, some basic guidelines can be established. Following the example of the revolutions in Eastern Europe, theorists and activists elsewhere often include under the heading civil society all

---

discussion and forms of autonomy and association not dominated by the power struggles characterising the state and economy (pp. 363, 427–9, 435, 453–4).

non-state institutions such as (1) the mass media of communication, including television, radio, film and the press (i.e., when they
are not controlled by the state); (2) educational institutions such as
crèches, schools, universities, museums, libraries, reading groups
and even monuments; (3) interest groups such as trade unions and
chambers of commerce; (4) churches and groups affiliated to
churches; (5) organised leisure and free-time activities such as
sports groups, clubs, neighbourhood and tenants associations, etc.
Crucially, some theorists include the economy, while others do not;
some include the private sphere of family and friends sometimes
also referred to as the *lifeworld*, while others do not. There is also
the important question of where one might place political parties.
Since these mediate between state and civil society, political parties
occupy a somewhat ambiguous position. Leaving these questions
aside for the moment, one might begin by saying that the term civil
society represents an ensemble of institutions, communication and
political action that is not reducible to any single sociological,
economic or political dimension. In Ernest Gellner's definition,

> Civil Society is that set of diverse non-governmental institutions
> which is strong enough to counterbalance the state and,
> while not preventing the state from fulfilling its role of keeper
> of peace and arbitrator between major interests, can neverthe-
> less prevent it from dominating and atomizing the rest of
> society.[3]

In this book I will use the term civil society in the broadest sense
covered by (1) to (5) above. For reasons which I make clear towards
the end of this Introduction, I include the economy and political
parties, while I have chosen not to include the private sphere of
family and friends. New forms of opposition and resistance have
indeed confirmed in a certain sense the feminist belief that 'the
private is political'. Nonetheless, my reading of recent struggles is
that they are attempts to reconstruct *public life* both in terms of state
and non-state institutions, without necessarily undermining the
private bases of intimacy, love and friendship. It is in this light that
arguments in favour of the political significance of friendship and
love seem somewhat unconvincing, and these will not be treated
here.[4] While political parties and the economy are included, this is

---

[3] Ernest Gellner, *Conditions of Liberty: Civil Society and its Rivals*, London:
Hamish Hamilton, 1994, p. 5.

only in a strictly qualified sense by implication. The qualification is
the following: while I would include both parties and the economy
in any empirical, historical or political sociological account of civil
society, there will be little direct reference to either the economy or
specific universities, reading groups, newspapers, churches, etc.
Instead, in what follows I will attempt to offer a *theoretical* analysis
of political action in civil society, where the terms public sphere,
community and recognition do not, as in functionalist analysis,
represent separate spheres or systems with independent logics
which mysteriously communicate their respective needs to each
other through codes.[5] Instead, these terms are used somewhat in a
manner akin to Carl Schmitt's definition of the political: not as a
sphere, but as a degree of intensity which can become acute in
specific moments of political life.

In chapter 2 it will be shown how Schmitt focuses on the potentially violent turn this degree of intensity can take with what he
refers to as a friend/enemy conflict. This attempt to distil the
essence of the political has been very important for my own work,

[4] Aristotle's *Politics* indicates that the political significance of friendship is
by no means a new argument. In 1972 Maurice Blanchot wrote a book entitled
The Politics of Friendship, and more recently there have been attempts by
Jacques Derrida (*Politics of Friendship*, London: Verso, 1997), Ulrich Beck and
Elisabeth Beck-Gernsheim (*The Normal Chaos of Love*, Cambridge: Polity, 1995)
and others to derive a political theory of friendship in opposition to Carl
Schmitt's notion of the friend/enemy conflict as the basis of a definition of the
political. However, I am in agreement with Hannah Arendt's notion that
'Love, by its very nature, is unworldly, and it is for this reason rather than its
rarity that it is not only apolitical but antipolitical, perhaps the most powerful of all antipolitical forces.' (*The Human Condition*, Chicago: University of
Chicago Press, 1958, pp. 241–2). The loyalty involved in politics is of a different nature than that inherent in love and friendship, since in the former it is
shaped by the political virtue of judgement, whereas in the latter it must be
simply unconditional. The problems inherent in the theoretical attempt to cast
politics in terms of unconditionality are taken up in the discussion of
Emmanuel Lévinas in chapter 5.

[5] Functionalists argue in various ways that an overall understanding of
social, political and economic life is not possible because of systemic complexity, and, in a Weberian vein, because of the differentiation of socio-political
processes brought about by inexorable rationalisation. This seems to be a weak
response to the difficulties of trying to analyse human action in abstraction from
structural and systemic phenomena like capital and legal codification. For a
detailed exposition of functionalism in the work of its most prominent theoreti-
cian, Niklas Luhmann, see Chris Thornhill, *The Theory of Politics in Modern
Germany*, Cambridge: Polity, 1999.

and has led me to adopt a theoretical-philosophical approach in this book rather than the usual political sociological or empirical/historical approaches to the question of civil society. But in Schmitt's writings, the friend/enemy dichotomy presents an oversimplified view which ignores how other, very different relations to the friend/enemy conflict can also crystallise in new institutions and modes of political action. Thus it will be argued that (a) the struggles to enact a politics of the public sphere, community and recognition take place in civil society in ways which are very inaccurately represented at the level of state as questions largely having to do with material interest, and (b) these struggles hint at the possibility of a democratic politics of self-government which might be fully realised given the appropriate economic foundation. Here a word of explanation may be useful to suggest how the rest of this book should be read: the argument will at times seem abstract because it does not make explicit reference to specific contexts like Chiapas, CND, Greenham Common, etc. But there is already an enormous body of primary and secondary literature on those specific struggles written by people who were there and observed and participated. What is still missing and needed is a theoretical account which draws out the implications of those events, which is exactly what the present study hopes to accomplish. As will hopefully become clear, the results point to a very different conceptual constellation than friend/enemy.

The choice not to analyse civil society in terms of function, system or sphere sets the current book apart from the approach of liberals like Gellner as well as the important contributions of other civil society theorists such as Jean Cohen and Andrew Arato. Cohen and Arato maintain that civil society first emerged in opposition to the feudal-aristocratic identification of society as a unified political order of assigned hierarchies. Influenced by the work of Weber, Parsons, Habermas and more recently systems theorists like Niklas Luhmann, Cohen and Arato and other theorists now argue that the historical process of modernisation results in increasing differentiation and rationalisation. These processes lead in turn to the emergence of autonomous social spheres which function according to distinct rationalities in the pursuit of incommensurable goals not reducible to a single over-arching standard of utility. In the writings of Cohen and Arato and other quasi-functionalist approaches, the separation between the state, on the one hand, and the social and economic institutions of civil society, on the other, creates possibilities for specifically modern forms of individual autonomy and group association. Cohen and Arato adopt a framework inspired by Gramsci and Tocqueville, with which they distinguish between the economy, economic society, civil society, political society and the state. They accept that relations between economy, civil society, political society and state cannot be absolutely separate, and that indeed there must be mediation between them. However, their normative emphasis, like that of many other civil society theorists, is on the greatest possible separation of spheres, since according to their account the logic of action in the civil sphere is inherently freer of constraint due to the instrumental logic of action governing the economy and political sphere. Writing with both the experiences of Western European political protest and the reform movements in Eastern Europe in mind, they argue that 'the actors of political and economic society are directly involved with state power and economic production, which they seek to control and manage. They cannot afford to subordinate strategic and instrumental criteria to the normative integration and open-ended communication characteristic of civil society.'[6]

Cohen and Arato and a number of other theorists have been extremely important in demonstrating how both the flourishing of NSMs in post-1968 Western Europe and the tremendous interest sparked by the opposition movements in Eastern Europe have contributed to sustained theoretical and practical interest in civil society. But just as I will not be looking at specific universities, reading groups, newspapers, churches, etc., I will also not offer a detailed critique of Habermas, Cohen and Arato, Touraine, Melucci, etc., or anybody else who has contributed to the exten-

---

[6] Jean Cohen and Andrew Arato, *Civil Society and Political Theory*, Cambridge: MIT Press, 1992, p. ix. The functionalist implications of Cohen and Arato's work is developed by Dirk Richter, 'Zivilgesellschaft – Probleme einer Utopie in der Moderne', in Rolf Eickelpasch and Armin Nassehi (eds), *Utopie und Moderne*, Frankfurt: Suhrkamp, 1996, pp. 181–7. See also Nicos Mouzelis, 'Modernity, Late Development and Civil Society', in John A. Hall (ed.), *Civil Society: Theory, History, Comparison*, Cambridge: Polity, 1995, pp. 225–6; Slavko Splichal, 'From Civil Society to Information Society?', in Slavko Splichal (ed.), *Information Society and Civil Society: Contemporary Perspectives on the Changing World Order*, Indiana: Purdue University Press, 1994, pp. 68–9.

sive debates and literature on the subject.[7] Apart from the fact that that has already been done, it is not the aim of this book. After having briefly sketched how Eastern Europe and the NSMs have brought the concept of civil society to the centre of theoretical attention, I want to mention two additional reasons for the renewed interest in civil society, which will be examined in sections I to II below. Then in section III, I will explain why and how I propose to construct a theoretical-philosophical defence of the concept without relying on or making explicit reference to the usual sociological or historical approaches to the study of civil society.

I

First, in the wake of the post-World War II crises of electoral participation in Western European and North American democracies, citizen apathy and voter disaffection with institutional political parties and politics seemed to confirm the blatantly pessimistic prognoses of the elite theorists Mosca, Pareto and Schumpeter. The elitists argue that the abyss between civil society and the political class will always be an unbridgeable gulf, and that as a consequence parliamentary elections are more likely to resemble plebiscites of largely symbolic and populist character rather than anything that could be described in more favourable terms as the articulate expression of the people's will or the 'general will'. Theorists and activists searched for an intellectual tradition within Western political culture which suggested ways of stemming the

[7] Very useful historical overviews are offered by Krishan Kumar, 'Civil Society: an Inquiry into the Usefulness of an Historical Term', in *The British Journal of Sociology*, 44 (1993), pp. 375–95; Norberto Bobbio, 'Gramsci and the Concept of Civil Society' in John Keane (ed.), *Civil Society and the State: New European Perspectives*, London: Verso, 1988, pp. 73–100; John Keane, *Democracy and Civil Society*, London: Verso, 1988; Adam Seligman, *The Idea of Civil Society*, New York: The Free Press, 1992; Jean L. Cohen, *Class and Civil Society: the Limits of Marxian Class Theory*, Amherst: MIT Press, 1982; Keith Tester, *Civil Society*, London: Routledge, 1992; Victor M. Perez-Diaz, *The Return of Civil Society: the Emergence of Democratic Spain*, Cambridge: Harvard University Press, 1993, and a very good book by Mark Neocleous, *Administering Civil Society: Towards a Theory of State Power*, London: Macmillan, 1996. For readers of Italian, there is an excellent collection of essays edited by Pierpaolo Donati, entitled *La società civile in Italia*, Milan: Mondadori, 1997. The introduction and first chapter by the editor are especially good.

populist and plebiscitary tendencies in parliamentary democracies which, far from being the paranoid fears of nostalgic intellectuals, had actually helped provoke the devastating crises of the 1920s and 1930s. The result has been the rediscovery since the early 1980s of a number of thinkers with ostensibly few common concerns such as Montesquieu, Ferguson, Hegel, Tocqueville and Gramsci. Despite marked differences in approach, these thinkers argue that because of the limited number of public political offices, only a very small number of people can at any one time actually be directly involved in state-level political institutions. It follows that political institutions at the state level can only function democratically if the institutions of civil society foster a culture of public criticism, democratic accountability of power and participation. Ferguson and Tocqueville warn of the de-politicising tendencies of modern commercially-oriented societies. On the basis of their readings of Montesquieu, they argue that if there is not a richly-articulated set of *corps intermédiaires* to stem the de-politicising tendencies inherent in a way of life organised almost exclusively around the family and commerce, the modern state will be in a position to orchestrate a kind of tyranny over an atomised civil society which would have been unthinkable under feudal political arrangements. This argument constitutes an implicit attack on the social contract tradition of political theory, in which isolated individuals in a postulated pre-political 'state of nature' miraculously join to renounce their pre-political freedoms in order to confer the use of legitimate force on the modern state. Instead, writers like Ferguson and Tocqueville convincingly demonstrate that in a democratic society, the relationship between the individual and the state must be mediated by a network of intermediate institutions. These institutions are entrusted with precisely that task assigned to civil society by Gellner in the quotation above, i.e., with the task of preventing the state 'from dominating and atomizing the rest of society'.[8]

[8] Similarly, Franz Neumann argued that 'Political liberty can only be realised in human *action*, i.e., to the extent that man determines the scope and methods of political power. A monarch or dictator can give him freedom – and can just as easily take it way from him ... The democratic political system is the only one which institutionalises the activist element in political freedom. It institutionalises the possibility for men to realise their freedom and *overcome their separation from political power*' (my emphases). Neumann, 'Zum Begriff der politischen Freiheit' (1953), in Herbert Marcuse (ed.), *Demokratischer und*

Moving on to the post-World War II period, the legal theorist Franz Neumann argued that beyond voting once every four or six years, it is necessary to institutionalise daily political engagement in order to safeguard political liberty. That is, since the state already has the monopoly of legitimate use of force within a given territory, it is important to contest state power in order to limit that use of force to areas of acceptable intervention. This means that freedom does not consist simply in freedom from coercion or merely being 'left alone'. Individuals must actively contest the state in all spheres of its activity, in order that they can enjoy an authentic private life alongside their public activity. Having to flee Germany during the 1930s informed Neumann's belief that if the state is not contested under modern conditions, it tends to extend its sphere of jurisdiction – and even become total. Thus one has to engage in politics in order to have a sphere that is not invaded by the logic of state colonialisation. Although somewhat paradoxical, to put Neumann's argument in republican terms, a 'virtuous' electorate best shows its loyalty to the principle of the state as the guardian of the general will by contesting the state. Only in this way does the state remain permeable to all interests and perspectives in civil society without becoming the instrument of its most powerful interests.

Tocqueville's suspicion about state tyranny was confirmed by the experience of political authoritarianism in Europe in the 1920s and 1930s: if the majority is either unwilling to exercise or is prevented from exercising its rights of assembly, freedom of information and freedom of expression, then activist minorities in extremist or populist parties backed by powerful private interests are in a position to usurp state power and transform the state into a coercive apparatus directed against the general will.[9] If 'fear and manipulation turn a people into a mob',[10] then the power granted to the modern state could transform the will of the people into the will of the mob in the name of popular sovereignty in times of crisis. This seems to be one of the important lessons of he 1920s and 1930s. Neumann and more recent political theorists like Gellner, Cohen and Arato and Habermas thus place fundamental impor-

---

autoritärer Staat: Studien zur politischen Theorie, Munich: Fischer Verlag, 1970, p. 126.
    [9] Neumann, 'Zum Begriff der politischen Freiheit', pp. 125–30.
    [10] *Ibid.,* p. 134.

tance on the necessity of an active role for the sphere of institutions mediating between individual and state for democratic politics, which has since 1989 been characterised as the 'rebirth of civil society'. The separation between state and civil society in the work of Cohen and Arato, Habermas and others is thus credited with (1) preventing the identification of individual and state which is the essence of totalitarianism, (2) providing the distance between political power and the struggle for wealth without which politics tends to degenerate into clientelism, (3) offering the institutional framework within which apathy and electoral abstention characteristic of commercial societies can be forestalled and perhaps even reversed and (4) offering a potential theoretical way out of the seemingly quite limited parameters for conceptualising politics set by the liberalism vs. communitarianism debates.[11]

The liberal vs. communitarian debates signal one set of possible responses to the crises of apathy and political legitimacy of the post-World War II period. There is an extensive literature on these debates, and the arguments of the respective sides will not be rehearsed here. With a number of important exceptions, both sides tend to distort their opponent's position, such that largely caricatural versions of liberalism and the political significance of community have emerged. While there is undoubtedly a plurality of possible liberalisms and communitarianisms, these debates have not been successful in developing an incisive analysis of the problems and possible solutions to the dilemmas of democratic theory and praxis which civil society theorists have attempted to carry forward. There is nonetheless an important political dimension to community which civil society theorists cannot ignore, and which will be examined in chapter 4 of this book outside the parameters of the liberalism-communitarianism debate. The decision to omit a discussion of these debates despite the political importance of community is guided by the belief that both positions are unsatisfactory. Although mutual misrepresentation has obscured rather than illuminated the problems confronted by both sides, there are serious limits to even the hypothetically best possible version of each position. I will briefly explain why this is so.

Despite the richness of permutation offered by different versions of liberalism, none adequately rise to the challenge posed

---

[11] Habermas, *Faktizität und Geltung*, pp. 215–16.

by theorists like Neumann and Habermas concerning the necessity of citizen participation in public affairs for democratic politics. Whether framed in terms of the precedence of the right over the good, or the need to take rights seriously, there is a deep suspicion of any theory of positive freedom in liberal theory. Thus if liberals are willing to accept a certain measure of justified praise for raising compelling arguments against core republican and communitarian arguments, they must also accept that they have no compelling answers to questions concerning the link between political action and political freedom. Moreover, where liberalism has been philosophically rigorous it has, with few exceptions, been sociologically naive in the extreme. This means that representatives of liberal thought have been unable or unwilling to explain how the liberal freedoms of expression and assembly undermined by social, economic and political power structures might be corrected within a liberal framework. In historical and empirical terms, this is precisely the point at which liberalism becomes parasitical on other doctrines for its own survival, and in the main this means parasitical on the redistributive and reformist practices of social democracy. The attempt to skirt this issue by saying that liberalism is perfectly justified in borrowing from social democratic and republican beliefs is only made at the price of having to abandon what is distinctive about liberalism.[12]

Similarly, there is no single version of communitarianism against which liberal arguments can be deployed. But compared to different communitarian arguments in favour of a common good, or a set of political and ethical virtues, or a communally-rooted identity, Hegel's theory of state and civil society is much more sociologically sophisticated and modern. Indeed, communitarian arguments have contributed to the renewed interest in Hegel's ideas on the struggle for recognition in civil society. This is because Hegel manages to incorporate the romantic critique of the Enlightenment and liberalism which has been taken up in new guise by contemporary communitarians into the broader framework of his theory of capitalism, the emergence of civil law, bureaucratic administration and the modern state. Thus unlike

---

[12] Of course there are liberal thinkers such as Piero Gobetti, L.T. Hobhouse and Franceso Saverio Merlino who make it virtually impossible to generalise about liberalism. Typically, however, the ideas of these thinkers are glaringly absent in the liberalism-communitarianism debates.

most contemporary communitarians, Hegel is not loath to talk about the exploitative, conflictual and plural character of modern civil societies, whereas unlike most liberals he retains a notion of positive freedom and a non-contractual conception of politics. Contemporary communitarian theory is quick to acknowledge its classical republican, romantic and Hegelian foundations without, however, seriously considering what might by now be outdated in those traditions. With regard to classical republicanism and political romanticism, this is clearly the idea of a common good or general will, with the organic metaphors and metaphysical presuppositions that this idea implies. With regard to Hegel it is a theory of positive liberty which must culminate in the state, which is a point I will return to below.

But it is in fact with Hegel that the theory of the modern state and civil society is first developed systematically, and it is not possible to understand the revolution in social and political thought in relation to state and civil society without understanding Hegel and in particular Hegel's critique of Kant. Thus the first chapter of this book will attempt to briefly reconstruct the relevant political ideas in Kant and Hegel for a theoretical understanding of civil society. In chapter 1 Hegel's position will be elaborated, along with Feuerbach and Marx's critique of Hegel. In chapter 5 I will return to Hegel in order to critically examine the political significance of recognition. The obvious problems in the liberalism-communitarianism debate as well as the inadequacies of much recent theorising about civil society indicate that far from being an outdated piece of intellectual history, the tradition of modern German critical political theory focusing on Kant, Hegel, Feuerbach and Marx is still necessary for an adequate understanding of the state as well as contemporary civil society. Moreover, the best aspects of this tradition are developed in the twentieth century by thinkers such as Max Weber, Carl Schmitt, T.W. Adorno and particularly Walter Benjamin and Hannah Arendt. Thus I have found it necessary to grapple with the ideas of these thinkers throughout the book. I hasten to add that the reception of their work here is critical and not in any way intended as a new canon or authority for political theory. Nevertheless, a careful examination of the work of these writers is much more important for a correct understanding of civil society than a great deal of contemporary social and political theory in general, and certainly more than the liberalism-communitarianism debate in particular.

Despite its many shortcomings, however, the liberalism-communitarianism debate has raised a series of important questions for civil society theorists. For example, how does one begin to think about a theory of political freedom without reducing freedom to some version of state protection of individuals from one another, on the one hand, and without presupposing some form of pre-modern (if such a community *ever* existed) type of homogenous community, on the other? A key step towards an answer has centred on the idea of the public sphere in civil society. The public sphere had a major impact both in the dissident movements in Eastern Europe, and in Western European and North American debates on the role of new social movements in civil society. As long as democracy is understood in ideal terms as collective self-government, the public sphere emerges as a key foil against the clientelistic nature of liberal parasitism on social democracy and corporatism.

In broad terms, under capitalism private interests tend to be integrated into the state apparatus in one of two ways. The first is likely to be some form of corporatism in which the state acts in conjunction with organised labour and the interests of capital to negotiate the compromise between labour and capital in extra-parliamentary fora, as was prevalent in England in the 1970s and in Germany and parts of Scandinavia in the 1970s and 1980s. The second form of integration into the apparatus of the state can take shape as a historic bloc in Gramsci's sense, i.e., joining the interests of key figures in the state with those in the economy, the media, business schools, the universities, etc., once again, however, in extra-parliamentary fora. In both cases, the public sphere is circumvented and the democratic ideal of transparency is undermined. In such cases the state patently fails to institutionalise a dialogue between the different actors in civil society and thereby fails to function as a liberal state should – as a *neutral* arbitrator between competing conceptions of the good. Neutrality requires that there be a public sphere in which all individuals and points of view can attain visibility, and from which these groups can have an equal share in being the authors of the laws that collectively govern them. There are three important points to be made about the public sphere in this regard which emerge in the discussion in chapter 3: (1) the public sphere need not necessarily presuppose an organic unity between the groups and individuals which are active in it; (2) its existence, and therewith the possibility of genuine neutrality, does depend on the political action of groups and individuals who can recognise themselves as the authors of the laws that govern them; and (3) genuine neutrality means to the largest possible extent enacting a form of politics beyond power, violence and interest. Thus the emphasis on the public sphere amongst civil society theorists can be regarded as a potential way out of the theoretical straitjacket imposed by the communitarian-liberalism impasse.

II

Secondly, the rise of civil society to theoretical prominence in recent years has been accompanied by a parallel surge in interest in globalisation. This interest has been accompanied by the increasing awareness that the territorially-located nation-state will not play the pre-eminent role in political life in the twenty-first century which it did in the eighteenth, nineteenth and twentieth, which in its turn has led to the call for an international or global civil society to take up the challenge of global politics.[13] It is becoming clear that the sovereignty of the national state will not in the long run be able to coexist with a fully globalised (rather than merely international) economy, but it is not at all clear what new forms of conflict mediation will emerge to replace national states. It is normally argued that the modern state assumes its most influential expression in secular and republican form as a result of the French and American Revolutions of the eighteenth century. Thus in historical terms, the idea of the sovereign nation-state with a monopoly on the use of legitimate force within the boundaries of a given territory is a relatively recent phenomenon, and by extension, likely to give way to new forms of political authority if a truly global economy

[13] Reinhart Kößler and Henning Melber, *Chancen internationaler Zivilgesellschaft*, Frankfurt: Suhrkamp, 1993; Michael Walzer (ed.), *Toward a Global Civil Society*, Oxford: Berghan Books, 1995; Martin Shaw, *Civil Society and the Media in Global Crises: Representing Distant Violence*, London: Pinter, 1996; Justin Rosenberg, *The Empire of Civil Society: a Critique of the Realist Theory of International Relations*, London: Verso, 1994. These are just a few of the recent books about the possibilities and likely problems with a global civil society. There have also been a large number of articles about the subject.

develops.[14] In the Preface to the 1961 edition of *Der Begriff des Politischen* (*The Concept of the Political*), Carl Schmitt argued that the post-World War II economic order created a political environment in which the state in its existing form might not be able to survive. He already saw that the international trading system was undermining the state's capacity to make decisions on the basis of strictly political criteria, and that as a consequence the national state as the decisive political decision-making unit was perhaps entering its twilight. Schmitt's predictions have been proved correct in large measure with the rise of international financial institutions like the World Bank and the International Monetary Fund (IMF). It has become clear that powerful internationally-organised economic interests can perform a kind of referendum on the policies of various countries (and of developing countries in particular). Under the current international system of private capital investment, low inflation rates and a strong currency become the criteria to determine whether or not a country qualifies for the loans and investment it needs to develop a stable material infrastructure. The threat of financial sanctions can induce governments to cut unemployment and housing benefit, health services, public transport, pensions, etc. in order to reduce inflation or bolster the strength of the national currency. The World Bank and other such international financial institutions are in a position to impose such

[14] This likelihood was already foreshadowed by the development of the nation-state itself. The creation of a sovereign political authority within the boundaries of what are now recognised as the individual nation-states of Europe and North America was inseparable from the need to create a legal framework for the regulation of a single national market for labour and capital. Male and then universal suffrage within this state was acquired in a series of struggles which had very ambivalent consequences. On the one hand suffrage provided the framework for a certain degree of control over economic and political processes. On the other hand the right to vote was also granted because it would have been impossible to draft citizens into the army without giving them the suffrage as well. The possibility of drafting citizens into the military was then of course utilised to the full in World Wars I and II. There is of course far more to the story than the necessity to find a suitable legal-military framework for the expansion of capital. For example, the aspiration to self-government on the part of Poles, Greeks and Irish against Russian, Turkish and English imperialism contained a democratic dynamic that cannot simply be equated with economic interest. It is noteworthy that the current movement towards a unified Europe seems to be largely bereft of such democratic aspirations, especially on the part of the economic and political interests driving the process forward.

measures even when these might be economically inappropriate for the country in question. If pushed to an extreme, this economic leverage can virtually eliminate the option of a political choice to live with the economic consequences of democratic participation and accountability at the neighbourhood, local, regional and state levels of decision-making. Much time is needed for citizens to acquire a sufficient understanding of the issues arising at all of these levels, and much time is also required in order for collective decision-making in a variety of contexts to be more than merely symbolic. All of this is time that is not spent working towards the consolidation of low inflation rates and a competitive national currency. This conflict of interests poses the issue of the need to choose between the political values of participation, transparency and accountability, on the one hand, and the economic and technical imperatives of economic growth, efficiency, and overconsumption, on the other.

In the critique of sovereignty and state violence in chapter 2, it will be argued that the time proper to politics is different from the time of the economy, and that it is only really in the former that humans distinguish themselves from animals and machines. This is a point I will return to briefly in section III below. For now, however, it must be emphasised that the globalisation of the economy after the political and economic experience of colonialisation and de-colonialisation has led to a situation in which virtually no country can opt out of the international trading system. This is a system which, due to the continued military and cultural hegemony of the United States, is obviously far more than a system of 'fair' trade or 'free' markets. It enforces very definite models of economic development, cultural expression, consumption patterns and conflict mediation. Recent history demonstrates that conflict must be reckoned with in the many instances where these imposed models square uneasily with the existing cultural norms. Thus while globalisation seems in some senses to have established itself in economic terms for the present, there has been no obvious political response to problems like fundamentalism, ethnic violence, and chronic underdevelopment. It is in this context that ideologically-charged terminology like the 'End of History' and the 'New World Order' are completely inadequate for explaining new forms of conflict and the persistence of old problems in new forms.

The Gulf War and the renewal of violence in the Balkans,

Ruwanda, Kurdistan, Algeria and elsewhere have underscored the urgency of finding supra-national institutions for conflict mediation. Wars in these regions have raised a number of urgent theoretical and practical questions about the limits to which a potential future world political community would be willing to tolerate 'ethnic cleansing', torture and related crimes simply because they are committed within the arbitrary boundaries of nation-state sovereignty. These conflicts have also contributed to the rise of population migrations which in the long term will not be solved by respecting existing state boundaries. The crises of repression, homelessness, disease and famine created by political conflicts whose origins in large measure are traceable to arbitrarily fixed boundaries – once again especially clear in developing countries with a colonial past – demand mediating institutions with a framework capable of addressing the international dimension of the problems in question. And while the work of the United Nations (UN) has been admirable in many respects, it finds itself time and again constrained to work around powerful state and economic interests which undermine UN peacekeeping and refugee operations. The Gulf War demonstrates how easily powerful interests can circumvent UN control, and just how precarious the so-called 'New World Order' is. Far from 'making the world safe for democracy', the innumerable conflicts in the post-Cold War world indicate that the problems of world peace and environmental safety simply go beyond the boundaries of the nation-state.

It is in this context that much hope has been aroused by the global civil society represented at least in outline by the growing number of Non- and Quasi-Governmental Organisations (NGOs and QUANGOs) and the international dimension of the peace, gay rights, indigenous peoples, feminist, environmental, and other movements.[15] However, there are two principal obstacles to the possible spread and development of these groups and movements into a well-articulated network of institutions capable of resolving international problems within a framework of global solidarity. The first is the persistence of the sovereignty of the nation-state. Despite the challenges of globalisation and the construction of the European Union and other supra-national political institutions, the

---

[15] Kößler and Melber, *Chancen internationaler Zivilgesellschaft*, pp. 58, 137–40.

state continues to play a decisive role in international politics. In normal cases, states still have a fundamental role in controlling populations by deciding who is and who is not free to enter their countries, which obviously poses severe limits to international co-operation in instances of conflict. Moreover, the crisis in the Balkans in the late 1990s suggests that in exceptional cases, states play an important role in defining and persecuting ethnic or otherwise defined 'enemies'. The second problem facing the formation of an international civil society is the continued political and economic domination of global capitalism. Any form of global civil society will require a material basis in which questions of investment and distribution are not determined by which country needs hard currency so much that it is willing to accept nucelar waste from another country or willing to destroy its environment for the sake of short-term economic competitivity. This material basis is also not going to be created according to which country can provide the cheapest and most disciplined labour force. At present, capital is free within certain limitations to move all over the world according to the principles of regulated markets as stipulated by the General Agreement on Tariffs and Trade (GATT) and its successor treaties, while the movement of labour is still strictly controlled by individual states. Within the framework of international competition, this means that the state cannot function as an arena for the expression of a plurality of viewpoints, but is instead largely occupied with regulating and disciplining the labour force for the needs of foreign and domestic capital, without which it would have no material basis for either its repressive or legitimate functions. As such, attention has turned to civil society as the sphere of possible democratic self-government. The argument in the present book, which I will introduce below, is that civil society *could* indeed *become* such a sphere. This will depend on a number of factors which I will sketch briefly in section III below before going on to the detailed case for civil society to be made in the rest of this book.

III

As stated at the outset, despite the rise to sociological attention of NSMs in Western Europe and the theoretical implications of the opposition movements in Eastern Europe culminating in the events of 1989, this book will not focus on NSMs, Eastern Europe, the manifest problems with the liberalism-communitarianism debate or the challenges to the state posed by globalisation. It attempts, rather, to theorise the significance of these phenomena in conjunction with another theoretical question which has also recently assumed prominence: that of defining the nature and boundaries of the political. If one may speak of political democracy, equality and liberty, one must also be able at least to attempt to define or specify what is particular about politics as distinct from economics, administration, redistribution, technology and consumption. The present book thus attempts to theorise both (1) the renewed interest in civil society and (2) the theoretical desirability of re-thinking the political at a time when the discourses and practices of globalisation and economic and technical rationality threaten the demise of politics – if not of power and domination. Originally this study intended to focus on civil society and Eastern Europe, NSMs and globalisation. But it became clear that such a project was not necessary. Excellent work in this area has already been done by Melucci, Touraine, Cohen and Arato, Pelcynski, and others.[16] Moreover, unless one has actually been active in dissident groups in Eastern Europe, or has been involved in a new social movement elsewhere, anything one might write about those subjects will be largely derivative. Thus while Melucci, Touraine, Cohen and Arato et al. have analysed civil society, Eastern Europe, and NSMs, this book attempts to provide a meta-analysis of those studies by drawing out the theoretical and philosophical implications of their work, and combining these with an analysis of the limits of Marxism and liberalism for furnishing the bases of an adequate theoretical understanding of either the state or contemporary civil society. My reading of recent events is that the struggles described by sociologists as the renewal or rebirth of civil society are in various ways arguments for a different kind of politics as well as a redefinition of the political in order to negotiate the possible bases of a new political praxis. This redefinition of the political centres on three key

---

[16] The work of Neil Stammers on new social movements, civil society, rights, and power has also been a key development in this regard. See his 'Social Movements, Power, Rights: Towards a Reconstruction of Global Civil Society from Below?', paper for the Regional Conference on social movements, 8–10 September 1997, Tel-Aviv, Israel, available from the author at the University of Sussex on permission.

concepts which will be analysed in chapters 3, 4 and 5: the public sphere, community and recognition.

In important respects the current book represents an attempt to further the project begun with *Radical Theories: Paths Beyond Marxism and Social Democracy* (Manchester University Press, 1994). In that book I attempted to demonstrate three things. First, that capitalism and democracy are irreconcilable. As an economic system, capitalism creates too many inequalities in wealth and power to make anything like political democracy possible. As a civilisation, capitalism flourishes best where it can harness fear, greed, and an utter disrespect for human life which is incompatible with democracy. Secondly, the attempt to abolish capitalism via the state fails. In historical terms it fails in its reformist form as social democracy, since social democracy is chronically undermined by capital flight and the inequalities created by capitalism, which it cannot tackle because it is fundamentally dependent on the capitalist economy for its own functioning. The failure of the 1981 Mitterand government to enact its social democratic programme offers a key example. In general the history of social democracy bears this out time and again wherever it manages to retain power long enough to even attempt to reform capitalism.[17] The attempt to abolish capitalism via the state also fails in its revolutionary form as Leninism, which patently concentrates too much power in the party–state apparatus. The history of the Soviet Union and the peoples' democracies of Eastern Europe offers convincing demonstration of this argument. And finally, I argue that the answer to the riddle of democracy suggests that it must be based on some form of non-statist socialism. In *Radical Theories*, I argue that by weaving together different strands of guild socialist, anarchist and green socialist theory, it is possible to sketch the institutional contours of such an economy. *Sovereign States or Political Communities?* attempts to carry the argument in *Radical Theories* forward, by arguing that if democracy is to be realised on the material basis of a non-statist socialist economy, one must also consider carefully how conflict is going to be medi-

---

[17] This is to say nothing of social democratic support for national war efforts in 1914 (apart from the Italian Socialist Party, which has recently itself disappeared as a result of its involvement in the *Tangentopoli* bribes and kickbacks scandal), and the role of the German SPD in bloodily crushing the council republics in Berlin and Munich after the World War I.

ated in non-statist terms, and the possibilities for this, in turn, are suggested by the subjects taken up in chapters 3 to 5. One must be clear on this issue: while it could offer the *basis* for a genuinely democratic self-governing civil society, non-statist socialism is not synonymous with democracy or civil society. This is where the importance of re-thinking the political becomes decisive, and it is in this task that the work of Kant, Hegel, Feuerbach, Marx, Schmitt, Benjamin, Adorno and Arendt have been extremely important. Thus the focus of this book will be that of formulating the politics of non-statist socialism as an attempt to develop further the implications of the analysis in *Radical Theories* for democratic theory. The central agrument of that book about the crucial link between non-statist socialism and democracy will not be repeated here, but must nonetheless be borne in mind as the key premise for the current work. The current work starts with the premise that the material basis of socialism will make democratic politics *possible*, but it is not itself politics.

One might ask why it is necessary to separate the arguments for non-statist socialism as the material basis of democracy conceived as self-government, on the one hand, from the arguments for the possible forms of the political which that democracy might assume, on the other. Is not socialism after all a political theory? The argument in this book is that, strictly speaking, it is not, no more than Leninism and liberalism are, and no more than Marxism is by implication only. The ideas of the public sphere, community and recognition imply a political praxis of solidarity and resistance, but also of courage, insight, the ability to forgive, and other non-instrumental modes of action. Solidarity and resistance can be assimilated to the experience of class exploitation, class interest and, more recently, to certain dimensions of the NSMs. Nonetheless, courage in a political sense and the ability to forgive are not reducible to questions of class or to interest. Thus the question of economic interest has to be to the greatest possible extent solved or, so to speak, neutralised, so that other, freer forms of human interaction become possible. These other freer, more creative forms of human praxis are explored in chapters 3 to 5 in this book as politics.

A careful analysis of liberalism, social democracy, syndicalism and Marxism-Leninism in power leads to the conclusion that the attempt to make interest the basis of politics is unsatisfactory and reductionist. In liberal terms, it in practice reduces democracy to the institutional mechanisms of administering the compromise between different social classes. Sometimes this works with a limited degree of harmony, sometimes it does not, and at other times it gives way all too quickly to more authoritarian political forms.[18] In Leninist terms, interest posits a direct chain of representation between class–party–state, where class interest assumes organisational form as party, and the party then stages a military conquest of state power. If one remains commited to a materialist explanation of social and historical phenomena as Marxists would urge, then one would have to say that there is a materialist explanation for Stalinism and other personality cults in the history of state socialism. That is, that the logic of representation of interest is likely to go a step further, i.e., to class–party–state–leader: Stalinism cannot simply be written off as a deviation from Marxism-Leninism. And whereas syndicalism offers no theory of the political other than the by itself inadequate notion of worker control of the workplace, social democracy offers a more anodyne version of the personality cult, as was seen once again in the English parliamentary elections of 1997![19]

In the chapters to come the theoretical-philosophical analysis of civil society converges with the normative-utopian defence of the political. This argument can be summarised as follows: Not only is there a latent political dimension to various aspects of action in contemporary civil societies that seeks articulation but is frustrated by existing political and economic institutions; the latter are structurally beset with authoritarian tendencies which strongly suggest that they should be changed if we want the word 'democracy' to have more than an ideological significance. The focus in the reconstructive chapters following the brief historical account of state and civil society in chapter 1 and the critique of the state in chapter 2 represents an attempt to re-think the

---

[18] With the failure of monetarism, and more recently the crisis of Fordism, and in the face of the uncertainties of globalisation and the possibilities of an ultra-competitive new world hegemonic order, a recurrence of authoritarian politics canot be excluded. For a convincing account of why this may be so, see Alain Lipietz, *Towards a New Economic Order*, Cambridge: Polity, 1992, chapters 1–4.

[19] This comparison is intentionally exaggerated. Yet the point remains that social democratic electoral politics trade on some of the same personality cults that characterise more authoritarian leadership styles.

political beyond the categories of interest, sovereign power and the ritual of voting for leaders. Again, this is not to negate the importance of material interests, and to repeat, that is why a fully-developed form of non-statist socialism is necessary for the full emergence of a new concept and praxis of the political. The reduction of democracy to questions of interest, power and the right to privacy furnishes an inadequate conception of the political, which, historically, has yielded various forms of catastrophe. Strangely, the catastrophes of the twentieth century seem to have brought little in the way of new thinking about the political, as 'economic miracles' of one sort or another have deflected energy and attention away from politics in the sense defended in this book.[20] The prodigious contribution to political thought made by Hannah Arendt is of course one of the fortunate exceptions to this, and her influence on the conception of politics worked out in the following pages is enormous. Indeed, if anything is achieved here, it might be the demonstration that non-statist socialism with a modified form of Arendtian politics offers a theory of the political with important practical implications. Just as Arendt's theory of politics is far too rarefied in its dismissal of the 'social question', so too is the virtual obsession with the social question in other theories a neglect of the political. The attempt to incorporate important aspects of Arendt's ideas into a political theory of civil society is an attempt to outline a concrete political utopia as an alternative to praying for the next economic miracle. The reader may well object at various points to what seems to be an untenable confusion of the theoretical and normative levels of analysis. At times I do consciously disentangle these levels, while at other times I do not, in the belief that both recent history and the theoretical implications of the debates on civil society seen in the light of Arendt's political thought suggest that there is a utopian content to contemporary political practice which is struggling towards articulation against capitalism and the existing

---

[20] The reference here is to the so-called economic miracles in Germany (*Wirtschaftswunder*) and Italy (*miracolo economico*) in the post-World War II period. There would be a lot to say about the nature of these 'miracles', but here I would only remark that they were relatively short and in both cases helped cause the large-scale disenchantment with capitalism which contributed to the student and worker revolts of 1968–69. They did not provide the stable foundation for future capitalist development, as the turbulent 1970s in both countries were to show.

state. My main hope is that the argument presented here will be plausible enough to make the utopian potential of the present stand out, since it is this present which suggests that the real is radical and the radical is real.[21]

[21] In addition to concluding the Introduction with this paraphrasing of Hegel's remark in the Preface to *The Philosophy of Right*, I would like to quote Max Horkheimer. With reference to what seemed to be the utopian nature of critical theory and its ostensible lack of wide-ranging popular support, he states: 'Dialectical theory does not exercise critique merely on the basis of an idea ... As long as thought has not fully won the day, it can never fall safe in the shadow of any form of power. Thought requires independence. And if the concepts of thought, which arise from social movements, seem vain and hopeless today because there is not much more behind them than their scattered followers, the truth will one day emerge. That is because the goal of a rational society, which today admittedly seems to be real only in the imagination, is actually rooted in the mind of every human being.' (Max Horkheimer, Appendix to 'Traditionelle und kritische Theorie', 1937, in *Traditionelle und kritische Theorie: Vier Aufsätze*, Frankfurt: Fischer Verlag, 1970, pp. 62–3)

1

Civil society and the origins of modern political theory

The form of intercourse determined by the existing productive forces at all previous historical stages, and in its turn determining these, is *civil society* ... Already here we see how this civil society is the true source and stage of all history, and how absurd is the conception of history held hitherto, which neglects the real relationships and confines itself to the high-sounding dramas of princes and states.

Marx and Engels, 'The German Ideology', their emphasis

This chapter traces the theoretical bases of civil society as they emerge in Marx's critique of the state and other forms of alienation such as religion, alienated labour and commodity fetishism. It will be argued that Marx arrives at his analysis of the separation of state and civil society by way of a complete critique of all institutions in which human relations become reified. This will entail a very brief look at the Enlightenment critique of Absolutism and religion before turning to both Marx's reading of Feuerbach and his interpretation of the Hegelian state as the most complete theoretical defence of alienated political power. The discussion in this chapter will serve to introduce the historical background to contemporary theoretical debates on civil society, and set the stage for the more focused critical analysis of the state and sovereignty in chapter 2, where the analyses of Weber, Schmitt and Benjamin will be used to demonstrate why the modern state can be considered an authoritarian political institution whose authority has recently been challenged by civil society.

The historical background

It is often argued that prior to the emergence of civil society, private property and the household constituted the basic unit of Western European economies. There are divergent opinions between economic historians as to exactly when this role was first usurped by the mercantile economy and then the international capitalist market economy. Karl Polanyi maintains that by the sixteenth century markets began to take on an important role in organising economic life. For other historians it seems to be clear that the household-based economy played the central role in organising the economy from the time of Aristotle's Greece until the end of the eighteenth century. Nonetheless, there is fairly broad agreement that until the beginning of Absolutism in Western Europe, what we call the economy was primarily organised either on the principles of reciprocity or householding, or some combination of both.[1]

Classical Greek society was organised on the basis of individuals organised in households, the eligible males of which led parallel lives as citizens who constituted the political community or *polis*. The household economy was sustained by slaves, women, craftsmen and foreigners that had no political rights; the institution served as a means for the satisfaction of daily material needs and to make a political sphere of truly autonomous action possible for the male citizens. Households combined to form villages, which in turn joined to form the *he koinonia politike* as the association aiming at the highest good within the Greek world existing as an end in itself. The rise of the city-state meant that in addition to his private life, the Greek citizen received his second life – his *bios politikos* – constitutive of which were action (praxis) and speech (lexis), from which everything 'merely necessary' was excluded. Though slaves, women, craftsmen and foreigners outside the *polis* were obviously also physically capable of speech, they were excluded from a way of life in which speech and discussion are the core of politics. It is here within the Western tradition of politics that the antecedents of the idea of a critical public and civil society are found. Bound up with its conditions of existence at this time was the strict separation

---

[1] Karl Polanyi, *The Great Transformation: the Political and Economic Foundations of Our Time*, Boston: Beacon Press, 1957 (1944), pp. 53–4; Utz Haltern, *Bürgerliche Gesellschaft: sozialtheoretische und sozialhistorische Aspekte*, Darmstadt Wissenschaftliche Buchgesellschaft, 1985, pp. 7–8.

of the *polis* and the household economy. There were of course non-economic institutions and schools in the classical world. But there was no civil society as we understand the term in its modern-Hegelian conception: as a sphere of market exchange, trade unions, churches, museums, libraries, universities, charities, mass media, etc., to mediate between the private world of individual households and the political community of citizens.[2]

Aristotle considers property important insofar as it guarantees the minimum of necessities to make the good life possible, though for him the acquisition of property is not to be confused with the good life itself. The good life centres instead on the cultivation of a range of virtues. In Greek life these tended to be qualities like courage, honesty, insight and loyalty which the individual could only develop within the context of concerted action with others in the ongoing preservation of a way of life based on praxis and lexis. In historical terms, this fostered the theatrical representation of politics on the stages of the classical world, since the existence of the virtues could only be attested to by a politically informed public. Thus a world held in common with its own issues and problems was given dramatic expression in a way that was intelligible and meaningful to all observers of the performance. According to Hegel, however, the 'common world' portrayed on the classical stage and the dramatic representation of the clash between the different virtues of that world became increasingly difficult to sustain. Existing bonds were torn asunder by the eruption of the principles of individualism and subjectivity represented by Socratic reasoning, Christianity and the rise of modern capitalism. Luther's version of Christianity was particularly adept at driving a wedge between social and political conceptions of truth and obligation, lived on earth, and religious conceptions of morality and ethics, which each individual experienced alone in a private relation with God. It is thus unsurprising that the Church was a rival to secular political authority until the various religious wars culminating in the Treaty of Westphalia (1648) provided Bodin and Hobbes with the theoretical justification of Absolutism as the only guarantor of peace.[3]

The period of classical Absolutism runs roughly from the Treaty

[2] Hannah Arendt, *The Human Condition*, Chicago: University of Chicago Press, 1958, pp. 24–5.

[3] Reinhart Koselleck, *Kritik und Krise: Eine Studie zur Pathogenese der bürgerlichen Welt* (7th edn). Frankfurt: Suhrkamp, 1992 (1st edn 1959), chapter 1.

of Westphalia until 1789, when, in the aftermath of the struggles of the English Civil War, the French Revolution decisively toppled absolutism in the name of the sovereignty of the people and the natural rights of equal citizens. The period is decisively marked by the concentration of military and political power in supra-religious state institutions which sought to divest the warring factions of Christianity and the nobility of their various claims to political authority. At the same time however, the autonomy of other important corporate bodies such as Guilds and Communes eroded as power was concentrated in the absolutist state. Initially there were attempts to integrate the city-states and communes with the emerging national state on a confederal basis. Thus town governments played an important role in the religious wars in France; both the Huguenots and the Catholic League supported the idea of semi-autonomous political federations within a united kingdom. Both groups defended the idea that towns should continue to elect their own jurors and magistrates. In Holland the Dutch Revolt (1565–81) inspired the belief that a confederation on the Swiss model might offer possibilities for local democracy within some overarching political framework of state sovereignty. Antony Black notes that the radically different outcomes of the sovereignty debate in France and Holland are mirrored in the opposed doctrines of Bodin and Althusius. Whereas Bodin defends a unitary notion of sovereignty which does not share ultimate power with town governments, guilds, the nobility or even parliaments, Althusius regards cities and provinces as public associations with their own spheres of competence in local administration, education, religious matters and trade practices. This contrast between French and Dutch thinking on the state should not be overdrawn, however, since it is Montesquieu in France who in 1748 defends the importance of *pouvoirs intermédiaires* in *The Spirit of the Laws*.[4]

The struggle between the increasing claims of state power versus the demand for self-government at the village, town and regional level was fought with particular vehemence in Germany, where the supporters of the guild towns defended the power of the communes against encroaching state power. The antecedents for

---

[4] Antony Black, *Guilds and Civil Society in European Political Thought from the Twelfth Century to the Present*, London: Methuen, 1984, pp. 145–6; Quentin Skinner, *The Foundations of Modern Political Thought*, Vol. II, Cambridge: CUP, 1978, pp. 204–5, 213–16.

this existed in the practice of the *Genossenschaftsrecht* (co-operative law) of the guilds which stipulated the norms of conduct and procedures for conflict resolution of a precedent-based *ad hoc* nature in opposition to the more rigidly stipulated written codes of Roman law. This is to stress that though we now take for granted that all citizens should have equal rights before the state, it is only relatively recently that the state emerged as the pre-eminent political institution for setting the terms of equality and freedom. Prior to the centralisation of state power which received its first major impetus under Absolutism, guilds, communes, universities and other associations defended the rights of their individual members in forms of association largely independent from any overarching political authority, even if in theory the members of these association were to varying degrees prepared to pay taxes, receive a certain amount of military protection, and maybe even concede the king's claim to rule by divine right. But corporate structure was too diverse, and norms of participation and corporate membership too variegated to embrace all of society under a general category of right and law. Insofar as they constituted a network of self-governing bodies, the corporations of the late feudal and early absolutist period represented a clear forerunner of our modern notions of civil society.[5]

In addition to centralising political power, absolutism suppressed religious conflict across Europe through the near complete separation of moral discourse from political discourse, and the almost complete exclusion of questions of ethics from considerations of state action. Precedents for this position could be clearly found in Machiavelli's reflections on politics in *The Prince*. The situation first changed with Locke's *Essay Concerning Human Understanding*, in which Locke challenged monarchical privilege by arguing that citizens had to declare their private views in public in

[5] Koselleck, *Kritik und Krise*, pp. 12–14; Otto Von Gierke, 'Über die Geschichte des Majoritätsprinzips' in Berndt Guggenberger and Claus Offe (eds), *An den Grenzen der Mehrheitsdemokratie: Politik und Soziologie der Mehrheitsregel Opladen*: Westdeutscher Verlag, 1984, pp. 24–5, 32–3; Black, *Guilds and Civil Society*, pp. 146–9. Thus Antony Black reminds us that in reference to the corporation, 'The importance of the concept was that it provided a ready and respectable means of conceptualizing the kingdom or nation-state as an entity *without* immediate reference to royal authority. Since corporations were so very diverse in structure, it would make no sense at all to say that, for the corporation of the realm to hang together, it must be governed by a king' (his emphasis, p. 149).

the form of general moral laws. Only in this way would it be possible to then subject these views to the scrutiny of other citizens, in order to determine if they conformed to the requisite universality to make them morally valid. Since under Absolutism citizens were denied access to political power, the critique of state power initially took shape as a moral critique informed by the universal postulates of natural law. This universality stood in stark contrast to the concentration of political power in state institutions:

> Completely excluded from politics, the men of society were forced to meet in 'apolitical' places: on the stock exchange or in coffee houses, or in the academies where new fields of research were opening up without directly threatening the political/eccesiastical authority of the Sorbonne, or in the clubs where they had no recognised right to speak but spoke instead of the ruling powers, or in the salons, in which spirit could flourish untrammelled by the official rules which prevailed in the chancelleries, or in the libraries and literary societies, in which art and science rather than state politics were pursued. Thus the institutions of the new society grew under the cover of the Absolutist state. Their tasks, whether promoted by the state or not, were 'social', and constituted a parallel set of institutions.[6]

Koselleck's reference to the stock exchange alludes amongst other things to the belief that despite reservations about the political implications of the end of the household economy expressed by Rousseau and Ferguson, commerce seemed to be a better alternative to war. But if putting an end to religious conflict seemed to legitimise absolutist state power, Enlightenment thought challenged the Absolutist state's right to dominate the rest of society as the price worth paying for peace. The Enlightenment critique of Absolutism thus developed both as a demand for transparency against state secrecy and as a clear rejection of Machiavelli in favour of the complementarity of politics and morality. The demand for transparency and the insistence on the mutually reinforcing pursuits of morality and politics is most clearly discernible in the works of Rousseau and Kant.

---

[6] Koselleck, Kritik und Krise, p. 53. With the obvious exception of the stock exchange, Koselleck's depiction of this period in France is in some ways suggestive of conditions obtaining in Eastern Europe in the period following the Prague Spring and leading up to the 'Velvet Revolutions' of 1989.

In marked contrast to the justification of state sovereignty by the defenders of Absolutism, Rousseau conceives of the dependence of each on all and all on each as the basis of popular sovereignty and political freedom. Thus he supports the idea that mutual dependence requires absolute transparency between individual wills to each other. Democratic politics depends vitally on the moral imperative that secrets and organised partial wills can not undermine transparency; otherwise, Rousseau insists, the General Will cannot emerge. In his usage, the General Will contains a truth content beyond the sum of individual wills; while the latter can at times yield erroneous decisions, the former is always right. Thus the General Will is not the mere result of the individual's decision to renounce violence in return for legal provision that violence must not be done to the individual – it is much more than the notion of the government of laws rather than just the opinions and privileges of men suggested by the term Rechtstaat. Instead, the implication of Rousseau's argument is that popular sovereignty presupposes the unity of morality and politics that makes democracy possible and the state legitimate. As such, the emergence from the state of nature to forge the fictive social contract making all subsequent contracts valid can not be derived from logic or actual political experience. It rests on an anthropologically based conception of a universal human political being whose autonomy is inseparable from the autonomy of other members of the political community. Rousseau concludes that it is possible for each individual to enter the political community and remain as free as they were before joining. Indeed, this individual is now freer due to the moral education one only receives as a citizen.[7]

Kant agrees with Rousseau's ideas on the unity of morality and politics and is also convinced that universally valid moral principles can be derived for all rational and autonomous individual wills. These beliefs inform Kant's implicit critique of Absolutism and his insistence that political power be transparent to a critical public. In the preface to the 1788 edition of his *Critique of Practical Reason* he confidently declares that:

> Ours is the age of critique, to which everything must be subjected. Religion and legislation may wish to avoid this by

[7] Jean-Jacques Rousseau, *Du contrat social* (*The Social Contract*), Paris: Éditions Garnier frères, 1960, p. 243 (start of chapter 6); Claude Gautier, *L'invention de la société civile*, Paris: PUF, 1993, p. 276; Koselleck, *Kritik und Krise*, pp. 135–6.

virtue of their holiness and regality. But in so doing they bring justified suspicion upon themselves, and must forego any claims to the respect that reason concedes to only those that can pass the test of free and open examination.[8]

Kant develops his ideas on the complementarity of morals and politics in his conception of the public sphere (*Publizität*), with which he hopes to refute Hobbes's principle that authority rather than truth is the source of law. Kant argues that practical reason yields general principles according to which the moral autonomy of individuals can be reconciled with the political necessity of binding all individuals as a collectivity within a just legal order. Just as in Rousseau's formulation, individual wills can join to form a collective will, without this process resulting in an encroachment upon individual freedom. Kant is committed to the ideal that the sphere of morally autonomous individuals can be linked to the political community of legal citizens through the mediation process achieved by public debate. Anticipating Jürgen Habermas's theory of communicative action, Kant insists that although it is extremely difficult for an individual to transcend their state of ignorance by themselves, a *critical public* can do just this by openly exchanging views and opinions.[9]

Two principles inform Kant's idea of a critical public mediating between morally autonomous individuals and the political sphere: (1) that the individuals comprising that public are endowed with a rational will independent of all empirically existing institutions and individual experience; and (2) that critical reasoning and exchange of information and opinion can only take place in the realm of freedom, i.e., not in the workplace, scientific laboratory, or other contexts where a chain of command is more apposite than an assembly of equals. Thus to the extent that Kant quite openly excludes women, children and salaried workers from

---

[8] Immanuel Kant, *Kritik der praktischen Vernunft* (*Critique of Practical Reason*), quoted in Koselleck, Kritik und Krise, p. 101.

[9] Immanuel Kant, 'Was heisst Aufklärung?', in *Schriften zur Anthropologie, Geschichtsphilosophie, Politik und Pädagogik*, I, Frankfurt: Suhrkamp, 1977, p. 54: 'It is thus difficult for each individual to emerge out of his almost natural state of immaturity . . . But that a public can become enlightened (*sich selbst aufkläre*) is, on the other hand, possible. In fact, when this public is given the necessary freedom it is almost inevitable' (my emphases). Hans Reiss has edited a vey good collection of Kant's political writings in English which includes the essays on 'Enlightenment' and 'Perpetual Peace'. See Hans Reiss (ed.), *Kant: Political Writings*, Cambridge: CUP, 1970.

the public sphere and political participation because of their lack of economic independence, his view of politics is in some respects 'classical' in the Greek sense.[10] Though the authority of experts should not be challenged in their respective fields, all economically autonomous citizens can assemble on an equal basis in the public sphere where they mutually enlighten each other. In the first instance the expert makes private use of his reason and is an unquestioned authority; in the second he speaks to the world as an equal among equals.[11]

Fundamental to Kant's view of *Publizität* as the basis for mediation between the private sphere of morally autonomous individuals and the political sphere (or civil society – civil society and state were synonymous until Hegel[12]) is his insistence, rooted in natural law, on the priority of the private sphere as constitutive of the public sphere. This corresponds to his distinction between morality and legality, and his simultaneously held conviction that morally autonomous wills exist prior to individual experience of life and the binding contractual association which brings civil society into existence. Thus like other natural law theorists, Kant deploys a version of the state of nature argument to explain the political sovereignty of the polity. But since for him morally autonomous individuals exist prior to the formation of civil society, it is quite possible to conceive of moral politicians but not

[10] At the same time, however, he stresses the necessity to mediate between moral individuals and the state. In so doing he distinguishes his position from both the theorists of absolutism like Bodin and Hobbes and the Machiavellian tradition of clasical republicanism, without retreating to Locke's defence of merely negative liberty. Kant, 'Was heisst Aufklärung?', p. 55.

[11] Kant, 'Was heisst Aufklärung?', p. 57.

[12] Norberto Bobbio, 'Gramsci and the Concept of Civil Society', in John Keane (ed.), *Civil Society and the State*, London: Verso, pp. 73–100. Bobbio traces the evolution in thinking about the state from the social contract distinction between the state of nature and civil society to the Hegelian triad of family, civil society and state which Marx and then Gramsci take up in their political writings.

[13] Immanuel Kant, 'Zum ewigen Frieden' ('Perpetual Peace'), in *Schriften zur Anthropologie*, pp. 243–4: 'There is thus no objective (i.e. theoretical) conflict between morality and politics. In subjective terms on the other hand (thanks to the self-seeking tendencies of men which, however, because they are not based on rational maxims cannot be termed praxis) it does exist and might always remain ... True politics (*die wahre Politik*) cannot take a single step without having honoured morality. If politics is indeed a difficult art, the unity of morality and politics is not an art in any sense' (my translation). Kant's distinction

necessarily, on the contrary, of the existence of political moralists.[13] The right to property, marriage, and family is a *natural* right deducible from practical reason. The origins of civil society, by contrast, by which Kant means the state, have to be traced to the *fictitious* moment when the state of nature is abandoned in order to form civil society. Kant concedes that philosophically this moment is a (necessary) construction of practical reason, and in actual historical terms always a moment of the violent imposition of a new political order. Thus while Kant sets up an opposition between morality and legality, within the terms set out in his political thought morally autonomous individuals need civil society to protect their natural rights, and they are only free to the extent that they continously assemble as a critical public mediating between a private sphere of natural rights and the ultimately violently founded political authority which legally guarantees those rights. It is in this context that Kant's theory of *Publizität* must be considered an important precursor to subsequent theories of civil society and the public sphere which view speech and action as crucial for the functioning of democracy.[14]

Kant makes clear that all actions that can not be reconciled with the principle of free, open public discussion can not be reconciled with the principle of *Publizität*. He insists on the need to mediate between the truths of morality and ethics (*Tugendlehre*, or theory of virtue) and the legal functioning of politics (*Rechtslehre*, or theory of law). The potentially radical implications of this position which Kant does not fully develop lie in the intimate relationship he posits between the validity of a moral maxim or a law and its reception by a critical public:

> The maxim which cannot be said aloud, without resulting in the immediate frustration of my aim, that is, as something which must be kept secret in order to succeed and to which I cannot openly commit myself without inevitably provoking the resistance of all against my position, can stem from nothing other than the fact that it offends all into resistance against me

between the objective basis of morality and the art of politics is important here and is central to Hegel's critique of Kant.

[14] Kant, 'Zum ewigen Frieden', p. 231, and 'Über den Gemeinspruch: Das mag in der Theorie richtig sein, aber taugt nicht in der Praxis', in *Schriften zur Anthropologie*, pp. 145–51; Habermas, *Strukturwandel der Öffentlichkeit*, p. 190; Otfried Höffe, *Immanuel Kant*, Munich: C. Beck, 1992, pp. 223–5.

because of its universal (that is to say a *priori*) unjustness which
threatens everyone.[15]

This postulate also informs Kant's notion that violent civil disobedience is never justified – only public discussion can be used to
mediate between the natural rights (private) of individuals and
the positive laws (public) enacted by a state tracing its sovereignty to the fictional original contract. He argues that it would
be absurd and ultimately self-defeating to declare one's intentions
to overthrow the state, and in any case such action would violate
the principle that one should never have to hide one's position
from others. Kant's position would appear to enjoin members of
the reasoning public to 'suffer in non-silence' while the sovereign
state continues to enjoy a monopoly on authority and force. Kant
of course sees this as a problem insofar as it suggests that his
proposal for mediating between the demands of morality and
legality seems to founder on the reality of state power. As a tentative response to this problem, he proposes that all maxims
resulting from the deliberations of the critical public should be in
accordance with law: the indispensable task of political action is,
after all, the necessity of harmonising the at times conflicting
projects of individual wills under a single authority acceptable to
all. By employing the word 'task' rather than 'duty' or 'law', Kant
is in effect granting that there is always likely to be a discrepancy
between the claims of authority, on the one hand, and the
freedom of the critical public, on the other, that does not admit of
a definitive theoretical solution. But if the claims of the public can
only be redeemed through *Publizität*, and if these claims acquire
universal validity through discussion, they then attain a discursive truth content making a change in the law a moral imperative.
Kant seems to hope that over time, *Publizität* would eventually
make the contrasting claims between morality and politics virtually non-existent. Discussion in the public sphere would thus
eventually disprove Hobbes's claim that authority and not truth
is the source of law, and authority would in turn acquire a moral

---

[15] Kant, 'Zum ewigen Frieden', p. 241. Thus on the same page Kant maintains that the principle of *Publizität* is both ethical and legal: '*nicht bloss als
ethisch (zur Tugendlehre gehörig) sondern auch juridisch (das Recht der Menschen
angehend)*'. Here there are strong parallels between Kant and Vaclav Havel's
'notion of living in truth', which became a cornerstone of Czech dissident action
in civil society contributing to the 'Velvet Revolution' of 1989–90.

and ethical status that it does not have under various forms of
state authoritarianism.[16]

Hegel and Marx on civil society

In *The Philosophy of Right* (1821) Hegel argues that the state of
nature is an abstraction, and that the movement of objective spirit
(*Geist*) through human institutions can be analysed in the
moments of the family, civil society and the state. Following his
reading of the Scottish Enlightenment thinkers and the econo-
mists David Ricardo and J.B. Say, Hegel comes to the conclusion
that Kant's notion of *Publizität* needs substantial revision. By the
time of his later political writings, Hegel has a far more negative
assessment of the critical public which Kant thinks can mediate
between morality and politics. Thus in *The Philosophy of Right*,
Hegel substitutes the idea of *Publizität* with the idea of 'public
opinion'. This substitution registers and distils socio-economic
changes in European society at the level of political theory which
to Hegel seemed to cast major doubt on the viability of Kant's
political philosophy. Whereas Kant employs the distinction
between our natural rights in the state of nature and our public
rights furnished by civil society, Hegel argues that the entire state
of nature idea with its corresponding notion of the (admittedly
fictional) contractual basis of the state has to be abandoned. Hegel
believes that Kant's political philosophy corresponded to a period
in which the economic reproduction of society could still be
considered a private activity which occurred within well-defined
boundaries. For Hegel, Kant's reasoning suggested that although
it was true that the economy had broken the boundaries of the
family, economic growth and development were still largely a
matter of land ownership (although he of course admitted that
professionals and intellectuals without land were independent
because of their knowledge). Hegel's reading of Smith, Ferguson,
Hume, Ricardo and Say convinced him that this period was now
over and that the economy had assumed a breadth hitherto
unknown in Europe which burst previous restrictions on
economic forces asunder. This expansion of economic forces had
completely changed the notion of the private sphere and civil

---

[16] Kant, 'Zum ewigen Frieden', pp. 250–1.

society, and challenged the integrity of the state in unprecedented ways.[17] While it was previously possible to subsume the economy under the category of the private and identify the civil sphere as the state, Hegel's political philosophy registers the expansion of the economy in a period where it comes to include and even dominate civil society. Thus for Hegel civil society, which was once synonymous with the state and excluded the economy, now includes the economy, while the state emerges as a separate political sphere. Meanwhile the family, which was increasingly deprived of its economic foundations, is relegated to what is left of the by now emaciated private sphere.[18]

The considerable reduction of the private sphere to family life corresponds to a tremendous expansion of the intermediate sphere of civil society. In marked contrast to the formulation in Kant's theory, however, Hegel's civil sphere is no longer in any position either to act as an assembled public in dialogue with the state, or to have a decisive impact on the formulation of law. Hegel perceives that the expansion of the economic forces of society reduces the scope of any critical public to the much more passive idea of public opinion. For Hegel, however, public opinion does not even manage to find a proper place within civil society alongside the 'system of needs' (the economy), the administration of justice, or the police and corporations. Although it is part of civil society insofar as it emanates from the representative bodies assigned to the business class, agricultural class and universal class of civil servants, for Hegel public opinion cannot in any way be mistaken with the Kantian idea of a critical public acting as a potential control on state power or source of ethical input for the political system. On the contrary, within the relatively small space consecrated to the subject in the pages of *The*

---

[17] Thus *The Philosophy of Right* provides a theoretical version of the Prussian reforms designed to allow the German bourgeoisie a certain degree of economic liberty while at the same time ensuring that ultimate power lay with the state. For the historicalbackground to these reforms see Reinhart Koselleck, *Preußen zwischen Reform und Revolution: allgemeines Landrecht, Verwaltung und soziale Bewegung von 1791 bis 1848 (Prussia Between Reform and Revolution)*, Stuttgart: Ernst Klett, 1967, and Jonathan Spencer, 'State and Civil Society in Prussia: Thoughts on a New Edition of Reinhart Koselleck's *Preußen zwischen Reform und Revolution*', *The Journal of Modern History*, March–December 1985, pp. 284–9.

[18] G.W.F. Hegel, *Grundlinien der Philosophie des Rechts* (2nd edn), Frankfurt: Suhrkamp, 1989, paragraph 257, pp. 398–9.

Philosophy of Right, public opinion fulfils the function of integrating dissent from above by the state.[19]

Hegel is convinced that Kant falsely poses the question of how politics and morals could be united, since for Hegel they are distinct moments of ethical life in its totality which emerge in the movement of objective spirit. Moreover, and in many ways anticipating Marx, Hegel argues that civil society is far too riven by economic competition and alienation for there to be any *Publizität* in Kant's sense. This situation was to some extent offset by the existence of corporate bodies in civil society, which gave individuals the chance to participate in important kinds of collective decision-making. These corporate bodies do indeed play an important role in the *The Philosophy of Right*, as they are the 'ethical root' of the state within civil society. However, this in no way alters Hegel's view that only the state can act as the 'reality of the ethical idea'. The good of individuals and the good of the state are separate things; the state has its own 'concrete existence' that does not depend on the maxims informing moral individual behaviour.[20] In paragraph 257 of *The Philosophy of Right* Hegel warns that:

> If the state is confused with civil society, and if its specific end is laid down as the security of property and personal freedom, then the *interest of individuals as such* becomes the ultimate end of their association, and it follows that membership in the state is something optional. But the state's relation to the individual is quite different from this. Since the state is mind objectified, it is only as one of its members that the individual himself has objectivity, genuine individuality and an ethical life (*Sittlichkeit*). *Unity* as such is the true content and aim of the individual, whose ultimate purpose is to lead a universal life (*allgemeines Leben*).[21]

Thus Hegel insists that the security of property and personal freedom are matters related to what he refers to as abstract right and the administration of justice (both in civil society), but they cannot be the basis of the state. The state is the reality or actuality

---

[19] Hegel, *Grundlinien*, paragraph 315, pp. 482–3; Habermas, *Strukturwandel der Öffentlichkeit*, pp. 198–9.

[20] Hegel, *Grundlinien*, paragraph 337, pp. 501–2; Habermas, *Strukturwandel der Öffentlichkeit*, pp. 200–1.

[21] Hegel, *Grundlinien*, paragraph 257, p. 399 (his emphases); for the Knox translation which is only slightly different see p. 156 the of T.M. Knox edition of *The Philosophy of Right*, Cambridge: CUP, 1967, p. 156.

(*Wirklichkeit*) of the ethical idea, and as such cannot be confused with a work of art or a social contract. Instead it is 'mind objectified', objective spirit, which quite simply 'exists in the world'.[22]

It is precisely this ontological defence of the integrity of the state that Ludwig Feuerbach and Marx reject and which prompts them to seek the real source of politics in our daily activity in civil society. In his critique of Hegel, Feuerbach asserts that the state must be subjected to the same humanist interpretation which he employs in his anthropological analysis of religion. In *The Essence of Christianity*, Feuerbach maintains that in religion humans project all of their potentially realisable qualities onto a being which they then worship in rituals and practices which degrade them. In the process, they prevent the actual development in themselves of those very same human qualities which they bestowed upon the other-worldly beings they create in religion. Thus God is omniscient, omnipotent, immortal, benign and forgiving, etc., while humans are weak, dumb, fearful and egotistical. In thinking this way and organising social and political life around this 'fallen' conception of humankind, humans contribute to the realisation of their own worst qualities, while God is ascribed all that is creative, strong and loving. Moving now from religion to philosophy, Feuerbach argues that Hegel projects onto the state all the qualities needed to make modern society democratic, harmonious, solidaristic and cohesive, when in fact these are the characteristics of people living and working together in civil society. For Feuerbach the fact that life in civil society is not always a harmonious process requires creative intervention in the form of new values and institutions. Hence the move from religion to philosophy is not enough: the realisation of a truly human world would have to make the further step to politics.[23]

Feuerbach struggles with the Kantian notion that since everyone's experience of life is different, one can only derive moral precepts from a principle prior to experience and making experi-

---

[22] Hegel, *Grundlinien*, paragraph 258 ('*Der Staat ist kein Kunstwerk, er steht in der Welt*'), p. 404.
[23] Ludwig Feuerbach, *Das Wesen des Christentums* (*The Essence of Christianity*, 2nd edn), Berlin: Akademie Verlag, 1984, pp. 45–74; Karl Marx, 'Kritik des Hegelschen Staatsrechts (Critique of Hegel's Theory of the State)', in Eike Henning, Joachim Hirsch, Hemut Reichelt and Gert Schäfer (eds), *Karl Marx, Friedrich Engels: Staatstheorie*, Frankfurt: Ullstein, 1974, p. 72.

ence itself possible, which for Kant is the rational will. Kant hopes
that if political life is decisively shaped by the maxims resulting
from the deliberations of the publicly assembled ensemble of rational wills, then it will indeed be possible to harmonise the projects
of individual wills under a single authority in accordance with the
demands of a universal morality. In response, Feuerbach radi-
calises the idea of *Publizität* as a means of mediating the truths of
morality with the necessity to adjudicate conflicts (politics). He
does this by stripping *Publizität* of the preconditions which restrict
Kant's public sphere to property-owning adult males. Feuerbach
approvingly cites a letter Goethe sent to Schiller, in which Goethe
says that 'only united *people*' (my emphasis) can know nature, and
'only united *people*' (my emphasis) love what is human. Feuerbach
seeks to follow Goethe in stripping away the preconditions of what
counts as universal (i.e., something prior to experience), and
stresses the many-sidedness of experience captured in Goethe's
usage of the term 'people' against the far more restricted experien-
tial sphere of the rational will. Feuerbach thus argues for making
experience itself the basis of the universality of the human species
(*Gattung*) regardless of gender, property and age, and he makes
this far broader conception of universality the basis of his conception of political democracy. In 'The Critique of Hegel's
Philosophy', Feuerbach suggests that in the communication of one
person's experience to the listening other, human language mediates diverse subjectivities without the necessity of abstractions like
the trancendental ego or absolute spirit. In this way a community
of equals with diverse subjectivities can collectively decide their
affairs.[24]

Feuerbach argues further that Hegel's idealist philosophy is
basically a logically-argued form of theology framed in philosophical terms. Just as the starting point of theology is a transcendent
God whose existence precedes human existence, Hegel separates
thought from humans and reduces humans to emanations of
thought. Hegel's absolute spirit thus exists prior to its earthly,
phenomenological manifestations in art, religion and philosophy,
while his objective spirit exists prior to its phenomenological manifestations such as the family, state and civil society. The Hegelian
system thus manages to alienate the essence of nature from nature

[24] Ludwig Feuerbach, 'Kritik der Hegelschen Philosophie' (1839), in
Philosophische Kritiken und Grundsätze, 1839–1846, Leipzig: Reclam, 1966, p. 35.

itself, the essence of humans from real living humans, and the essence of thought from thinking. Fundamentally important for Feuerbach's argument and its significance for society is the idea that to this extent, Hegel also separates politics as the clash of divergent interests from the state. As shown above, Hegel insists that the ends of the state cannot be confused with those of civil society. This is a consequence of Hegel's attempt to explain human institutions as concrete manifestations of an abstraction, i.e., the Idea. This meant that in practice humans could never realise themselves but only abstractions of themselves. Feuerbach thus maintains that philosophical idealism needs to be challenged by anthropological materialism. The realisation of religion thus entailed the dissolving of religion into real individuals united by the boundless love which under the rule of religion had been an attribute of God, while the realisation of democracy entailed the dissolving of the state into real universal individuals in civil society deciding how to manage their collective affairs. If idealism postulated that history, religion and the state had been subjects and humans were predicates, anthropological materialism demanded that the speaking, working, loving human individual be the subject making art, religion, history and politics. As a consequence, the state had to be understood as a human creation – a political community and a constantly evolving political project – and not as 'mind objectified'. Feuerbach concludes that when conceived as the latter, the state could inflict the same violence and torture on people that idealist philosophy did to our minds.[25]

This critique of the state as alienated political power is the focus of the young Marx's rejection of Hegel. Although he agrees with Feuerbach in principle, Marx argues that in relying on generic notions like 'species-being' and 'the people', Feuerbach does not go far enough in assailing Hegelian abstraction. What was needed was both a theoretical and empirical investigation of how the private appropriation of socially created wealth brought social classes into open conflict, thus making the state necessary. Nonetheless, Marx is convinced that Feuerbach did show how the fetishism of God in religion was closely related to the fetishism of the state in Hegel; in

[25] Ludwig Feuerbach, 'Vorläufige Thesen zur Reformation der Philosophie (Preliminary Theses for the Reformation of Philosophy)', in *Philosophische Kritiken und Grundsätze*, pp. 187–90, and 'Grunsätze der Philosophie der Zukunft' (1843), p. 231.

both cases humans project attributes of themselves onto institutions that then appropriate those energies at the expense of the humans from which they emanated. For Marx, the critique of heaven leads to the critique of life on earth. That is, the critique of religion necessarily leads to philosophy, and philosophy in turn leads to the critique of law, the state, and 'all relations' in which people are humiliated and enslaved. This critique is precisely what Marx undertakes in his early political writings of 1843–44, and especially in the *Critique of Hegel's Theory of the State, On the Jewish Question, The Holy Family* and *The Economic and Philosophical Manuscripts of 1844.*[26]

In the *Critique of Hegel's Theory of the State,* Marx acknowledges Hegel's importance in recognising the separation of the state and civil society as the hallmark of modernity. He nonetheless criticises Hegel for supposing that the modern state effectively creates political unity out of the conflicts which consume civil society. Marx was particularly struck by paragraph 308 of Hegel's *The Philosophy of Right.* Here Hegel conjures up the image of a complex and richly articulated civil society comprised of associations, communities, corporations, etc., drawing their origins from the mediaeval communes. Referring back to his own paragraph 251, Hegel is also quite willing to ascribe to these institutions an explicitly political function, even though they are active outside the state. Indeed, in *The Philosophy of Right* it is within these institutions in civil society that individuals have concrete existence and political experience. By extension, the political representation of associations, communities and corporations in public affairs has to take place on the basis of the particular interests and activities proper to those institutions.

Once again, however, Hegel dismisses the idea of a generic *Publizität* of rational wills that is not connected to some form of lived daily experience. He opposes universal malehood suffrage as a merely symbolic method of aggregating individual opinions. Marx objects that if people with concrete social, political and economic existence cannot be represented individually, then why could not *civil society itself* be the basis of politics? In asking this question Marx thinks to have the grounds to refute Hegel, for in invoking the necessity of the state, Hegel is in effect admitting that both state and civil society in their existing forms, i.e., as separately

[26] Karl Marx, 'Einleitung zur Kritik der Hegelschen Rechtsphilosophie' (1844), in Henning *et al., Staatstheorie,* pp. 101–2.

existing spheres, are expressions of alienated power. Reading Hegel alerts Marx to the marked shift that had occurred since the Middle Ages, when associations, communities, corporations and guilds did have substantial political power. At this time, however, it was what Marx calls the 'democracy of unfreedom', since public life was based on the feudal political privileges of certain individuals which were openly exercised at the expense of others. Here state and civil society were not separated. The separation of state and civil society diagnosed by Hegel marks the passing of political control of the economy under the democracy of unfreedom, to the freedom of trade from political constraints which guilds and corporations could previously impose on economic interests. Hegel attempts to show that as mind objectified, the modern state successfully assures the continued integrity of politics in ways superior to the guilds and corporations. Marx counters that in effect, trade had been liberated from politics, and politics was liberated from civil society, i.e., politics became the alienated state where all people were supposedly represented on an equal basis. Marx agrees with Hegel that real representation can only happen on the basis of what individuals are and do. He then objects that it is precisely this that cannot take place when state and civil society are separated as they are in the pages of The Philosophy of Right. Hegel may want to attack Kant's view of Publizität as abstract, atomistic, and therefore superficial, but by justifying the necessity of separating state and civil society, Hegel denies the very possibility of real democracy, i.e., a self-governing civil society where politics is integrated into existing institutions on a truly democratic basis, rather than the 'democracy of unfreedom' in new guise as the modern state.[27]

In contrast to both the 'democracy of unfreedom' and the modern state separated from civil society, Marx envisages a radical democracy of a wholly new type. He first begins arguing for such a politics by stressing the importance but crucial limitations of what he referred to as political emancipation. Marx expresses this idea in 'On the Jewish Question' as a part of his critique of religious freedom in his debate with Bruno Bauer: 'the emancipation of the state from religion is not the emancipation of real people from reli-

[27] Hegel, Grundlinien, paragraphs 308–9; Marx, 'Kritik des Hegelschen Staatsrechts', pp. 68–72; Karl Marx and Friedrich Engels, 'Die heilige Familie (The Holy Family)', ibid. Henning et al. p. 130.

gion'.[28] That is, in officially tolerating all religions the state ostensibly becomes free of religion, while people continue projecting their best qualities onto abstract, other-worldly essences. Moreover, Marx clearly sees that under pevailing capitalist social and economic institutions, the more the state becomes free and neutral, the more the citizen becomes enslaved and biased. Marx's early writings demonstrate that the state, as an expression of relations between individuals, reaches its apogee as alienated political power in the very articulation of its neutrality. In its role as mere guarantor of individual freedom to do anything that does not inflict injury on others, the state becomes the purest expression of a relation of sheer interest and egotism between people. Just as the state substantially augments its own freedom to exercise sovereign power by washing its hands of particular religions (and guarantees thereby that religion would reign amongst people), it ensures the ongoing preservation of a very specific kind of civil society which appears 'natural' and therefore eternal and unalterable to its participants. But this is in fact a civil society in which a person's possession or lack of property becomes the fullest expression of their being or the source of their exclusion.[29]

By washing its hands of any particular conception of the good, honour, etc., the modern state in conjunction with the capitalist economy acts as guarantor for a civil society based on legalised exploitation. This becomes possible when a specific version of state neutrality simultaneously protects individuals from each other, without having to uphold any specific conception of morality. For Marx, the mechanism by which this occurs is the supposed neutrality involved when one person has to sell their labour power to another in order to survive. No one is actually forced to sell their labour power to anybody else; all relations between individuals are thus constituted on the basis of freely contracting individuals protected in free exchanges by a state that has freed itself of all the particularity that had characterised feudal political relations:

> The political revolution therefore abolished the political character of civil society. It divided civil society into its most basic component parts, that is, individuals, on the one hand, and the

[28] Karl Marx, 'Zur Judenfrage (On the Jewish Question)', in Henning *et al.*, Staatstheorie, p. 84.
[29] Marx, 'Zur Judenfrage', p. 87.

material and intellectual elements which formed the lived experience and civil condition that shaped their lives, on the other ...
Political emancipation was at one and the same time the emancipation of civil society from politics or even the appearance of its having a universal content.[30]

The emancipation of civil society from politics is at the same time the emancipation of the state from the lived content of people's lives in civil society. For Marx this means above all that representation in the state bears little resemblence to the daily experience of labour as the means by which humans create themselves and actively change their world. For Marx, the inability of the labouring person to recognise themselves in the legal concept of the citizen reached an unprecedented high point in the separation of state and civil society in post-French Revolution Europe and North America. He diagnoses a parallel process taking place in civil society itself, as individuals became increasingly alienated, which, in Marx's terms, means that they become increasingly incapable of recognising their energies and creative activity in either the products they make or the wages they received in return for their labour power. Under such conditions, the ostensible neutrality of the state finds its parallel in the ostensible exchange of equivalents embodied in the labour contract; behind the first is the repression of the police and bureaucracy, while behind the second is the legalised plunder of labour by the power of capital. Marx pursues this idea at length in the *Economic and Philosophical Manuscripts of 1844*, where he sketches his theories of commodity fetishism and alienation as direct extensions of his reflections on the separation of state and civil society.[31]

In these notes of 1844 Marx explains how the energies of our labouring activity come back to us in virtually unrecognised forms as money and commodities after their conversion from use value into exchange value.[32] Over time, the transformation of productive

---

[30] Marx, 'Zur Judenfrage', pp. 91–2.

[31] Karl Marx, *Ökonomisch–philosophische Manuskripte vom Jahre 1844 (Economic and Philosophical Manuscripts of 1844)*, Leipzig: Reclam, 1988, pp. 241–2.

[32] Thus in the 1844 *Manuscripts* Marx denounces the credit system as a merely cosmetic attempt to end the power of person over person, and return power to the individuals that labour and create. Indeed, as the essence of the banking system the credit system represented an even more extreme and infamous system of power than anyone suspected. It could not in any way be confused with a genuine return (*Rückkehr*) of the individual to him or herself and thereby to their fellows.

labour into commodities for exchange rather than use places manufactured goods into a circulation process which attains a life and
power of its own when fuelled by the logic of capital accumulation.
In losing sight of the fact that we make these commodities
ourselves, we attribute to them the same divine qualities which we
confer upon the Gods of our religions. Once in circulation as
anonymous forces, commodities assume magic qualities and capacities to alter the world and relations between people. While the
state guarantees peace and democracy in political heaven,
commodities make us happy, safe and secure despite the daily hell
of exploitation and alienation at work. Relations between people
assume the form of relations between *things*, when in fact it is only
concerted human action which can secure a political space for
freedom.[33]

Thus in his early writings Marx remains largely true to the
Feuerbachian critique of religion and the state, and then proceeds
further to uncover similar processes at work in the labour process
under capitalism. These insights would soon lead Marx and Engels
to declare in *The German Ideology* that neither the state nor religion,
but civil society is the real stage of human history.[34] However, they
also admit in this slightly later work of 1845–46 that they analyse
the relationship between humanity and nature, not the relationship
between citizens or the relationship between state and civil society.
Yet the exploration of these very relations is necessarily critical to
any project of addressing the problems of fetishism, alienation and
reification, and asking the political question, what different kinds
of democracy are possible? If Marx and Engels were correct to
locate civil society as the true theatre of human history, they were
not able to outline the principles of an appropriate theory of a
specifically political form of action for a civil society emancipated
from capitalism. They could not do this, for they reasoned that the
end of religion was tied to the end of the material conditions that
gave rise to religion, while the end of politics was tied to the end of
the material relations in civil society that gave rise to politics. For
Marx and Engels it is at this point that humans would be truly free
to hunt, fish, debate, etc. The crucial flaw in this vision and its
implicit understanding of civil society is that there is no theory of

[33] Marx, *Ökonomisch–philosophische Manuskripte*, pp. 160, 228, 232, 235, 241.
[34] Karl Marx and Friedrich Engels, 'Die deutsche Ideologie (The German
Ideology)' in Henning *et al.*, *Staatstheorie*, p. 158.

the public sphere, community or recognition to bind humans in a form of association beyond the need to produce in common. Since the end of private property would mark the end of the need for the state and politics, emancipation would be realised as the emancipation of civil society from politics in its hitherto existing form (i.e., from politics conceived and practised in a naive Kantian or specious Hegelian way).[35] But apart from the fleeting remarks on the subject that Marx offers in the 1843–44 writings and the very brief sketch outlined on the basis of the Paris Commune, Marx and Engels suggest no concrete or theoretical vision of how politics might be organised in positive terms.[36]

The following chapters of this book seek precisely to fill this lacuna in the work of Marx and Engels through a redefinition of the political on the bases suggested by recent theory and practice concerned with civil society. In so doing, I will attempt to re-examine some of the problems posed by Marx and Engels, though from a very different standpoint. This will come in the form of the following argument: if the emancipation from religion is perhaps possible through the elimination of the conditions that give rise to religion, and if the emancipation from economic exploitation might be realised by changing the conditions that give rise to alienated labour, there can be no definitive emancipation from politics if there is to be freedom from political authoritarianism. It might be immediately objected: is this not simply the old republican defence of positive freedom harnessed to the slogan of civil society which has characterised post-1968 and post-1989 political discourse? It is not, because as Hegel says in The Philosophy of Right, 'civil society is the creation of the modern world': the historical reconstruction of the theory of civil society in this chapter has attempted not only to show that the political virtues of classical (and by implication Renaissance) republicanism are inappropriate for modern civil societies, but also to suggest that the latter offer a unique space for political action that the former did not know.[37]

Hegel's political philosophy shows that any unmediated rela-

---

[35] Marx and Engels, 'Die deutsche Ideologie', p. 158; Marx, Ökonomisch-philosophische Manuskripte, pp. 226–7.

[36] For a discussion of the ideas on democracy in the 1843–44 writings and the Paris Commune, see the Introduction to the author's Radical Theories.

[37] Hegel, Grundlinien, addition to paragraph 182.

tionship between citizen and *polis* of the classical Greek kind is no longer possible, and that attempts to create this kind of unity are likely to fail, as the Terror during the French Revolution suggested. A critique of Hegel picking up some of Marx's ideas but going beyond Marx might run as follows: the emergence of civil society not only signifies the historical reality of the emancipation of civil society from politics in Marx's terms, but also suggests the possibility of a future emancipation of civil society from capitalism to a new kind of politics. Classical and subsequent versions of republicanism are predicated on the explicit exclusion of most individuals from the public sphere, which meant that in these regimes, politics entailed a largely repressive dimension centred on protecting the privileges of the élite group who qualified as citizens. But the modern revolutions signify the possibility for a historically new, non-repressive and anti-authoritarian form of enacting politics. Its realisation depends on the greatest possible neutralisation of material need – made possible by an unprecedented development in the productive forces making a socialist economy an objective possibility, and the invention of correspondingly expansive political forms, such as those suggested later by the appearance of revolutionary councils in the Paris Commune, the Russian Revolution, and thereafter in the revolts of 1956 in Hungary, 1968–69 in Italy and France, and 1989 in Eastern Europe, to name only the most famous of such examples. That is, the possibility of a non-instrumental and non-authoritarian practice of politics for *all* citizens arises with the emergence of civil society and modern forms of political economy. Thus the immediate question to be addressed is, how might the elimination of material necessity be squared with the appropriate forms of politics, which is by implication to raise two questions which come up in various ways throughout the rest of this book: what is the role of the modern state in unnecessarily reifying political authoritarianism, and what other forms of democracy are possible? In order to begin to answer these questions, it is useful to analyse Weber, Schmitt and Benjamin on the modern state, and this will be the focus of chapter 2.

2

Violence and the state

All significant concepts of the modern theory of the state are secularised theological concepts.

Carl Schmitt, *Political Theology*

The famous sovereignty of political bodies has always been an illusion, which, moreover, can be maintained only by the instruments of violence, that is, with essentially non-political means. Under human conditions, which are determined by the fact that not man but men live on the earth, freedom and sovereignty are so little identical that they cannot exist simultaneously. Where men wish to be sovereign, as individuals or as groups, they must submit to the oppression of the will, be this the individual will with which I force myself, or the 'general will' of an organized group. If men wish to be free, it is precisely sovereignty they must renounce.

Hannah Arendt, 'What is Freedom?'

The last chapter sought to provide the historical background necessary for a theoretical understanding of political action in contemporary civil societies. Amongst the relevant ideas was that a reformulation of the question of how to make the public sphere and ethics (Kant) rather than merely authority (Hobbes) the basis of politics, might indicate what different kinds of democracy are possible in civil society beyond the limited forms which Hegel ascribes to corporations and other intermediate bodies. This line of questioning led further to Feuerbach's critique of Hegel and Marx's critique of Feuerbach, and it was seen that Marx finally locates civil society as the true theatre of human history. It was also demonstrated that while Marx is correct in this assessment of civil society, the deeply non-political strain in his thinking prevents him from adequately exploring the question of what different kinds of politics are possible for a self-governing, i.e., democratic civil society. By way of an analysis of Weber, Schmitt and Benjamin, this chapter seeks to demonstrate that the institutions of the modern state do not offer an adequate framework for debating this question either. As the quote above from Arendt suggests, the idea of sovereignty neither substitutes the rule of universal legal principles for the arbitrary rule of individuals, nor adequately stipulates the boundaries within which equal citizens might decide by which values and institutions they choose to live. The political history of states since the French Revolution shows that sovereignty in practice is beset with structurally authoritarian and populist tendencies which are antithetical to the idea of democracy as self-government.[1] The argument in this chapter seeks to link the populist and demagogic tendencies of the modern state to the idea and practice of sovereignty, especially when sovereignty is postulated as the only possible basis of law. It will be shown that there is an implicit authoritarianism in a conception of the political essentially rooted in power, violence and theology and that these, in turn, find their most dangerous application in the institutions of the state conceived as a sovereign body.

It will be argued further that this violent foundation can only be legitimated in plebiscitarian terms, that is, by reducing citizenship to the technical procedure of saying 'yes or no' to various party appeals. This in effect reduces citizens to the means through which the organised will of an electorally/militarily successful party comes to exert power over civil society, which in turn reduces the political action in civil society to *interests* which can be represented. The transformation of political action into the institutional structures of class compromise, i.e., of representing different material interests, is extremely difficult to avoid in the absence of the appropriate forms of socialist economy to prevent the functional subordination of all things political to the imperatives of survival. By contrast, the rise of civil society to theoretical and practical

---

[1] The political history of authoritarian statism culminating with National Socialist, fascist, Francoist and Stalinist regimes in Germany, Italy, Spain and Russia in the 1930s foreshadowed more recent instances of the abuse of sovereign power in Greece and Portugal in the 1970s and even more recent abuses in Latin America, Africa, Serbia and elsewhere.

significance in recent years indicates that there are possibilities for enacting the political which elude the logic of interest, which are at present misrepresented to the point of unrecognisability by the existing institutions of 'representative' government. These possibilities are suggested by the forms of participation to be analysed in chapters 3 to 5, which require the active presence of citizens who together constitute a space for non-determined, non-instrumental action. Thus chapters 3 to 5 examine the possibility of creating a political space of appearances for words and deeds which cannot be represented as such, but are articulated and enacted by speakers, and heard and seen by citizens. In anticipation of the argument to be developed in the course of the chapters to follow, Arendt's notion that 'not man but men live on the earth' challenges the idea that all political decision-making must culminate at the peak of a vertical chain of command (people-party-state power), and posits instead the possibility of a horizontal model of collective authority (collective self-government). Before this argument can be made, however, it must first be demonstrated that the ideas of law and the state are indeed theological when erected on the foundation of sovereignty. Weber, Schmitt and Benjamin provide the basis of this argument, and it is to their ideas on the modern state that we now turn. The exposition of their ideas is not meant as an exercise in intellectual history, but rather to show how the modern state functions in ways which are inimical to politics understood as an ongoing project and continually changing praxis, i.e., as a form of democracy. Thus the critique of the metaphysics of presence implied by the discourses and practices of sovereignty in this chapter will be followed by a phenomenology of non-foundationalist politics of action in civil society in chapters 3 to 5.[2]

Political theology or wordly politics?

Feuerbach and Marx's objections to Hegel's theory of the state analysed in chapter 1 form the background to most subsequent theorising on the state. Whereas Feuerbach and Marx reject the state as an inadequate vehicle for democracy, Max Weber concludes that the evolution of political centralisation in Western

---

[2] Carlos Castoriadis, *L'institution imaginaire de la société*, Paris: Seuil, 1975, pp. 127, 131; and pp. 354–69; Maurice Blanchot, *L'éspace littéraire*, Paris Gallimard, 1955, pp. 265, 328.

Europe and North America represented an inexorable process which we could perhaps understand, but which we were relatively powerless to change. Weber's writings on the state indicate that far from serving as the most appropriate vehicle for democratic self-government, the modern state is prone to latent authoritarianism which in times of crisis become manifest. Though Marx was not able to develop a theoretical alternative to the state, his writings on Bonapartism reveal an acute awareness of the problem of state violence. Marx also anticipates the potentially dictatorial nature of the state when he remarks in reference to the Paris Commune that 'the working class cannot lay hold of the ready-made state machinery and wield it for its own purposes'. He maintains that this is so because in conjunction with modern capitalism, neither the state nor law are expressions of a human species-being which transcend the diverse conflicts raging in civil society betweeen capitalists and workers, men and women, etc. to enact a political community of citizens equally empowered for collective self-government.

Beyond the Marxist analysis of the state's dependence on capital accumulation, the state must also be understood in terms of the discourses that legitimate state violence and other forms of domination which are possible with a wide variety of possible modes of production.[3] In his cogent analysis of legal/rational domination, Weber hints at the core of violence at the centre of the discourses that seek to provide legitimation for the state. In addition to his study of Protestantism, Weber is probably most well known for his theory of rationalisation, which forms part of his *Herrschaftssoziologie* (sociology of domination). In 'Politics as a Vocation', Weber distinguishes between 'politics' and 'the state'. He argues that the former can assume the widest conceivable variety of forms, so that politics is involved in a union's conduct of a strike, in a company's strategy for increasing its number of customers, etc. But while politics in the sense of strategic action can thus be said to form part of virtually all human activities, the state represents a very specific set of institutions with very specific means at its disposal. Since politics covers so many diverse spheres of action and can be pursued through a plethora of

---

[3] Indeed, one might even speak of an original state or *Urstaat* as Giles Deleuze and Félix Guattari, borrowing from the German word, do; this state pre-dates capitalist forms of economy. They expound their argument in *Capitalisme et schizophrénie: L'anti-Oedipe*, Paris: Éditions de Minuit, 1973, pp. 257–60.

means, Weber insists that the state is simply that set of institutions which have the monopoly on the legitimate use of physical force and violence within a given geographical territory. Weber approvingly cites Trotsky's comment at Brest-Litovsk that all states are founded on violence, and concludes that if politics is ultimately a struggle for power which can take many forms, the modern state is the result of a specifically modern and Western rationalisation process culminating in the legitimation of force through legal norms.[4]

Without ever actually acknowledging any express debt to Nietzsche, Weber came to this conclusion by way of a genealogical study of different forms of domination, of which the modern state was the most recent and perfected expression. In *The Genealogy of Morals*, Nietzsche explains that what interested him was the chain of seemingly unrelated institutions and ideas through which a concept assumes different forms of articulation over time. This had been the project first embarked upon in *Beyond Good and Evil* and continued in the *Genealogy* in the direction of the posthumous *Will to Power*. Already in the *Genealogy*, however, Nietzsche thought he had located struggle and the will to power as the originating drive beyond all subsequent manifestations of that basic drive, which acquired different guises at different junctions in the historical evolution of various cultures. In the *Genealogy* he maintains that the will to power embodied in different concepts and institutions can be discovered by conducting a path of investigation analogous to that of looking behind the terms 'good' and 'evil'. In direct opposition to Kant's notion that it is possible for all rational transcendental subjects to arrive at a set of moral truths which constitute the good in universals equally applicable to all of those subjects, Nietzsche argues that 'good' always means *conducive* to the way of life and vital instincts of a small minority. If dominant, this minority manages to impose *its* conception of the good in accordance with its vital instincts as universally good, i.e. good for all members of the society. This is the case whether or not that group is aware of its will to dominate and have its version of the good triumph over others.[5]

---

[4] Max Weber, 'Politik als Beruf' ('Politics as a Vocation'), in Johannes Winkelmann (ed.), *Gesammelte politische Schriften*, 5th edn, Tübingen: J.C.B. Mohr, 1988, pp. 505–6, and see also Weber's *Staatssoziologie*, Berlin: Duncker and Humblot, 1966, pp. 27–8. Weber's analysis of rationalisation and the relationship between law and domination can be found in English translation in Weber's *Economy and Society*.

[5] Deleuze and Guattari, *Capitalisme et schizophrénie*, pp. 224–7.

For Nietzsche this genealogy of ideas about morality is most obviously traceable in religious conceptions of good, bad, and worldly asceticism. Yet for him it is no less true of notions like the categorical imperative, law and democracy. What is significant in the modern period, however, is that whereas previous hierarchies were straightforwardly legitimated in various caste and aristocratic forms where relations of domination were more or less apparent, the age of 'democracy' ushers in a new form of minority power which has to be legitimated in the name of 'the people', or the masses. Thus in the French Revolution, the Jacobins and their supporters were able to topple the absolute monarchy in the name of equality and the 'rights of man and citizen', when in fact relations of hierarchy and domination had merely assumed a new form with the consolidation of bourgeois hegemony over feudal-aristocratic privilege. Thus unsurprisingly the Jacobins continued rather than reversed the centralisation of state power undertaken by Absolutism which, as we saw in the last chapter, reached an apogee in the period following the Treaty of Westphalia before assuming republican form in France in 1789. Unlike Marx, however, who argues that the contradiction between formally equal rights and manifest inequality has its origins in a mode of production which is condemned to crisis and eventual extinction, Nietzsche is more concerned to demonstrate that in the modern world, the vital instincts of the emerging dominators is articulated in the language of would-be 'objective' human or natural sciences: morality, ethics, economics, jurisprudence, etc. Naturally, this meant that those who disagreed with the 'truths' of science were dangerous. Fundamental to this analysis was the thesis that modern society is certainly no more democratic in terms of power sharing than any other age. Instead, a socio-political hierarchy based on the penchant for the values of leisure, luxury, privilege and honour had given way to one based on the values of worldly asceticism, utility, predictability and calculation. Those individuals deeply possessed of the later virtues (however stupid they were in Nietzsche's eyes) would henceforth exercise their will to power in the name of universal discourses like popular sovereignty and democracy.[6]

This view of modern forms of domination is clearly seen in Weber's sociological reflections on the state, law and the plebisci-

---

[6] Friedrich Nietzsche, *Zur Genealogie der Moral* (*The Genealogy of Morals*, originally published in Leipzig, 1887), Munich: Goldmann, 1983, part 2, section 12, pp. 64–5.

tary tendencies of parliamentary democracy in the epoch of mass parties. He distinguishes between what he refers to as three 'pure' forms of domination, which represent three ideal types or categories that in some form tend to be present in all social formations where power is legitimated. Though analytically distinct, Weber maintains that mixed forms normally appear in actual historical circumstances. In all cases, however, he argues that forms of domination changed primarily in terms of how they were understood and accepted by the dominated. Thus Weber follows Nietzsche, for whom power and struggle are constants throughout history, and opposes Kant, for whom history demonstrates the general tendency of the species towards greater rationality and individual autonomy. In remaining more faithful to Nietzsche than Kant, Weber would have been extremely reluctant to pronounce upon the relative merits of different social formations in terms of better/worse or more/less democratic. Instead, Weber clearly saw that the rationalisation process culminating in the civilisation of contract, calculation, predictable conditions of exchange, and instrumental rationality brought entirely new threats to human freedom on an unprecedented scale. To this extent, he incorporates both Nietzsche and the ideas of the sociologist Georg Simmel on capitalism and money to analyse the forms of rationality embodied in modern law and economic organisation. Proceeding in a genealogical vein, Weber sees that the critical dimension of reason conceived of as autonomy by Kant and other Enlightenment thinkers was gradually replaced by a very particular form of rationality linked to the logic of capital during the course of the nineteenth century. The resulting form of rationality could no longer effectively be linked to the Enlightenment project of creating the material and cultural bases for human emancipation from physical need and socio-political alienation as a precondition for creative individual development. Rather, in clear anticipation of the Frankfurt School theorists and Michel Foucault, Weber demonstrates that reason had been 'decoupled' from critique. If during the Enlightenment it was possible to enlist reason in the battle against religion, mythology and other forms of ideology in the name of freedom and autonomy, by the time of Weber's writing this was no longer the case. As a result, no rational justification of norms, values or possible alternative forms of political organisation was possible; rationality became synonymous with efficiency and interest, while autonomy became synonymous with security. The emergence of a closed system of instrumental and administrative rationality seemed to follow as an inexorable consequence.[7]

In developing his sociology of domination, Weber distinguishes between (1) charismatic, (2) traditional and (3) rational/legal forms of legitimation. The legitimation of charismatic domination is based on the personal aura of a leader whose legitimacy resides in some special power that separates him or her from the rest of society and confers the right to make important decisions upon that person. Thus prophets and seers, or poets like Homer, wield legitimate power because of their unique ability to explain the origins and future direction of a society by virtue of extraordinary poetic or magical talents. Traditional domination is invested in those groups or individuals who ensure continuity between past and present on the basis of custom or accumulated cultural heritage, i.e., as in the notion of the rule of the royal families or elders who were seen to embody the sanctity of tradition and precedent. Finally, rational/legal domination is based on formal rules and codes which provide to the greatest extent possible for uniform criteria to make decisions binding on all legal subjects regardless of the particularities of their individual circumstances. It is this third form of authority which is of particular interest for the critique of state violence in this chapter.[8]

Two crucial points emerge from Weber's analysis: (1) that domination is not eradicated over time but rather changes form, and (2) that this process of increasingly rationalised forms of domination culminates in the monopoly of legitimate force within a given territory in the institutions of the modern state. In the last chapter it is argued that this development was accompanied by the gradual and finally complete erosion of any notion of differentiated rights or privileges based on membership in pre-state organisations like guilds, churches or other civic associations. All people were eventually forced to be members of the same mass electorate under the principle of majority rule. The analysis of Rousseau in chapter 2

[7] Max Weber, *Soziologische Grundbegriffe*, Tübingen: J.C.B. Mohr, 1960, pp. 44–5; Georg Simmel, *Die Philosophie des Geldes* (*The Philosophy of Money*, 1900), Frankfurt: Suhrkamp, 1989, part 4; Raymond Morrow, 'Mannheim and the Early Frankfurt School', in Ashe Horowitz and Terry Maley (eds), *The Barbarism of Reason: Max Weber and the Twilight of Enlightenment*, Toronto: University of Toronto Press, 1994, pp. 183–4.

[8] Weber, *Staatssoziologie*, pp. 99–110.

attempts to show that the notion of majority rule can only work as a functioning political principle if there is a more fundamental principle to bind minorities to the outcomes of elections and decision-making processes taken by majorities. Within the populist framework of a general will or some other such metaphysics of higher unity, this principle is almost inevitably going to be some version of sovereignty. Moreover, where politics is seen as a function of interests and interest aggregation and representation, the logic of sovereignty as the means for overcoming a division in interests is more than likely articulated in the language of indivisible unity and practised as suppression of plurality.[9]

The idea of sovereignty in its various manifestations is usually traceable to the (in temporal terms, fictional) founding of the political community. This moment is often represented as the single and irrevocable decision in which all members of society agree upon the decision to leave the state of nature. This decision binds them to accept all subsequent political decisions regardless of their outcomes. The supposed participation and re-living of this founding act – recreated in various forms of ideological celebrations of state – then becomes the legitimating discourse invoked to reconcile, by force if need be, minorities to majority decisions. Hobbes, Rousseau, Kant and others recognise the founding moment legitimating subsequent use of legitimate force as a necessary fiction, i.e., as a necessary 'as if' that makes the law binding and the state sovereign above the electoral fluctuations of minorities and majorities. It is, so to speak, the contract to render all future contracts valid. Unlike the absolute monarchies making sure that the warring religious and aristocratic factions within a given territory did not destroy each other, more modern rational/legal domination must secure leadership changes through an electoral mechanism, which in historical terms evolved in a process in which restrictions on voting were gradually eliminated during the period spanning the 1848 revolutions until World War I (or later in countries like France and Italy). These changes in the direction of a mass electorate bring with them the danger of what Weber calls Caesarism, which combines the most insidious characteristics of charismatic and legal/rational forms of domination at one and the same time. In clear anticipation of the populist demagogy characterising Weimar and then National Socialist Germany, Weber

9 Deleuze and Guattari, *Capitalisme et schizophrénie*, pp. 300–1.

argues that the modern state needs *both* of these forms of legitimation in order to guarantee propitious conditions for capitalist
growth and accumulation (rational/legal), on the one hand, and
leadership based on a direct appeal to the largely powerless masses
(charismatic), on the other.[10]

Insofar as it is based on some notion beyond majorities and
minorities, the phenomenon of Caesarism is directly related to the
concept of sovereignty. In times of crisis, when the origins and
future life of the state are in question, a charismatic figure could
appeal above minorities and majorities to some unifying principle
ultimately beyond normal politics, i.e., principles such as nation,
race or security of the state. Recourse to such manoeuvres is most
obvious in instances of authoritarian regimes like those of Hitler
and Mussolini, which might appear to be exceptional cases.
Weber's analysis shows that the exception proves the rule: because
crises of government can result in the suspension of normal major-
ity/minority politics at any time, there has to be some legally
guaranteed mechanism to go beyond the normal functioning of the
law, back to the violent founding moment of sovereignty. In relatively trouble-free times, the law can ensure the protection of
individual and minority rights. In moments when the suspension
of these rights occurs, however, the incoherence of the idea of
sovereign law as a neutral or impartial mechanism of adjudicating
conflict becomes evident. Equality of citizenship and equal protection under the law can then abruptly give way to wiretapping,
searching on suspicion and the suspension of constitutionally
'guaranteed' rights. For now the point to bear in mind is that the
Caesarist figure is a stark reminder that it is people and not laws
that govern, however much domination in the age of mass parties
appears to be based on universally valid rational and legal norms.
Characteristic of Caesarism is the combination of the first and third
of Weber's ideal types of domination. Weber identifies this combination in the person of the demagogue, who relies on both
charisma and legal authority to incarnate the principle of sovereignty in a crisis situation. Rather than applying merely to the
obvious cases of German and Italian Fascism, Weber's insights can
be usefully invoked to analyse the political tactics of De Gaulle,
Thatcher and other leaders operating under so-called 'normal' situ-

[10] Weber, *Staatssoziologie*, pp. 74–5.

ations.[11] Thus in developing these ideas in a decidedly authoritarian direction, Carl Schmitt was merely drawing out and affirming the full implications of Weber's analysis, as we shall see below.[12]

Put in context, Weber's analysis of the crisis in the political legitimacy of the state pointed to a more general crisis in modern Western culture related to the loss of meaning which accompanied the steady rationalisation of all areas of life. This rationalisation created a schism within purposive action between issues of value rationality like freedom and autonomy, on the one hand, and issues concerning instrumental rationality like technical progress and economic growth, on the other (*Wert/Zweck Rationalität*). The general trend towards the differentiation of spheres of social life according to different rationalities finds its institutional expression in the increasing separation of the tools of production from the workers who used them, the transfer of citizen responsibility for defence to the full-time staff of the professional army, the separation of the means of administration from the elected representatives of the public, etc. This later phenomenon in particular had reached an acute stage of development. Rather than being a means of giving expression to the views of the various groups comprising civil society on questions of solidarity, freedom and autonomy, parliament had to content itself with controlling executive power in key areas of public administration. This reflected a shift in the electorate and the dramatic transformation of the public sphere.[13]

[11] Numerous examples could be cited in this context, such as the harassment of Martin Luther King and other outspoken defenders of peace and negotiation in the American civil rights movement in the 1960s, the establishment of the GLADIO network of state terrorism across Europe during the Cold War, and measures taken during the 1984–85 miners' strike which resulted in large-scale intimidation and harassment of wide sectors of British society. Of course this is only the tip of an iceberg of innumerable examples. The massive deployment of state security forces in the fight against terrorism in Italy and Germany in the 1970s also provoked a series of rights abuses which are only now beginning to come to light, and which, in the Italian case, now strongly suggest collaboration between the mafia and the Christian Democrats, the then leading party of the ruling coalition.

[12] Weber, *Staatssoziologie*, pp. 27–9.

[13] As is well known, the uneasy tension between forms of bourgeois private law protecting the interests of private property and capital, on the one hand, and the social democratic redistributive provisions enshrined in the Weimar constitution, on the other, completely undermined the German Reichstag during that period, and helped prepare the political terrain for the Caesarist solution that was in the offing. See Carl Schmitt, *Die geistesgeschichtliche Lage des heutigen Parlamentarismus*, 8th edn (*The Crisis of Parliamentary Democracy*, 1923) Berlin: Duncker & Humblot, 1996.

Prior to the era of mass parties, political opinion was articulated by political clubs largely comprised of the nobility and educated élites of the bourgeoisie. For these people, politics was a part-time activity performed in addition to whatever economic or cultural interests this strata of Western European society cultivated. The progressive extension of the franchise resulted in the professionalisation of these clubs and their evolution towards our modern mass parties. Politics increasingly became a full-time profession for a much smaller core of people who, unlike their predecessors, relied on their salaries as a condition for a political career. If the public sphere had ever in reality been a mediating space between moral and political imperatives, it was now transformed from a forum for the exchange of ideas and opinions of a rather select group into an arena for the electoral competition of mass parties whose almost exclusive function was to attract votes. The competition for votes was a drive for control of the executive and its increasingly growing number of paid offices, which could provide a stable career and source of income for the party activist, who was no longer the independently wealthy member of the gentry, urban bourgeoisie or landed aristocracy. While this process was most accelerated in the United States where the party 'Boss' represented a direct analogy to the boss of an economically competitive firm, Weber argued that the same general trend was in evidence across Europe.[14]

The transformation of the political clubs which attempted to control executive power into mass electoral machines resulted in the increased attenuation of possible mediation between value and instrumental rationality. This was a direct consequence of the fact that the parties had abandoned even the pretence of transmitting moral and value concerns. They had no other real goal than the conquest of office, i.e., power, such that political success began to look more and more like a version of economic success mediated through the institution of plebiscitary elections. If economic activity is by its very nature dominated by largely non-moral, instrumental criteria, the assimilation of politics to modes of economic conduct has obvious implications: the marginalisation of value-related questions from the public sphere and the conflation of questions about freedom and autonomy with issues related to

[14] Weber, *Staatssoziologie*, pp. 57–9.

economic growth and technical progress. Whereas the former has to do with the political space for a very specific kind of action and possible relations between people within that space, the latter within a capitalist economy is centrally concerned with the relations between people and things and the accumulation of commodities over time. In brief anticipation of the discussion in the next chapter, a public sphere for freedom and autonomy in a political sense can best be negotiated by subjects with relatively few time constraints. By contrast, technical questions require technical solutions bound by temporal considerations about the satisfaction of material necessities. Thus at the most basic level we can negotiate what kinds of freedom and forms of democracy are posssible and desirable, whereas food and shelter must not be negotiated but simply provided. The economy is not a sphere for freedom or autonomy, though it is vital in making these possible. The question of the autonomy of the political conceived in terms of a space for action rendering certain kinds of human relations possible will be at the centre of chapters 3 to 5. The important point for the moment is that the space of the political is not to be confused with the time of the commodity, which is a point I will return to towards the end of this chapter. In the context of the present discussion, Weber's writings on law and rational/legal domination are fundamental for an understanding of how the modern state attempts to transform civil society, starting with the public sphere, into legitimation fodder for sovereign power.

Weber's writings are of great interest here because they attest to the process in which the increasingly difficult distinction between value and instrumental rationality was accompanied by the structural transformation of the public sphere chronicled by Jürgen Habermas. As rationality gradually became divorced from ethics and Publizität in a Kantian sense, it became increasingly difficult to argue for a yardstick to adjudicate different value positions. Thus there inevitably arose a potential moment of irreconcilability between attenuated value positions whose validity was gauged only in terms of power measured in terms of electoral success. But since electoral succcess and power had become the only recognised standards of validity, it was clear to Weber that conflict was an omnipresent possibility. That is, with the transformation of the public sphere and the legislature into fora for negotiating material interests, questions of ethics and values had been largely shut out of political life – and with them any possible negotiable criteria with which to mediate different political positions. This was especially dangerous within an institutional framework structured in vertical terms culminating in a non-negotiable, extra-political pinnacle: plurality and the possible mediation of plural positions was attenuated with the concentration of all legitimate force in the state. If the Middle Ages represented the 'democracy of unfreedom' in political terms, it at least offered the authority of countervailing institutions like churches, guilds, rival courts, corporations, etc. to limit the power of the state. By contrast, the modern state was empowered, through popular sovereignty, to make decisions of even existential import, such as commanding citizens to be ready to die in war. Weber believed that responsible behaviour by political leaders, parties, trade unions and other institutions mediating between state and civil society could hopefully prevent conflicts of a life-and-death nature within the legal jurisdiction of the state. However, what could one do with the person who said 'here I am, I can do no other', i.e., with the person within the sphere of state jurisdiction who refuses to let themselves be outvoted in a matter of existential importance? In the face of this dilemma, he pleaded for an ethic of responsibility to temper a value-centred ethics, lest an absolutely irreconcilable clash of value positions resulted in civil war, or, what Weber's student Carl Schmitt refers to as the 'state of exception'.

Schmitt largely concurs with Weber's work on the particular features distinguishing the modern state from previous forms of political association such as the absolute monarchy or forms of the caste system in India and China. But whereas Weber defines the modern state as the institution or set of institutions which possess a monopoly on the use of legitimate force within a given territory, Schmitt asks a further question: under what circumstances can this monopoly be called into action? In the light of the manifest failure of liberalism and parliamentary democracy during Weimar, Schmitt goes beyond his Weberian point of departure in pursuing the answer. In so doing he develops his ideas on the state of exception, the friend/foe distinction, and concludes that the origins of sovereignty are ultimately theological.[15]

As was seen above, Weber believes that in contrast to the state defined as the monopoly of legitimate force within a given terri-

---

[15] Weber, 'Politik als Beruf', pp. 559–60.

tory, 'the political' is too diffuse to be defined precisely. Schmitt argues that although 'the political' is certainly diffuse, there are nonetheless moments when 'normal' politics based on clashes of interest and opinion become instances of irreconcilable antagonism. In these moments neither law, contract nor a compromise between competing social or economic interests will mediate conflict, thus making a series of executive decisions necessary: our generally politicised existence assumes crystallised form as the conflict between 'friend and enemy' (*Freund/Feind*). This idea is clearly expressed in the first sentence of *Der Begriff des Politischen* (*The Concept of the Political*) (1932): 'The idea of the state presupposes the idea of the political'.[16] Although he does not say it as such, Schmitt's analysis signals that in order to mediate conflict in a democratic-pluralist rather than a merely functionally efficient way, the modern state will have to be supplanted by completely new political institutions. This possible interpretation of Schmitt is plausible when informed by a reading of Marx's 'Zur Judenfrage' ('On the Jewish Question'): whereas the modern state can absorb ethnic and socio-cultural identities from Judaism to contemporary forms of identity politics, and while it can integrate economic interests by means of corporatist or other social democratic compromises, the state is directly challenged by the political practice of self-government in civil society suggested by action in the public sphere, political community and diverse forms of recognition. But Schmitt dismisses the possibility of a political revolution of this kind in civil society, and indicates that some form of charismatic decisionism suggested by Weber's critique of bureaucracy will have to suffice as a 'realistic' interim measure to provide the state with some measure of ethical legitimacy. Thus rather than opting for the revolutionary implications of what is an accurate analysis of modern state–civil society relations, Schmitt retains Weber's notion that modern democracy is by nature plebiscitary. For Schmitt this means that in twentieth-century political life 'the people' can merely say yes or no to various political machines, but can never actually govern, administer or even deliberate as a critical public. This creates a situation in which questions have to be posed from above in a yes/no, either/or fashion which significantly curtails the possibilities for plurality of perspective.

[16] Carl Schmitt, *Der Begriff des Politischen* (1932), Berlin: Duncker & Humblot, 1963, p. 20.

For Schmitt the reason why the people can only say yes or no and can never be self-governing – *pace* the pluralist theories of G.D.H Cole and Harold Laski which Schmitt rejects in *The Concept of the Political* – is that the omnipresent *possibility* of life-and-death conflict necessitates the empowering of some single person or institution to make a decision when the law no longer suffices to peacefully regulate social life.[17] In stark contrast to Arendt's notion that 'not man but men live on the earth', i.e., that plurality, perspectival diversity and conflict constitute the political dimension of the human condition, Schmitt maintains that the yes or no of the people is needed to authorise an end to deliberation and negotiation and an end to the state of exception (*Ausnahmezustand*). He argues that this is the only way to restore a 'normal' state of affairs where legal norms can once again settle disputes. It is in a state of exception that the legally irreconcilable positions of friend and enemy lurch from omnipresent possibility to direct visibility, which for Schmitt means that the exception is the real truth behind the usually prevailing state of affairs, i.e., that prior to law is the political antagonism between different wills to power which had only been temporarily suspended in the founding act of sovereignty. Sovereignty is thus above the law, just as the will to power is prior to the law. Legally enacted sovereignty thus becomes, in the state of exception, the authority to settle a friend/enemy clash with the death of the latter. Here the state's monopoly of the legitimate use of force within a given territory could be used to destroy an internal opponent with all the technical means at its disposal. The historical precedent of this actually happening during the period of National Socialist dictatorship suggests that Schmitt's argument was anything but speculative, and that it only reflects the

[17] To this extent Schmitt sought to politically translate Martin Heidegger's remark in *Being and Time* (1927) that 'Still higher than reality itself is possibility'. See Martin Heidegger, *Sein und Zeit* (*Being and Time*, 1927), Tübingen: Max Niemeyer, 17th edn, 1993, p. 38. Heinrich Meier notes that despite some similar elements in their thinking and in their biographies – most glaringly their participation in the initial re-organisation of German educational and political life under the National Socialists followed by their distancing themselves from the Nazi Party – it is difficult to evaluate the extent to which Heidegger and Schmitt actually exchanged ideas and influenced one another. Despite allegations of their intellectual partnership, letters indicating some such exchange have been almost impossible to find. See Heinrich Meier, *Die Lehre Carl Schmitts: Vier Kapitel zur Unterscheidung politischer Theologie und politischer Philosophie*, Stuttgart: J.B. Metzler, 1994, pp. 205–6.

cogency of his analysis. The notion of going beyond the human world of politics (in the sense intended in chapters 3 to 5 of the present book) to the theological world of the sovereign, marks the decisive step toward eschatological conceptions of conflict. Weber and Schmitt are of key importance for a theoretical understanding of the permanent state of exception in the political conflict between state and civil society. In different ways they show that this conflict can always take an eschatological turn where there are sovereign states.[18]

In answer to the question, under what conditions can the state employ its monopoly on the legitimate use of force within a given territory to annihilate an opponent, Schmitt answers that this is a necessary step every time sovereignty is fundamentally jeopardised. It is the sovereignty of the state which, after all, guarantees social harmony above the clash of interests and opinions, and it is precisely in a moment of legally irreconcilable difference between friend and enemy that sovereignty is under attack. This leads Schmitt to the conclusion that prior to law there is the 'miracle' of law, or, that the law enacted by the sovereign state has its ultimate foundations in something non-legal, and indeed, non-worldly. Thus for Schmitt the pre-political, pre-legal injunction to obey is ultimately the miraculous, other-worldly presupposition of possible worldly injunctions to obey. He clearly formulates this position in *Political Theology* by arguing that the miracle is to theology exactly that which the state of exception is to law, i.e., that it is ultimately grounded in something mysterious, inexplicable and of a divine power. What is more, Schmitt does not fail to emphasise the theological resonance of legal categories like commandment, judgement, innocence, pardon and condemnation, and he argues further in this vein that all modern

---

[18] In footnote 29 of 'Grundrechte und Grundpflichten' (an essay of 1932, in relation to the ideas of Friedrich Naumann), Schmitt argues that the norms of the state should be regarded as a kind of catechism, and that this idea is in keeping with a long line of thinking about the state that goes back to Hegel. See Carl Schmitt, 'Grundrechte und Grundpflichten', in *Verfassungsrechtliche Aufsätze aus den Jahren 1924–1954: Materialien zu einer Verfassungslehre*, Berlin: Duncker & Humblot, 1954, p. 194. Also see *Der Begriff des Politischen*, pp. 27–8, 46; *Politische Theologie: Vier Kapitel zur Lehre von der Souveränität (Political Theology I: Four Chapters on the Concept of Sovereignty)* (1922), Berlin: Duncker & Humblot, 7th edn, 1996, p. 17; Christian Graf von Krockow: *Die Entscheidung: Eine Untersuchung über Ernst Jünger, Carl Schmitt, Martin Heidegger*, Frankfurt: Campus, 1990, pp. 64–5.

theories of state sovereignty are ultimately theological in the sense that they require at some level a belief in the miraculous and other-worldly for their earthly validity.[19]

From the theology of states to the politics of civil society

On the basis of his interpretation of Weber and the history of schisms within Christianity, Schmitt sees sovereignty as the necessary price for certainty and order in a world of sectarian and political conflict.[20] But the preceding analysis of Weber and Schmitt shows that the authoritarian tendencies of the modern state can be traced to modified forms of revelationary thought which, when imposed from above on civil society, do not guarantee peace or even security, to say nothing of freedom and democracy. It can on the contrary result in the violent suppression of the political in the name of the miracle, original social contract, restoration of the purity of the social body, etc. The possibility of preventing a state of exception from resulting in this kind of catastrophe surely turns on the rejection of the yes/no framework of plebiscitary politics. Subsequent chapters in this book propose what possible alternative conceptions of the political could be practised by drawing out the theoretical implications of recent forms of action in civil society. For the present it is important to emphasise that Weber's and Schmitt's analyses indicate that both the eschatology of religion and the politics of sovereignty can be traced back to the idea of revelation as the basis of a non-negotiable supra-political concept to be invoked in an instance of sectarian conflict. The idea of authority being in the last instance a question of revelation requires absolute, and if

[19] Schmitt, *Politische Theologie*, p. 43. It might be objected that although he excludes a democratic-pluralist approach to the question of a political conflict, Schmitt actually accepts the necessity of functional efficiency with a dose of charismatic legitimacy, and even endorses such a position against more eschatological ones. While the language of technical competence and efficiency may at first sight seem more benign, it is also clear that twentieth-century forms of mass extermination required the reduction of unique individuals to the status of numerical statistics to be dealt with in an administratively 'efficient' way.

[20] This religious background to Schmitt's understanding of law, politics and the state runs through all of his writings, but is especially clear in *Römischer Katholizismus und politische Form* (*Roman Catholicism and Political Form*, first published in 1923 by Jakob Hegner), Stuttgart: Klett-Cotta, 1984, pp. 14–15.

necessary terminal, rejection of the non-believer, whose non-belief is a permanent threat that must be dealt with through a series of resolute decisions. Within this framework there can be no space for politics understood as a distinctly human activity essential for human freedom. This is because the faithful–heretic/ friend–enemy dichotomies negate the flourishing of qualities like trust, courage, judgement and other *political*, as distinct from economic, religious or technical capacities. It is true that human affairs can suddenly change and former friends can become opponents. This is precisely why a non-theological, and non-technical political praxis is necessary: the technological-theological imperative to exterminate the enemy can assume an eschatological dynamic when armed with the language of sovereignty. The mediation of human conflict in human terms requires community, recognition and other institutions and political spaces which are cultivated in concerted action in the public sphere, and which are likely to be inappropriate in the economy (where technical and functional considerations are paramount), and, more importantly from the preceding analysis, in the church or state (where belief and submission to authority are the conditions of stable hierarchies and plebiscitary forms of legitimation).

If conflict is inevitably going to arise because 'men and not man inhabit the world', and if the state has historically proven to be a dangerous institution for mediating conflict, how are antagonisms in civil society going to be dealt with in a way that precludes the state of exception and the extra-political settlement of political disputes? At first glance, one might respond that the law can fulfil this role, which raises a series of related questions. Is law possible without the state? Or can difference be mediated without law? The answer to the last question is of course yes – where there is love and trust. But love and trust express a quality about a direct relationship enacted in non-instrumental forms of communication, whereas under modern capitalist forms of ownership, law and contract express a relationship between people mediated by land and objects like commodities. This is of course most obviously true in the ownership and sale of property. Yet this is no less true of the labour contract, when someone's energy and imagination are reified into the commodity of labour power, which is then bought and sold on the labour market like any other object (although with the important difference that machines can simply be turned on and off, whereas labour power has to be disciplined and monitored). Property represents an instance of relatively straightforward disposition over land and objects, while the labour contract illustrates the transformation of the social relationship between producers into that between buyers and sellers of the saleable commodity of labour via the legal sanction of contract. In this case, contract facilitates the transformation of a relation between people into a relation between things, while law protects this relation with the sanction of financial loss, imprisonment or even violence in cases of non-compliance with the terms of the contract. In what follows it will be argue that law and contract can, within the framework established by commodity production and commodity fetishism, actually impede relationships of mutual, if also at times agonistic, recognition between people.

It has been argued that Schmitt demonstrates that the exception proves the rule, and that the state confirms rather than points beyond the omnipresent possibility of irreconcilable antagonism. Similarly, contract can be interpreted as confirmation of the legal sanction given to an act of usurpation which at some point is likely to be contested. The arbitrariness of the act of usurpation may result in acts of defiance which in turn will require the protection of the usurped land, confiscated labour-power, etc., through force. The institutionalisation of a monopoly of the legitimate use of force in the state alone obscures the fact that the legal relations embodied in the institutions of property, the labour contract, and even marriage express relations of domination between people living in civil society. This is not to say that juridical norms are reducible to property relations. It is rather to say that the concentration of legitimate force in the sovereign state suggests the creation of a legal order to protect all citizens in return for their consenting (or being forced) to renounce violence so that they can all peacefully trade, build houses, establish relationships, etc. Legitimate force and law would then seem to be concentrated in the state, while the markets for land, labour power and love acquire a quasi-'natural' status in civil society that is merely safeguarded by law. But there is in fact nothing 'natural' about these relations of domination, which is precisely why they require positive law in order to be enforced. Hence one might distinguish between violent law-creating acts and the far more subtle form of violence suggested by law-preserving acts, as Walter Benjamin does in his 'On the Critique of Violence' (1921).[21] Benjamin is close to both Schmitt and Weber in regarding rational/legal forms of authority to be forms of domination. But whereas Weber and Schmitt consider law and the state to be absolutely indispensable for mediating conflict because life is always potentially violent, Benjamin rejects the state because of what he calls its mythical foundations. To this extent Benjamin is both approving but also critical of Nietzsche, especially insofar as he rejects Nietzsche's notion of 'the eternal recurrence' of all manifestations of the human spirit in different forms. Benjamin works with a very different conception of time, which has important consequences for his understanding of the political. He contrasts law, domination and manifest bloodletting violence, on the one hand, with divine, blood-sparing violence and justice, on the other. The key to this distinction is Benjamin's insistence that while rational secular law must stipulate universally applicable norms and sanctions for all like cases, justice is another matter entirely, since in reality every individual case is an exception. Thus the juridical-bureaucratic 'necessity' that there be order and hence a single authority imposing universally enforceable rules stands in opposition to the uniqueness of each individual's life, and closes off the different kinds of justice which the praxis of unique individuals acting together might make possible. For Benjamin, the latter has much more to do with *politics* in the sense of each person's particular existence and relation to others than *legality*, i.e., their supposed equality before the

---

[21] Benjamin's critique of law and the state draws on a series of diverse examples, such as territorial conquest through war, control over human life as typified by the death penalty, the role and function of the police, and the incoherence at the heart of right to strike laws. Walter Benjamin, 'Zur Kritik der Gewalt', in *Angelus Novus*, Frankfurt: Suhrkamp, 1988, pp. 42–3, 46–7, 52–3. This article is also contained in translation on pages 132–54 in the edited collection *One-Way Street and Other Writings*. War and conquest illustrate the most obvious cases where rights and law ultimately stem from actual or potential violence, such as in the case of the appropriation of native American land in North America in the name of life, liberty and the pursuit of happiness. See Steven T. Newcomb's 'The Evidence of Christian Nationalism in Federal Indian Law: the Doctrine of Discovery, Johnson v. McIntosh, and Plenary Power', in the *New York University Review of Law and Social Change*, 20 (1993), pp. 317–18.

constantly changing laws, regulations and statutes of the legal system.[22]

Benjamin maintains that the truth of the human world is thus not the eternal recurrence, but the absolute singularity of each experience. This draws attention to both the plebiscitary limitations of a politics focused on saying either yes or no to parties seeking power, on the one hand, and the equally drastic limitations for theorising the political offered by dichotomistic categories like friend/enemy, on the other. It also points to the political signifi- cance of language, memory and tragedy, where the latter can be understood both in the classical Greek sense of a clash of loyalties, and in the more conventional sense of the sheer inevitability of death.[23] The uniqueness of each person's path and possibility of irreconcilable obligations to different parties represents for Benjamin an absolute 'now' against the mythology of 'newness': the conflict between incommensurate values constitutes a perma- nent state of exception. As an ontological attribute of political relations between people, Benjamin's 'nowtime' (Jetztzeit) is at once unrepeatable and timeless, and incapable of formal-legal codifica- tion or representation. If the truth of the human world is not eternal recurrence, but the absolute state of exception represented by 'nowtime', the truth of the commodified world is apparent newness, clearly represented by changing styles of fashion. In the sense of its pretended newness, fashion can also be understood in the widest terms in Benjamin's usage to include leadership changes of established political parties competing for control of the state, as well as for all commodities placed in circulation and the commod- ity form itself.[24]

---

[22] Benjamin, 'Zur Kritik der Gewalt', pp. 46–7. This distinction between poli- tics and legality is of central significance in attempting to theorise how various forms of political action in contemporary civil societies challenge the represen- tative legitimacy of law and the state, and seek to articulate other possible forms of enacting public life. These will be explored in detail in chapters 3 to 5.

[23] Walter Benjamin, 'Über das Programm der kommenden Philosophie', in Angelus Novus, pp. 28–34. The political signficance of language, memory and tragedy is developed in somewhat cryptic but nonetheless highly suggestive terms in Ursprung des deutschen Trauerspiels (The Origins of German Tragic Drama, 1925), especially in the 'Epistemological Prologue', Frankfurt: Suhrkamp, 1978, pp. 9–39.

[24] Benjamin, 'Über den Begriff der Geschichte', in Michael Optiz (ed.), Walter Benjamin: Ein Lesebuch, Frankfurt: Suhrkamp, 1996, pp. 665–76.

The commodity form as fashion in the extended sense can thus embrace ideas in the form of books, or art in what Horkheimer and Adorno later called 'the culture industry'. Benjamin maintains that where the commodity form is at work Nietzsche is indeed correct – commodities promise newness but in fact spell the return of the same in new guise. Commodities circulate under socially opaque relations which contribute to their apparent timelessness, but in fact commodities have no time rather than timelessness. This is because they are in most cases manufactured with the express purpose of becoming obsolete. Planned obsolescence stands in rather obvious contrast to the uncertainty which governs individual lives and the fragility of the actual (now) time/moment of absolutely singular individuals. Looked at in the light of Weber and Schmitt's theses on the state, Benjamin's ideas suggest that it is important to distinguish between (1) the time of technology and the commodity, (2) the time of law, and the (3) (now) time of the political. These distinctions might help us understand the politics of civil society as something distinct from technology, administration, economics, etc., and thus shed light on possible directions towards a theory of the specificity of the political in non-Weberian/Schmittian terms. Such a theory would have important implications for the critique of the state at the centre of this chapter, and point beyond toward a possible non-statist theory of the political capable of drawing out the implications of manifestations of self-government in contemporary civil societies, which currently seek political recognition from the state.[25]

The eternal recurrence suggests that the human world is bound to similar repeating cycles such as those found in the natural world like the changing seasons or the inexorable pattern of daybreak, dusk, daybreak. In a related vein, a series of economic theories of democracy hold that the 'naturalness' of the natural world is mirrowed in the boom and bust of the business cycle, the 'laws' of supply and

---

[25] Walter Benjamin, *Das Passagen-Werk*, Volume I (edited by Rolf Tiedemann), Frankfurt: Suhrkamp, 1983, pp. 492–5. The relation between Benjamin's *Passagen-Werk* and his theories of time and politics is treated with flair and imagination by Martin Blobel in 'Polis und Kosmopolis: Naturrecht in der Zeit der nachrevolutionären Verzerrungen der Mimesis. Über Benjamins *Passagen-Werk*', unpublished doctoral thesis submitted in Philosophy at the Freie Universität, Berlin, in 1994. See in particular pages 40–2, 85, 197–8, 283, 320, 884–6.

demand, survival of the fittest under conditions of scarcity as the 'seed' of economic 'growth', etc., and, further, that politics is an expression of these natural drives and cycles.[26] The interests that people have as citizens at the level of political representation then become a function of the time constraints imposed by the natural cycles of boom and bust, supply and demand, survival of the fittest, etc., such that the satisfaction of the conditions of life is substituted for the political articulation of different possible *worlds*.[27] This distinction between life and world will be developed in detail in chapters 3 to 5. The important point to keep in mind in concluding the critique of the state in this chapter, is that the conditions of life, such as the satisfaction of hunger, thirst, the need for shelter, etc., are something we share to a greater or lesser extent with others within the constraints imposed by nature, such as the aging process. By contrast, the world we share with others is not shared in a way fundamentally determined by the rhythms of exclusively material and physical needs, nor is the world the inevitable site of friend/enemy conflicts. It is rather a space that is shared by different perspectives, where sharing is not one of equal parts which together constitute a whole. Whereas no individual can fully transcend the rhythms of physical need and aging, and is thereby subjected to a certain measure of inevitability and unfreedom, the world can change drastically from the moment a new perspective is introduced into the public sphere.

The conflation of economic necessity and political decision is at the heart of a misunderstanding between (a) the time of the commodity (a technical decision affecting the material and physical dimension of the life-cycle and its reproduction) and (b) the time of the political (existential decision in relation to the articulation of possible present and future relations between members of a political community). The scope of freedom involved in the first time is admittedly bound by the constraints of harvesting in accordance with natural cycles, curing the sick in accordance with time of likely incubation of disease, etc. But political time is not economic

---

[26] The best known of these is Anthony Downs, *An Economic Theory of Democracy*, New York: Harper & Row, 1957. There are many other versions of this thesis. In varying ways they collapse the distinction between politics and economic/technical concerns, and as such obscure the distinctness of political praxis.

[27] The distinction between life and world is at the heart of Hannah Arendt's political philosophy, and will be developed in far greater detail in the next chapter.

or natural time. Political time can be interpreted as the enacted but non-representable (now) time of the exception, but not the exception suggested by the failure of different versions of natural or positive law to mediate a friend–enemy conflict, as Schmitt would have it. Schmitt argues that outside of the framework of adjudication provided by natural and positive law there is only the friend and enemy distinction, which is far too simplistic. What he does prove, however, is that the time of law, however distinct from the time of the commodity, is still of a different order than the time of the political. Schmitt shows that within the framework of natural and positive law there is indeed no solution to a situation of irreconcilable antagonism, and further, that at that point recourse must be had to something prior to the law, i.e., which is his particular version of the political (friend/enemy). But in insisting that (a) the sovereign state should settle these conflicts, and that (b) the power of the sovereign state to settle states of exception is ultimately theological rather than political in origin, Schmitt manages to discredit the state as an acceptable solution to the problem of conflict after showing the inadequacy of law to play that role. This suggests that neither law nor the state in their present *form* offer the possibility of a *political* solution to conflict and perspectival pluralism, which is what the more radical expressions of dissent, opposition and resistance in contemporary civil societies confirm. Thus while Weber and Schmitt clearly demonstrate the various ways in which the modern state is highly problematic, Benjamin's ideas provide the beginnings of a framework for re-interpreting the political in the light of contemporary events.[28]

[28] A detailed discussion of natural, positive and exceptional law can be found in Carl Schmitt, *Über die drei Arten des rechtswissenschaftlichen Denkens* (*On the Three Forms of Legal Thought*) (1934), Berlin: Duncker & Humblot, 1993. Very briefly stated, one might summarise by saying that natural law tends to posit a set of rights such as the Rights of Man and Citizen in the French Revolution, which ascribe to all human beings certain rights solely on the basis of their humanity, i.e., rights that they are entitled to strictly on the grounds that they are human (natural) beings. The implication is that all members of the species should enjoy these rights. Positive law baldly affirms that we enjoy only those rights that are on the statutes, with the obvious implication that constitutions in Nazi Germany, Soviet Russia and racially segregated South Africa all stipulate in terms of positive law why some people quite obviously do not qualify as rights-bearing members of the political community. The notion of exceptional law has already been elaborated in this chapter in the discussion of Schmitt's conception of sovereignty and the state of exception.

On the one hand, arguments in support of natural law suppose that violent means are acceptable in the pursuit of a just end, i.e., such as the creation of a state of law or *Rechtsstaat*. Whether one is talking about the necessary fiction of the unanimous decision to leave the state of nature, or the necessity to act 'as if' majority decisions are just decisions, theories of natural law tend in some way or other to regard 'forcing someone to be free' to be an act of legitimate force.[29] On the other hand, arguments in support of positive law imply that any means employed in the pursuit of a certain agreed political end are legitimate (whether or not they be just), i.e., such as the decisions to enact racial separation laws such as the Jim Crow, Nuremberg or Apartheid laws: positive law is purely procedural and does not discriminate between good and bad laws. In both natural and positive cases, however, law is the expression of force rather than justice, or, as Benjamin puts it, both are mired in a utilitarian calculation about means and ends rather than justice as an absolute value. Just as force or any other means are justified to bring about the supposedly just ends stipulated by natural law, any means are justified in the execution of legally enacted decisions once law is defined as procedure. This indicates that the Weberian bifurcation of means and ends is also operative in the domain of law and the state, such that legalistic rationality is incapable of rendering a just outcome in many instances of legal ambiguity like the state of exception. Law is thus the expression of the means to achieve the end of socio-political order, but is not in itself a yardstick of justice. Schmitt simply omits the question of justice – and thereby the question of how to settle an antagonism when natural and positive law fail to reconcile implacably opposed starting positions. To the extent that this shows that prior to law there is the political, he is correct; to the extent that the political can be said to exhaust itself in the friend/enemy couple, he is mistaken. The critique of state violence undertaken in this chapter represents a first step towards

[29] This is not true of the particular theory of natural law developed by Ernst Bloch. He argues that natural law can not be used to justify property or the state, since if there was ever such a thing as a 'natural' state of humankind, it must surely have been stateless and classless. According to Bloch, these forms of domination only developed in the process of the historical evolution of Western European society towards capitalism. See Ernst Bloch, *Naturrecht und menschliche Würde* (*Natural Law and Human Dignity*, 1961), 2nd edn, Frankfurt: Suhrkamp, 1980, pp. 119–23.

the reconceptualisation of the political outside the parameters defined by the discourses of sovereignty.

This chapter has sought to demonstrate that these terms have been implicitly or manifestly either violent or theological. If this is so, it means that despite Feuerbach and Marx's incisive critiques of the state in general and the Hegelian state in particular analysed in chapter 1, our thinking about the state is still pre-modern, to say nothing of supposedly postmodern thinking! This chapter has also sought to establish that it might be possible to assimilate what is fruitful in Schmitt, i.e., that the time of the political is the time of the exception rather than the legal norm, but that one must move beyond Schmitt's reduction of the political to the friend/enemy distinction to confront the notion of 'exceptionality' in far more nuanced terms. In order to move beyond the critique of state violence towards a positive reconceptualisation of the political, it will be necessary to address questions of possible boundaries between state and civil society as well as the specificity of 'the time of the political', without falling back on notions like sovereignty, monopolies on legitimate force, or the state of exception conceived theologically.[30]

Anatole France's remark that the law forbids both rich and poor to sleep under the city bridges at night offers an apposite starting point for such a positive reconceptualisation of the political. This is a point about the ostensible neutrality of the law, which, by definition, has to be the same for all members of a political community if it is to be enacted as law rather than whim, privilege, tradition, etc. The injunction that both rich and poor must not sleep under public bridges at night challenges the liberal notion that freedom consists in doing what one wants, provided that one does not violate that same freedom of others. This particular law accomplished in fact a quite different result by requiring people to sleep in homes or shelters when their presence under a bridge at night would have in no way impinged upon someone else's freedom to sleep in their bed.[31] Rather than establishing a public sphere or the framework for mutual recognition between citizens, the law in this instance sets boundaries stipulating what kind of behaviour is *appropriate* in a

---

[30] Benjamin, 'Zur Kritik der Gewalt', pp. 42–3, also contained in translation in the edited collection *One-Way Street and Other Writings*.

[31] France's remark is cited by Benjamin towards the end of 'On the Critique of Violence'. See 'Zur Kritik der Gewalt', p. 61.

particular space. Boundaries in their turn signify (a) the norm, in terms of specifying what is mine, yours, ours and theirs, and (b) what happens in the case of a violation of the norm, i.e., what happens when I take what is yours, they take what is ours, etc. But they cannot pronounce on (c) the exception. Here the law functions as a means to the end of fixing a clearly established order demarcated by boundaries; it is not an end in itself. If order itself is considered to be a political end or value, then concentration of legitimate force in the sovereign state and the simultaneous exercise of power and relations of domination of civil society seems 'natural'. This raises once again the previous point about positive law, i.e., that there is in fact nothing 'natural' about these relations of domination, which is why they require positive law in order to be enforced. In anticipation of the argument to be developed in chapters 3 to 5, an important component of the argument developed in chapters 1 to 2 is that in a democratic society, where there is a specific form of action recognised as political, law must be transparent to – and perhaps even subordinate to – the exception: hence the decidedly political character of the faculty of judgement and a public sphere for its exercise. In a democratic society law must be transparent to the exception in ways that eschew both the 'democracy of unfreedom' characteristic of the explicitly religious Middle Ages (diagnosed by Marx) and the implicit political theology characteristic of the modern state (evident in the work of Schmitt).[32]

---

[32] The case of the right to strike provides a good example. Under industrial relations law in Europe, years of organised struggle have ensured that the right to unionise and strike is by and large legally guaranteed. At the same time, however, this right may be abrogated when it is deemed that 'things have gone too far', and that it is time to go back to work lest the competitivity of national industries be damaged (leaving aside for the moment the possible consequences of Maastricht and European union). Characteristically it will be argued in such a situation that the right to strike is a guaranteed economic right and that it can no longer be guaranteed when it becomes a general (political) strike aiming at a transformation of existing power relations. The right to strike is then likely to be met with the equally guaranteed right of the state to enforce a return to work with the threat of imprisonment or financial penalty for those who do not comply. The strike example is only a more dramatic case of a conflict inscribed within the ostensibly neutral terms of legal discourse, a discourse which in states of exception reveals itself to be anything but neutral. If we move from the specific example of the economic vs. the general strike to the more catastrophic question of how to reconcile individual liberty with legally guaranteed equality

The equally enforced prohibition not to sleep under the same bridge does not signify the reign of equality but rather its opposite for those without homes. The more important point is that because of the different times which define their parameters, there will never be an absolute transparency between action in civil society and political representation. This in itself constitutes a state of exception in permanence, since no norm can be discovered to reconcile the two times, just as no norm, legal or otherwise, will ever fully mediate individual freedom with the postulates of collective equality between citizens. The political problem implied by this irreconcilability is not so much that some have homes and others do not, some have work and others do not, etc., for this has always been so to varying degrees. But since the French Revolution the citizens of civil society demand both freedom and equality, which Hegel thought only possible within the boundaries set by the separation between civil society and state. However, both the simple positing of the boundary or the demanding of its abolition spells the triumph of violence – speculative or in practice – over the political conceived in its specifity as the time of the (permanent) exception. The critique of the state, law and violence in the name of the political is a defence of the specificity of the political as the truly human moment when individuals choose their own time against essentially mechanical and technical rhythms/ processes, on the one hand, and mythical/revelationary thinking, on the other. This means enacting a political praxis in which the exception attains the necessary visibility to dictate the rule. Recent political theory and practice concerned with civil society suggests that this is possible. The following chapters will explore the ways in which such a politics might come to more complete theoretical articulation.

---

for all citizens, we will see that in modern parliamentary democracies we are dealing with a state of exception in permanence, and it is a state of exception concerned with the boundary between state and civil society. See Benjamin, 'Zur Kritik der Gewalt', pp. 61–2.

3

The public sphere

> It has been in the nature of our tradition of political thought to be
> highly selective and to exclude from articulate conceptualization
> a great variety of authentic political experiences, among which
> we need not be surprised to find some of an even elementary
> nature.
>
> Hannah Arendt, *The Human Condition*

In chapter 1 we saw how Hegel criticises Kant's concept of the
public sphere mediating between assembled independent private
individuals and the state. Hegel refuses to concede such an important political role to *Publizität*, which he demotes to the category of
public opinion in *The Philosophy of Right*. In chapter 2 it was then
shown that the mediation between the state and *Publizität* in Kant's
political writings and criticised by Hegel becomes even more problematic with the enlarging of the franchise and the transformation
of the political societies and clubs of the former public sphere. In
the period roughly spanning the upheavals of 1848 to the World
War I and the Russian Revolution, these political associations were
transformed into modern professional mass parties competing for
control of the state in a process analysed first by Weber and then by
Habermas in *Strukturwandel der Öffentlichkeit* (*The Structural
Transformation of the Public Sphere*).[1] Weber analyses the rise of the

---

[1] Weber, *Staatssoziologie*, pp. 27, 70–5; Habermas, *Strukturwandel der
Öffentlichkeit*, pp. 212–14, 267–8, 307, and 320. Thirty years after the publication
of *Strukturwandel der Öffentlichkeit*, Habermas continued to rely on the analyses
of Weber (and by this time to a much reduced extent on Adorno) in his
assessment of the changes in the relation between the political system, the
public sphere and civil society. See *Faktizität und Geltung: Beiträge zur
Diskurstheorie des Rechts und des demokratischen Rechtstaats*, Frankfurt: Suhrkamp

modern state as part of a set of parallel developments characterised
by: a) the erosion of the political importance of the public sphere
with the rise of the mass parties and their function as vote-gather-
ing machines; b) the transition towards new forms of legitimation
of power based on the combination of plebiscitary and
rational/legal domination; c) the concentration of political power
in the state, where the state no longer resembles anything like
Hegel's ethical idea, but becomes the set of institutions with a
monopoly on the legitimate use of force within a given territory.
Thus the period from Kant to Weber is marked by the steady
erosion of recognised political power outside the state. It also
attests to the radical transformation of the notion of 'the political'
itself, making Schmitt's Nietzschean reading of Weber possible in
Der Begriff des Politischen (The Concept of the Political) of 1932. What
previously is a political sphere mediating between the private
sphere and the state disappears, while the political becomes largely
synonymous with party competition, state power and force. It was
also seen that the erosion of the public sphere as a non-statist political space in civil society and the consumation of the political in
administrative/technical terms is reflected in the writings of both
Weber and Schmitt as a political translation of Nietzsche's idea of
the decisiveness of the will. Weber argues that he who pursues
politics pursues power, while Schmitt regards the implacable
enmity of the friend/enemy distinction as irrefutable grounds for
state sovereignty and the eventual necessity of terminating the
political enemy.[2]

The aim of the present book, however, is not to reconstruct the

---

1992, pp. 402–3. Weber's analysis of the transformation of what Habermas
would later call the public sphere is the most systematic and historically accurate available. It is nonetheless extremely interesting to examine the analyses of
the same period by Alexis de Tocqueville (Democracy in America, 1835–40),
Vilfredo Pareto (Socialist Systems, 1902), Ortega y Gasset (The Revolt of the
Masses, 1929), and other liberal and conservative critics of the emerging 'mass
society'. Although in many ways these thinkers were reactionary and quite
obviously hostile to electoral reform, they were also accurate in concluding that
the specific ways in which 'democratisation' was occurring were inimical to a
non-instrumental view of the political. To this extent they clearly prefigure
themes in Joseph Schumpeter's controversial study Capitalism, Socialism and
Democracy (1942).

  [2] Weber, Politik als Beruf, p. 507; Schmitt, Der Begriff des Politischen, pp. 20,
26–8; Ekkehart Krippendorf, Staat und Krieg: Die historische Logik politischer
Unvernunft, Frankfurt: Suhrkamp, 1985, p. 202.

events which witnessed the transformation of these theoretical
dilemmas into the actual rise of authoritarian government across
large portions of Europe during the 1920s and 1930s, which has
already been ably chronicled by historians. The aim here is instead
to analyse how this transformation of the concept of the political
was able to triumph, and how the idea of 'the political' might be
reconceptualised in non-violent, non-sovereign terms, beginning in
this chapter with the idea of the public sphere in civil society. The
critique of the state at the centre of chapters 1 and 2 thus serves as
the background for the reconstructive chapters that now follow.
There is obviously a great deal at stake here, since Schmitt is
correct in one fundamentally important regard, i.e., to argue that
the exception proves the rule: authoritarian government is not a
pathology of transition periods, but rather an omnipresent possible
consequence wherever the concept of sovereignty itself is politically legitimate.[3]

   In the discussion that follows civil society includes all non-state
institutions including the economy[4] (see the definition of civil

[3] Franz Neumann remarks that one of the distinguishing features of
National Socialism in practice was that the function of the judge was transformed into that of a policeman. While the example of National Socialism
supposedly represents an exception to the 'normal' functioning of a *Rechtsstaat*,
Schmitt's analysis of Weber points to the conclusion that in modern parliamentary democracies the real leader is also always a judge. That is, even under the
normal functioning of a Rechtstaat, political leaders exercise both executive and
judicial power. This is typically the case in instances such as Weimar, where the
parliament's ability to make and propose laws is fundamentally undermined by
the degradation of politics to an institutionalised compromise between classes.
See Franz Neumann, *Die Herrschaft des Gesetzes*, Frankfurt: Suhrkamp, 1980, pp.
352–5; Carl Schmitt, *Die geistesgeschichtliche Lage des heutigen Parlamentarismus*
(1923), 8th edn, Berlin: Duncker & Humblot, 1996, pp. 18–19; Von Krockow, *Die
Entscheidung*, pp. 103–4. Schmitt is most acute when criticising liberal legal and
political institutions. What is attempted in this book is among other things an
exploration of how Schmitt's ideas might serve in the construction of a socialist
theory of the political against both liberalism and Schmitt's own far-right positions.
   [4] In so doing I retain the Hegelian and Marxist conception of civil society
against both non-Marxists like Tocqueville, Habermas, Arato and Cohen, etc.,
and a number of Marxists like Etienne Balibar, who like Habermas and Arato
and Cohen exclude the economy from civil society. See Habermas, *Faktizität und
Geltung*, pp. 443–5. For a critical discussion of the usage of the state/civil
society dichotomy within Marxist thinking see Etienne Balibar, 'Marx, le joker', in
Michel Delorme (ed.), *Rejouer le politique*, Paris: Éditions Galilée, 1981, pp.
149–52, and pp. 161–3.

society in the Introduction). As stated in the Introduction, however, no explicit analysis of empirically functioning capitalist or other economies will be presented here. But it is important at this juncture to insist that it is the exclusion of the economy in Cohen and Arato and other theorists which gives civil society in their usage a distinctly functionalist quality. Based on the theoretical interpretation of civil society offered in this book, the public sphere refers to a specifically political and communicative *network* within civil society. It is a network that can grow to such an extent that it actually challenges state authority, as was the case in Eastern Europe in 1989–90. In Schmittian terms, the public sphere, like community and recognition, indicates a degree of intensity rather than a precisely delineated sphere.[5] This distinguishes the approach here from other theoretical approaches, in which the public sphere within civil society normally mediates in modified functionalist terms between the state and the private sphere of family and friends sometimes referred to as the lifeworld.[6] I am purposely choosing not to adopt any of the prevalent quasi-functionalist approaches to analysing civil society, which in various ways tend to miss the radical potential of recent movements in civil society around the world by reducing the civil sphere to one of several functional units. This theoretical reduction is characterised by the extremely unconvincing argument that civil society is a site of radical contestation and at the same time, it can exist as a sphere alongside others like the economy and state, as if somehow linked yet separated from these. This is not only to largely misread the various forms of action, resistance and opposition in contemporary civil society, but it is also to fail to see the implications of the

[5] The analytical separation of economy, political society, civil society and state often serves civil society theorists in the project of unconvincing model-building in which it is difficult to see exactly what role civil society and political initiative are supposed to play. See Richter, 'Zivilgesellschaft – Probleme einer Utopie in der Moderne', pp. 177–87.

[6] Though the lifeworld has itself been defined in various ways, the writings of Alfred Schutz and Habermas offer perspectives on this concept with continuing relevance. See Jürgen Habermas, *Theorie des kommunikativen Handelns)*, Volume II, Part IV, 'System und Lebenswelt' Frankfurt: Suhrkamp, 1981, pp. 174–97, pp. 230–47, and Alfred Schutz and Thomas Luckmann, *Strukturen der Lebenswelt*, Frankfurt: Suhrkamp, 1979. On the frequent conceptual slippage between civil society, public sphere and lifeworld in the theoretical work of many civil society theorists, see Richter, 'Zivilgesellschaft – Probleme einer Utopie in der Moderne', p. 184.

critique of the state suggested by the various forms of praxis which have challenged the legitimacy of the state and political parties everywhere. The theoretical implications of these movements will be drawn out in this chapter. This chapter seeks to shed theoretical light on contemporary civil society and, at the same time, suggest the outlines of a non-statist theory of the political which recent political action in civil society already anticipates.

One of the most theoretically relevant issues suggested by political action to create a public sphere in actual empirical contexts, is the critique of the political party in its specific manifestation as a technically-conceived organised will to power. While this aspect was especially salient in the 'Velvet Revolutions' of 1989–90, it has been a factor in almost all instances where civil society challenges state authority. Party organisation and strategy can be seen as closely tied to a concept of the political rooted in interest and power, which, in its turn, is intrinsically linked to a particular concept of the state. Where the state is grounded in some version of the general will, it will be the task of the party to embody that will to the greatest extent possible: where material interests are not to the greatest possible extent neutralised, Rousseau's ideal of no factions inevitably gives way in practice to the domination of the successful party or coalition of parties. Thus every party is successful to the extent that it can become a single ruling party, i.e., to the extent that it can eliminate politics.

This chapter seeks to illuminate the seeming paradox of non-political political parties by attempting to develop the implications of the discussion in the last chapter further, and by exploring the contemporary relevance of Arendt's remarks above. One of the tentative conclusions from chapter 2 concerns the non-political character of state sovereignty. It was seen that in a crisis of political conflict or interpretative textual dispute, discourses of sovereignty and revelation theology share the common need to resort to a non-negotiable, unitary source of unquestionable authority beyond minority/majority deliberations. This prompts Schmitt to conclude that the idea of sovereignty is to the state what the miracle is to theology, such that there can be no discussion with those that dispute the authority of either. If sovereignty is unitary and indivisible, it has to stem from a single source which is itself indivisible: the (general) will. In reality the indivisibility of the general will is of course belied by the actual fragmentary and plural nature of the group or category in whose name sovereignty is exercised, i.e., 'the people', 'the party', 'the citizens', etc.

That sovereignty is thus incompatible with perspectival pluralism seems clear. In what follows it will be shown that (a) the suppression of the political inherent in the institutional practices of sovereignty constitutes the domination of 'the social' at the expense of the specifically political content of daily experience, as suggested by the quote from Arendt above. It will be argued further that (b) the political content of these experiences, unlike material interests, cannot be represented, but must be enacted by each individual citizen; what this means will become clear in the course of the discussion. The discussion of Nietzsche, Schmitt and Weber in the last chapter indicates a set of related tendencies within modern capitalist democracies contributing to the triumph of the social over the political, signified by: (1) the concentration of all legitimate political power in the state, (2) the reduction of the political to questions of the will and (3) the contradiction within the will itself between means and ends.[7] In this chapter it will be argued that the delineation of all spheres of action and experience outside the state as either private or social constitutes an attack both on the public sphere and the pluralistic dimension of public life, which various forms of political action in contem-

---

[7] Manfred Riedel notes that in his conception of contract, Kant was the first philosopher to consistently maintain the distinction betwen fact as an aspect of our daily empirical reality of objects and appearances, on the one hand, and norm, as a non-empirical idea of practical reason, on the other. Kant conceded that the original contract conferring legitimacy on the state had no empirical basis but was rather a norm with objective validity. Thus Riedel remarks that: 'Domination and communication on the one hand and compulsion and freedom on the other are for Kant no longer opposed to each other, but rather unified in the concept of legitimate domination (enabling everyone to exercise their freedom). Freedom, understood as the legislation of practical reason, demands for itself exercise of domination based on agreement, but in the form of legal compulsion. As such, the exercise of freedom by every individual is restricted to the conditions of its possible lawful agreement with the freedom of all other individuals'. Manfred Riedel, 'Transcendental Politics? Political Legitimacy and the Concept of Civil Society in Kant', in Reiner Schurmann (ed.), *The Public Realm: Essays on Discursive Types in Political Philosophy*, New York: State University of New York at Albany, 1989, p. 33. Under such conditions it is not difficult to see that other individuals will be perceived by the individual subject as obstacles to be overcome or annihilated. Thus the trajectory from Kant to Nietzsche's theory of the will and beyond to Weber's *Herrschaftssoziologie* (sociology of domination) clearly emerges.

porary civil societies challenge. This challenge comes in the form of attempts to institutionalise the political content of the public sphere, community and recognition, and it is to the first of these that we now turn.

The rise of the social and the response of the political

Our inability or refusal to recognise action outside the sphere of the state as political action is closely related to what Arendt calls 'the rise of the social', which she argues is a relatively recent phenomenon linked to the emergence of the modern state in the Weberian sense.[8] The modern state in the Weberian sense as a set of institutions with a monopoly on legitimate force was accompanied by the rise of modern mass political parties. The parties were entrusted with the task of mediating between the state and civil society in the specific sense of representing the interests of individuals in civil society at the level of the state. This, however, was to conflate the material interests of citizens with their experience of the political, and to thereby misrepresent civil society at the level of state as first and foremost a sphere of production, exchange and clashing interests rather than diverging perspectives. Since diverging perspectives cannot be represented as such but must be seen and heard, they require a space for speakers and listeners. By contrast, the representation of interests is a technical process best carried out through a vertical chain of command where diverse perspectives need to be to the greatest possible extent shut out. Parties thus translate the highly plural experience of the political that is bound to vary from individual to individual into the homogenous language of vote totals, where one vote distinguishes itself in no way from another. Parties cannot be blamed for this, since as Weber notes they are by nature designed to aggregate very generic preferences much in the way a private business enterprise uses advertising to attract potential customers in its competition with other firms. Like the private firm seeking to maximise profits, the party seeks access to institutional power; votes are the instrument which grants that access. Thus parties use people, by way of their votes, to get to power, which is very different from allowing a plurality of opinions and perspectives to achieve visibility. Where

---

[8] Arendt, *The Human Condition*, chapter 2.

revolution is not an option, whatever legal means that are required to gain votes must be a political good if the goal is to achieve power. Within the institutional framework assimilating the experience of the political to the experiences of making and manufacturing, politics is instrumental to the more fundamental goal of power, and the will to attain power becomes the political instinct *par excellence*.

In what follows it will first be shown how the will attained this pre-eminent stature in political theory/practice. Then it will be possible to see how efforts to create a public sphere constitute an attempt to enlarge a political space in opposition to the tyranny of the will institutionalised as party coalitions and states.[9] It will be recalled from chapter 1 that both Rousseau and Kant regarded the will as a centrally important political category in terms of legitimating political power. Rousseau is immediately associated with the distinction between the will of all as a summing of individual opinions, on the one hand, and the general will, where the latter is more than a simple aggregate but the very basis of sovereignty itself, on the other. The general will is somewhat akin to a common substance shared by all members of the political community despite contingently diverging opinions. As such, individuals lose none of their freedom in submitting to its dictates which could only also be, in the last anaysis, their own. In a related vein, Kant employs the concept of the will to distinguish between needs and interests. In discussing the question of individual autonomy, he characterises physical, sensual and other inclinations based on non-rational impulses as needs, while to him it is clear that when the will is dictated to by rational principles one could speak of interests. Both Rousseau's reconciliation of the individual and general will and Kant's theory of the autonomous individual regarded the faculty of the will as indivisible and 'beyond' the realm of experience; this is particularly clear in Kant's formulation of the will as part of a 'metaphysics' of morals. The 'freedom' of the will is thus not connected with any collective political experience of freedom rooted in concerted action, but has to do instead with an inner state of mind. Political theory thus registered a dramatic shift between two worlds separated by the experience of Christianity, i.e.,

---

[9] Weber, *Staatssoziologie*, pp. 51–3; Habermas, *Faktizität und Geltung*, p. 403; Brian Seitz, *The Trace of the Political*, Albany: State University of New York at Albany Press, 1995, p. 5.

between the Greek conception of freedom informed by the public
life of the *polis*, and a conception of freedom in the quasi-religious
sense as the free will to do the good/obey the law. Arendt notes
that political *philosophers* (as distinct from political theorists like
herself) became interested in the problem of freedom when
freedom was no longer immediately experienced as collective
action in the presence of others, but lived in the contemplation of
the possible presuppositions or *a priori* conditions of one's own
freedom, i.e., in a psychological examination of one's inner self.
Rousseau can be seen as the paradigm thinker of this trend;
revolted by what he saw around him, he retreats to the private
world of his 'confessions', 'solitary wanderings', etc. Here the individual can perhaps make some sense of his or her life in quiet
contemplation. Similarly, Kant enjoins us to abstract from experience, feeling, inclination and desires in order to allow the rational
will to formulate universally valid principles. This can be interpreted as an attempt to shut out all extraneous influences, in order
that the individual will be able to impose order and achieve
freedom from what Kant calls 'self-inflicted immaturity' in his
essay on the meaning of enlightenment.[10]

The political problem suggested in the writings of Rousseau,
Kant and other Enlightenment political thinkers is immediately
recognised by Hegel. Hegel sees that with the intellectual achieve-
ments of Machiavelli, Descartes and especially Kant, modernity
had overturned almost all previously held principles in the name
of will and subjectivity. But Hegel also perceives that if one starts
from the position of an isolated individual will seeking its autonomy and freedom, all other such wills will necessarily be
perceived as obstacles. Since the social contract was a manifest
fiction, the war of all against all would still win the day, and the
realisation of the state as an ethical idea would be impossible in
practice. In chapter 1 it is suggested that this line of reasoning
compels Hegel to argue that the integrity of the state can only be

---

[10] Hannah Arendt, *Between Past and Future*, New York: Penguin, 1954, pp.
157–63. Perhaps Machiavelli was the last great political thinker for whom
freedom was a matter concerning worldly forces like *virtù*, rather than a function of the individual rational will. Thereafter, and perhaps most
emblematically in the writings of the social contract theorists, political freedom
is not theorised on the basis of experience, but on the notion of a thought exper-
iment, i.e., the fictitious 'state of nature'.

maintained if the state is not confused with civil society – and especially not with the system of needs. Thus Hegel is fully aware of the need to develop a theory of intersubjective recognition. This would be necessary if there was ever to be a possible mediation between conflicting wills moving beyond the self-interest implicit in contract towards mutual understanding. He is also aware that the isolated individual will viewing all others as real or potential obstacles could only be what Hegel in *Die Phänomonologie des Geistes* (*The Phenomenology of Spirit*) calls an 'unhappy consciousness'. Hegel's theory of the state, which in large measure is a response both to Rousseau and Kant as well as Hegel's romantic contemporaries like Hölderlin, marks a watershed in our tradition of thinking about politics. One of the reasons why is because in thinking of possible responses to Hegel, neither Marx, Kierkegaard or Nietzsche – Hegel's most important opponents – are able adequately to refute Hegel on *specifically political grounds*. This is borne out by the lack of a Marxist theory of the political until Gramsci, on the one hand, and the refusal of Kierkegaard, Nietzsche and their respective critics to systematically address questions of the state and politics, on the other. In different ways both Kierkegaard and Nietzsche confirm Hegel's suspicion about the inevitable unhappiness of the isolated individual will. In clear anticipation of problems confronted by Freud, Kierkegaard and Nietzsche hint that the isolated will, when seeing other individuals as obstacles that thwart the ego's goals, is likely to either turn back against itself out of frustration, or seek individual aesthetic or religious solutions to human problems; the idea of a *political* project engaging different subjectivities in a common undertaking is not even seriously considered. When confronted with innumerable 'others', the individual will must reconcile itself to being outnumbered and alone; these others then tend to become 'the herd', the masses, the vulgar and those in bad faith. The absolute embracing and rejecting of Christianity in Kierkegaard and Nietzsche happens very much in terms dictated by Christian thinking itself, and in ways which support rather than challenge the Christian notion of freedom as free will.[11]

---

[11] G.W.F. Hegel, *Die Phänomenologie des Geistes* (1807), Stuttgart: Reklam, 1987, pp, 157–70; Karl Löwith, *Von Hegel zu Nietzsche*, Zurich: Europa Verlag, 1941, part 2.

Kierkegaard and Nietzsche are not central here, nor is there space to treat the range of their responses to the Hegelian dialectic. But in relation to the question of the relationship between the will as an individual/social entity on the one hand, and the political as a public/political concept on the other, a crucial hypothesis is raised. This hypothesis concerns the relationship between the political as an agonistic space of appearances, on the one hand, and the individual will, on the other. It could be formulated as follows: where there is no public sphere as a political space for individuals to clash, exchange views and come to mutual understandings as *citizens* – not as consumers, friends or workers – political issues will be supressed only to find their expression as *individual* social and *psychological* 'problems' which must be 'treated' clinically as pathologies of everyday life (i.e., difference which must be 'cured'). Politics and the very possibility of there being a plurality of perspectives rather than merely more or less successful strategies, depends on the existence or creation of a public sphere. Without such a sphere, there exists a strong tendency for genuinely political clashes of incommensurable values and energies to be treated as either material – i.e., democracy enacted as the institutionalisation of class compromise – or the social and psychological problems of isolated individuals.[12]

Thus there must be a public sphere where individuals in the political sense of *non-identical* equals can both agree and differ as citizens, in a forum where they are entirely exceptional and yet unqualified equals. Otherwise difference will tend to be judged as either (1) a superior/inferior performance in a competition where there are no different perspectives, but merely different levels in a hierarchy leading to the same place (success, however measured), or (2) a deviation that is in need of therapeutic cure of one kind or another.[13] Difference in both these cases is the likely result of activity in the economic and social institutions where equality is never fully attainable. Thus one is neither surprised to find that some

[12] This notion is well captured by the German expression for the public sphere, *Öffentlichkeit*, which indicates that the political nature of the public sphere is bound up with its open ('offen') character.
[13] Thus the rise of the social is intimately linked with the rise of the therapeutic social sciences, such as psyschology, psychiatry, psychoanalysis, criminology, social work, etc. See Deleuze and Guattari, *Capitalisme et Schizophrénie*, pp. 382–3.

people earn more money, are better athletes, worse cooks, more popular, better looking, etc., nor can one hope to achieve political equality in such performative contexts which tend to generate unequal outcomes.

By contrast, the political difference between non-identical equals is one of perspective rather than performance in a narrowly-conceived meritocratic sense, such that divergent opinions result in a more complete understanding of a common world inhabited from different standpoints. Where a public sphere is brought into existence and sustained through diverse perspectives, telling and listening become important political attributes in the knowledge process of finding out or discovering/uncovering. Where there is no public sphere within civil society for the political in the sense of collective action and speech by equal citizens, subjectivity is likely to be experienced as either an attribute of the will or a talent/liability (what we are wont to call personality). In this case subjectivity is largely restricted to artistic, social and economic activities. This spells the dominance of the social over the political: there are few possibilities to either experience the world politically as a public person, or explore the ways in which each individual's freedom is connected with the freedom of others. It is a small step from a situation where there are few possibilities to share words and deeds in the presence of others, to a situation in which other individuals are perceived as either impediments to our will and freedom, or the sources of our inner turmoil. In this case the role of the political essentially will be to empower the state with a monopoly of the legitimate use of force within a given territory to protect people from one another. Then political institutions cannot possibly function so as to sustain a public sphere or the ethical idea of a community of equals; democracy is thereby reduced to largely technical, economic or redistributive questions. Moreover, where the political bond between citizens has become this tenuous, it is not difficult to see that it is merely another short step from this situation of mutual suspicion to a friend/enemy conflict. In instances where freedom is merely economic and social, it is likely to be limited to individual choice in careers, friends and manufacturing brands. Without political freedom that goes beyond the protection of individuals from one another, one must reckon with the likelihood of an eventual state of exception of a bureaucratic-administrative nature stemming from the dominance of the social over the political. As will be suggested below, this might take the form of a kind of 'silent' state of exception.[14]

In the absence of a public sphere within civil society to share divergent perspectives of the world, other individuals cannot *tell* us anything; to a great extent we do not actually see them, nor do we need to. Since there are no authentically different perspectives but merely more or less 'successful' ones, telling must by and large be transformed into a form of advertising in a competitive struggle. In order for someone to be able to tell us something, we have to be in a position to experience what they communicate to us, not in terms of its usefulness for us or them, but rather in terms of what it says about the *world* that we inhabit together from different stand-points. When the precondition of freedom is conceived of as the legal framework within which individuals can pursue goods at the likely expense of other citizens' ability to attain similar goods, freedom itself becomes success in this competitive endeavour. Failure in this endeavour suggests more than simply lack of freedom, but actual guilt, since the will has not been exercised properly, as it should be or could have been. Sharing different perspectives is not possible; there is a dominant perspective, and the other perspectives get disciplined or punished.[15]

Insofar as listening and speaking make a common world seen from different perspectives possible, they raise the possibility of a non-violent and plural conception of the political. Institutionalised hierarchies reduce specific individuals to mere statistical importance,

[14] Arendt, The Human Condition, chapter 5; Walter Benjamin, 'Über Sprache überhaupt und über die Sprache des Menschens' (1916, 'Of Language in General and Human Language in Particular', now in the collection Illuminationen) in Michael Opitz (ed.), Walter Benjamin: Ein Lesebuch, Frankfurt: Suhrkamp, 1996, pp. 28–30, 40–2. Benjamin lays particular stress on the non-identity/incommensurability of the different languages of human expression including painting, poetry and politics.

[15] Thus a person can be guilty without even knowing they have committed a crime, nor even knowing what that crime might be. This is precisely what happens to Kafka's protagonist Joseph K. in The Trial, which can also be read as a tale about the rule of bureaucracy as the anonymous political form of domination exercised in the age of the social. On the relation between the rise of the social and the novel as an art form, Arendt notes that 'The astonishing flowering of poetry and music from the middle of the eighteenth century until almost the last third of the nineteenth century, accompanied by the rise of the novel, the only entirely social art form, coinciding with a no less striking decline of all the more public arts, especially architecture, is sufficient testimony to a close relationship between the social and the intimate'; Arendt, The Human Condition, p. 39.

to non-visibility, which is the most effective way of making them redundant or replaceable. We can only think of suppressing the political as part of a project to suppress the plural character of a world inhabited by different speakers, and, by extension, of suppressing forms of equality that recognise and institutionalise difference as a part of the political dimension of human action – and not simply an illness to be cured or a problem to be administered. The kind of equality in redistributive terms which is possible in response to social and economic exploitation is not synonymous with the political equality of citizens. Implicit in the former is that redistribution is a necessary administrative measure to counteract an imbalance in basic goods that all people want or need. Implicit in the latter is the tension between the radical non-identity and incommensurability of each individual life, on the one hand, and the simultaneous belonging to a community, on the other. The collapsing of these two distinct dimensions of equality into either (1) redistributive equality or (2) equality of opportunity with a relatively small degree of redistribution, is symptomatic of the dominance of the social over the political. This is a form of domination aiming at the suppression of the political; in institutional terms, it typically translates into the transformation of political struggles beyond recognition into questions of security and utility. Historically this project has been undertaken in the first instance as the attempt to abolish politics in favour of the 'administration of things' (state socialism in the former Soviet Union and its allies). Yet the eclipse of the political accompanying the structural transformation of the public sphere also signals the real possibility of the 'totally administered society' in the West in the second instance. In the absence of institutionalised political equality, the administered society is ill-equipped to deal with differences in perspective. Such a society will have to impose bureaucratic solutions on essentially political conflicts in the silence of central and local government offices rather than in the light of the public sphere. But if Habermas is correct in arguing that we can only speak of a public sphere where access is open to everyone, it follows that it is in the public sphere that conflict can be re-presented as a clash of incommensurable values between non-identical equals for *all* citizens.[16]

[16] Habermas, *Strukturwandel der Öfentlichkeit*, pp. 156, 203–4; *Faktizität und Geltung*, pp. 435–6; *Theorie des kommunikativen Handelns*, Volume II, Part IV, p. 230.

The possible recuperation of the political dimension of equality and the defence of the public sphere have thus become two intimately related dimensions of action in civil society. Both in Eastern and Western Europe and around the globe, there have been a myriad of attempts to re-think the political beyond the social-administrative straitjacket of representation usually institutionalised according to the logic of stages as interest–party–state. This form of interest representation inevitably spirals vertically and culminates in the state, since social interests are best administered in the absence of divergent perspectives. By contrast, the political space for the representation of incommensurable values is articulated horizontally so that the perspectives of non-identical equal citizens attain simultaneous visibility. Thus party and state complement each other as vehicles seeking to suspend the potentially limitless political space of the political, and transform it into a hierarchical chain of command.

In *On Revolution*, Arendt notes that if modern constitutions provide a public space for the representatives of the people, they do not do so for the people themselves. It was the political consequences of this problem that first preoccupied Tocqueville in *Democracy in America*, Weber in *Politics as a Vocation*, and then Habermas and other theorists today. A constant theme in Habermas's writings since the 1960s in conjunction with the transformation of the public sphere is the notion of 'legitimation crisis', which among other things involves the crisis which ensues when the meaning or sense of what we do becomes increasingly divorced from the structures and institutions that require us to persist in the repetition of that activity. In political terms, this has happened with regard to key institutions through which individuals in civil society normally articulate their needs and desires to the political system of interest representation. For example the activity of voting increasingly ceases to have sense for us to the extent that votes do not meaningfully translate our experience of the political into political representation. Where there is no public sphere for political rather than social (socio-economic), private, etc., experience, political institutions at the state level lose their legitimation to claim they represent the citizenry politically. There continues to exist a 'political system' for making and enforcing laws, regulating the process in which one party replaces another as the party / coalition of government, etc., but the link between the political system and the individual political actor becomes increasingly tenuous. To the extent that they aggregate economic, social and private rather than political interests, institutional political parties are confronted with an increasingly impossible task of bridging this gap between system and citizen. The result in almost all Western European and North American polities has been either widespread voter disaffection and apathy, or the rise of populist anti-system movements. The latter are often defenders of some kind of implicit or explicit racist ideology such as the National Front in France, with the obviously dangerous implications for democractic politics that these movements carry. In the following section of this chapter it will be argued that the possible reconstruction of the public sphere of civil society will depend on our ability to recuperate for the public sphere 'the great variety of authentic political experiences' which our tradition of political thought has excluded.[17] It might then be possible to start thinking about how we might create specifically political representative institutions alongside the social, economic and private representative institutions we currently have. In chapter 4 on community and chapter 5 on recognition, it will be argued further that what is specifically political in this endeavour is the reconstruction of the meaning or sense of what we are doing, which is a political rather than a social or private matter. In making this argument I will be relying on Arendt's distinctions between both the 'social' and the 'political', on the one hand, and between 'life' and 'the world', on the other. These distinctions will now be elucidated below.[18]

The public sphere

Action and experience

In the last chapter it was mooted that production, politics and other spheres of human endeavour suggested distinct experiences of time. Thus it follows that perhaps time itself is not simply a homogeneous medium of individual experience. As a consequence it is

---

[17] Arendt, *The Human Condition*, pp. 238–9.
[18] Arendt, *On Revolution*, p. 238; Habermas, *Faktizität und Geltung*, pp. 402–3. Arendt's distinction between life and world is certainly influenced by her reading of Heidegger's phenomenological-ontological account of worldliness in *Sein und Zeit* (1927). Arendt gives the Heideggerian concept of 'the world' a thoroughly political dimension, however, which is underscored by Dana Villa in *Arendt and Heidegger: The Fate of the Political*, Princeton: Princeton University Press, 1996.

possible to think that both the time required in production, and the perspective of the individual worker in the production process, are different than the time implied by the equality of non-identical equals in the public sphere. This is not an argument sanctioning in any way a view of economic life based on the notion 'laws' of supply and demand or business 'cycles'. Rather, the aim of the discussion in the last chapter is to attempt to disentangle the discourses of the political from the economic and other fields as Schmitt tries to do, though without accepting Schmitt's definition of politics. Thus it was suggested in chapter 2 that the timing involved in harvesting, crop rotation, attempting to co-ordinate supply and demand, etc., is of a different order from that involved in political questions concerning the public sphere and issues of community, conflict and recognition. It was also seen how Benjamin applied Nietzsche's idea of the eternal return to commodity production and especially fashion, so that commodities can be analysed as ever-recurring manifestations of surplus value promising novelty in each only apparently new guise. Benjamin notes that Marx accurately depicts the capitalist economy as an endless accumulation process, such that the end result of hours and hours of labour appears to be a gigantic accumulation of goods.[19]

However, rather than seeing paths to emancipatory politics in terms of redefining the political to include the labour process and class exploitation, Arendt correctly maintains that the labour process – however organised – will always be governed by technical and means/ends considerations which distinguish 'labour' and 'work' from what she refers to as the political activity of 'action'.[20] That is, whether privately or collectively controlled, the means of production can ultimately only serve to reproduce the necessities of life. This is in no way unimportant; it is, in a literal sense, vital. Moreover, the central thesis of the present book is that from a

[19] Karl Marx, *Das Kapital* (*Capital*), Volume I, in MEW (*Marx-Engels Werke*), Volume 23 Berlin: Akademischer Verlag, 1955, p. 49; Oscar Negt and Alexander Kluge, *Öffentlichkeit und Erfahrung: Zur Organisationsanalyse von bürgerlicher und proletarischer Öffentlichkeit* (*The Public Sphere and Experience*, 5th edn), Frankfurt: Suhrkamp, 1977, p. 225; Benjamin, *Das Passagen-Werk* (*The Paris Arcades Project*, 1927–40), 2 vols Frankfurt: Suhrkamp, pp. 800–23.

[20] Arendt distinguishes between labour, which is immediately bound up with producing the necessities of life, on the one hand, and work, which includes individual creative projects embodied in works of art, on the other. See *The Human Condition*, chapters 3 and 4.

modified Arendtian perspective, some kind of collective control of the economy is indeed necessary, so that a specifically political space of a non-violent and non-sovereign nature can emerge amidst the technical and material processes governing the life-cycle and the preponderance of social and private concerns over all others. The variegated attempts to sustain a public sphere in contemporary civil societies can thus be seen as attempts to oppose the structural tendencies of existing institutions to transform *political* struggles into questions of interest representation from the narrow standpoints of 'identity politics' and political correctness. The only Arendtian caveat in this context would be that collective control of the economy might make politics and a public sphere possible, but these are, strictly speaking, nonetheless separate issues. To confuse them is to confuse the exigencies of labour and work with the political praxis of action. The former is concerned with the material necessities of *life* and the life-cycle, while the latter is concerned with the *world* and the possibility of creating a space of appearances for absolutely single and exceptional acts by people. Thus for Arendt the processes of making, producing and producing for reproductive purposes imply a different kind of time and perspective from the time and perspective of non-identical individual actions and words that cannot be manufactured, reproduced or represented – but only debated, cherished, honoured and remembered.

Marx is indeed correct in remarking that the worst architect distinguishes him or herself from the most intelligent bee by knowing and planning in advance what is going to be built. But to this Marx could have added that there is something fundamentally human that separates any person acting politically from *all* architects and bees in their private, socio-economic or instinctual capacity – a difference between life-preserving activity and world-changing action. It is certainly conceivable that plant reproduction, the cycle of changing seasons, etc., in short *life* can go on without humans. But there can be no *world* without the kind of political action that sustains a space for individuals with different perspectives to come together, tell different sides of the collective story of humankind, and thereby reach some sort of understanding of the *sense* of the world. In order for these different perspectives to constitute a history rather than a mere concatenation of events, there have to be listeners who in their presence preserve the space that make telling and remembering possible. From the perspective of the political understood in this worldly sense, it is not really so important whether one considers life to be a creation of God or a process of natural evolution, or the result of mechanical economic laws and necessities. In each case, freedom is strictly circumscribed by forces external to human intervention. The world, however, is a human creation that is never completed and which is, on the contrary, dependent upon humans for its ongoing preservation. Its precariousness consists in the omnipresent possibility of its elimination. Its promise consists in the possibility of new beginnings which, in the modern era, have been fleetingly brought to fruition in revolutions.[21]

The world and revolution

The new beginnings offered by modern revolutions are closely linked with the sudden opening up of political spheres and public spaces rather than the transfer of power that the revolutions bring about. The tragic legacy of what Arendt calls 'the lost revolutionary tradition', is that these spaces have tended to close up again once the transfer of power is completed and the bureaucratic imperatives of the social (administration) gain the upper hand over the political (action). This becomes clear when observing the recurrent appearance of the ideal of *Öffentlichkeit* that thrives in the writing of constitutions, formation of councils and organising of resistance etc., which characterise modern revolutionary situations. The closing down of public spaces is intimately linked with the success of the strategic project to 'seize power' which, as the Jacobins and Bolsheviks proved, is best organised by a political party. Through their strategic action, vanguard parties manage to take advantage of revolutionary situations in which a constellation of class and other social forces cease for a moment to be congealed as oppressive order. The 're-setting in motion' of this previously congealed picture opens up a public space, making visible just how arbitrary and unjust existing power relations in civil society are at that particular moment, or, in other words, how false, one-sided and senseless the institutional representation of actual events had been up until the revolution. Previously-existing power relations were unjust and arbitrary to the extent that they made hierarchy and the

---

[21] Arendt, *The Human Condition*, chapter 3; *On Revolution*, chapter 6.

rule of the few over the many appear the 'natural' condition of humans living together, when in fact the human condition made possible by people living together bears witness to an ongoing political project and continual transformation subject to abrupt changes.[22]

For Arendt the demands for 'liberty, equality and fraternity' and 'all power to the soviets' in the French and Russian revolutions symbolise attempts to translate the lived experience of equality into political institutions. Authentic political experiences which up until the revolutions had been considered merely private or sectarian issues finally received a hearing and thus achieved visibility.[23] The extremeness of the revolutionary situation was at the same time the basis of its political radicality; evolution belies the myth of political inequality by making visible the incommensurability of different energies and perspectives which challenge existing hierarchies as a disparate yet united bloc. The crucial point in relation to civil society/state relations and contemporary politics is that although these groups and individuals could *act* politically, they could not, in their disparateness, *rule*, which was and continues to be the social/administrative function of parties and states. Hence revolutionary parties are able to manipulate these situations in their favour and seize power. The seizure of power then inevitably closes down the momentarily public spaces of diverse perspectives opened up by the revolutionary situation; the successful parties

[22] In *The Human Condition* Arendt remarks that the tendency to accept political rule by the few as normal rather than a state of exception goes all the way back to Plato and Aristotle: 'Escape from the frailty of human affairs into the solidity of quiet and order has in fact so much to recommend it that the greater part of political philosophy since Plato could easily be interpreted as various attempts to find theoretical foundations and practical ways for an escape from politics altogether. The hallmark of all such escapes is the concept of rule, that is, the notion that men can lawfully and politically live together only when some are entitled to command and others are forced to obey' (p. 222).

[23] Negt and Kluge, *Öffentlichkeit und Erfahrung*, pp. 21–6; Oscar Negt and Alexander Kluge, *Geschichte und Eigensinn (History and Stubbornness)*, II: *Deutschland als Produktionsöffentlichkeit* (1981), Frankfurt: Suhrkamp, 1993, pp. 526, 548, and *Geschichte und Eigensinn, III: Gewalt des Zusammenhangs*, Frankfurt: Suhrkamp, pp. 1234–7. Negt and Kluge's Benjamin-inspired theory of the public sphere has not received enough attention in the English-speaking world. For an overly critical view, see Frederic Jameson, 'On Negt and Kluge', in *October*, 46 (1988). Issue 46 of *October* (1988) is dedicated to their work and includes translated sections of *Öffentlichkeit und Erfahrung*.

then proceed to reinstate the congealed hierarchies of rulership under new forms. Since the American and French revolutions this tended to mean rule by a single party or a party system. Thus the 'success' of party strategy was at the same time the triumph of instrumental over political considerations. In terms of the dynamic that makes power constellations cohere, the 'victory' of the organisational form of the party signalled the triumph of the will to power and of the spread of the experience of time and perspective peculiar to manufacturing activities. In political terms it meant the triumph of the social.[24]

The idea of seizing and transforming makes absolute sense in terms of the transformation of the raw material of nature to satisfy human material needs; there is indeed an ineliminable element of violence and even rage in such activities. But the yes/no, more/less criteria of manufacturing and production can only have a very limited role in a sphere for other virtues, i.e., in a sphere primarily for debating, honouring and remembering unique acts of insight, courage and trust. Here rule in the sovereign political sense and violence in the productive-transformational sense mentioned above are not only not appropriate – they are likely to spell the colonisation of the public sphere.[25] Rule and violence are appropriate in contexts where the means linking a given strategy are likely to produce success, and where the conditions of success are then reproduced to intensify the form of gain particularly involved in the pursuit of that given end (the execution of a central economic plan or the accumulation of capital are possible examples). Indeed, one might argue that in activities of this kind, rule, hierarchy and even intimidation are likely to be conducive to success in strictly means/ends terms. The criteria of success and failure are clear, i.e.,

---

[24] Arendt, *The Human Condition*, p. 190; *On Revolution*, pp. 268–9.

[25] Thus the way in which we conceive of political freedom in the future is closely linked to how we relate to the events of the past. Contrary to a 'common sense' view, it may even be the case that the past is more open to change and re-evaluation than the immediate future, especially where the latter is overdetermined by the material necessities of the life process, i.e., where capitalism and the logic of capital work to shut down the political spaces of the public sphere. See Arendt, 'Thoughts on Politics and Revolution', in *Crises of the Republic*, New York: Harvester, 1972, pp. 212–15; *Elemente und Ursprünge totaler Herrschaft (Origins of Totalitarianism*, 1951), Munich: Piper, 1986, pp. 239–66; and *Love and St. Augustine* (1929), Chicago: University of Chicago Press, 1996, pp. 15, 52–3.

as capital, money, property, prizes, status, etc. But in a political space shared by non-identical though equal citizens, there can not be success as such, nor can there be accumulation on the basis of other models suggested by different fields of human endeavour such as economics or householding. In contrast to these, the freedom inherent in politics stems from the action of self-disclosure which takes place in a space of political visibility, the outcome of which can never be predicted, and whose course can take many different, unforeseeable turns depending on how others in that space act. Thus the will and its vital life exigencies of domination and subordination inevitably clash with the worldly exigencies of the perspectival pluralism of simultaneous and mutual political visibility. In this clash, the will can only triumph with the elimination of politics. A modified Arendtian perspective on contemporary politics suggests that this is what political parties struggling for control of the state seek to do, to the detriment of the self-governing aspirations articulated from diverse quarters of civil society.[26]

As an organised collectivity of wills, the successful party (or coalition of parties) can utilise the technical means at its disposal akin to those employed in manufacturing and other semi-violent activities to consolidate its rule. But rule has more to do with the concerns of life than those of the world. Since the concerns of the world can never be completely repressed or ever fully eliminated by the concerns of life as long as people act politically, the will cannot be everywhere triumphant and has to eventually turn back on itself. It is, in its isolation, almost blind, i.e., deprived of other perspectives. In order to achieve state power, the will's criteria of reality has to be based on the *intensity* of the individual or party will in question; here lack of perspective is actually a positive attribute, insofar as this lack serves the instrumental goal of gaining power by blocking out the complexity introduced by the presence of other views. The faculty of *judgement*, by contrast, can only be cultivated by way of an examination of a plurality of stand-

---

[26] Barbara Cassin, 'Grecs et Romans: les paradigmes de l'antiquité chez Arendt et Heidegger', in Miguel Abensour and Christine Buci-Glucksmann (eds), *Ontologie et Politique: Actes de Colloque Hannah Arendt*, Paris: Éditions Tierce, 1989, pp. 31–3. These aspirations to self-government characterised KOR and other sectors of the Polish opposition to party rule prior to the fall of communism.

points, which make judgement and comparison more than arbitrary opinion. Since intensity serves the organised will of the party best to the extent that it shuts out plurality and ambiguity, it is harnessed by the party in a forward direction towards the prize of state power. The cultivation of judgement requires a different kind of vision and a different understanding of experience. Because it is dependent on other perspectives, those who exercise judgement in a political sense see that they are not free in isolation and, by extension, that the world which they help sustain is going to exist even when they as individuals die; this is not to say that they will be forgotten, and as such they will still be part of the world – if not of life.[27]

As an instrumentally organised collectivity of wills, political parties demonstrate that it is possible to organise an attempt to suppress the world in the name of life. They do this in various ways, regardless of whether they are alone at the summit of a single-party system or whether they work together in coalitions in conjunction with opposition parties in parliamentary systems. Whether they be parties of the left or right, parliamentary parties have a more or less equal hand in the defence and administrative representation of the experiences linked to labour (and to a much less extent, work[28]), to the almost total neglect of other more political, i.e., action-oriented ones. This is of course most obvious in the glorification of labour under state socialist regimes, but true too of contemporary parliamentary regimes in which the language of

[27] Hence in *The Human Condition* (pp. 55–6) Arendt writes: 'There is perhaps no clearer testimony to the loss of the public realm in the modern age than the almost complete loss of authentic concern with immortality, a loss somewhat overshadowed by the simutaneous loss of the metaphysical concern with eternity ... Under modern conditions, it is indeed so unlikely that anybody should earnestly aspire to an earthly immortality that we probably are justified in thinking that it is nothing but vanity.' But it is not merely vanity: although life and the concerns of life must move forward and at some point die, the world can be made larger to the extent that new perspectives become visible in the public sphere through acts of remembering the past and the temporarily forgotten. To the extent that political action sustains the world as a countervailing political space against the dictates of the will, political action can create a space for the immortality of worldly acts and individuals.

[28] Arendt comments that from the standpoint of making a living, every activity unconnected with labour must be considered a hobby rather than the work of an artist (*The Human Condition*, p. 128).

progress and welfare span the left–right spectrum. Arendt explains this in terms of two worlds separated by the experience of Christianity. While the Greek political world knew of immortality on earth in the *polis*, Christian civilisation speaks of immortality in other-worldly terms, and with the gradual erosion of Christian faith we can no longer even imagine immortality in heaven. Apart from fleetingly in the experience of modern revolutions and then again very recently with the 'rebirth of civil society', it was difficult to envisage a possible recuperation of the worldly experience of immortality, which had for centuries ceased to be a lived political reality. Schmitt's ideas suggest that where the theological dimension of Christian political culture triumphs, earthly *immortality* of a Greek lineage ceases to be an option. In this case, parties become the caretakers of *longevity* practised through the hymns to economic growth, order and stability that they preach to the electorate from the pulpits of the state.

However, longevity is experienced individually as a futile desire to prolong that which must ultimately culminate in death – individual life. As a populist institution, the modern socialist and capitalist states function so as to prevent the emergence of a public sphere capable of forestalling direct appeals from party leaders to 'the people', who are transformed from participants in the public sphere to isolated individuals of a 'massified' electorate. Politically this means that in the absence of a public sphere, isolated citizens can only hope for material progress and technical innovation to postpone the arrival of the inevitable final day, and politics is reduced to the choice of voting for the party which most convincingly claims to be able to deliver this extension of the life process. This engenders the frustration likely to ensue from the intuition of the impossibility of indefinitely-extending longevity, which, in turn, exacerbates the rage experienced by the prospect of there always being more in terms of wealth, property, capital, years, etc. to acquire, such that isolated individuals can never be at rest or free. Within this political constellation, it is unsurprising that parties across the left-right spectrum compete to present themselves as the most plausible vehicles to deliver on the promise of the greatest lifespan for the greatest number. Here progress consists in everybody's right to an equal chance to attain a bourgeois lifestyle and enjoy the 'best things in life', while politics and the concerns of the world are consigned to aesthetic protest or theological reflection.[29]

The attempt to contest the state's monopoly of political legitimacy and to sustain a public sphere in opposition to the state is best illustrated with the example of revolutionary councils, which spontaneously appear in almost every revolutionary situation since the American and French revolutions. Councils were of course especially important in the Russian revolutions of 1905 and 1917. But the history of radical council activity really spans the entire period from the Paris Commune of 1870 to the Spanish Civil War and beyond to the Budapest uprising of 1956, the Prague Spring of 1968, and the organised resistance to state socialist rule in European Europe culminating in the 'Velvet Revolutions' of 1989.[30] The power of the council experience lies in the act that rather than attempting to seize power, councils strive to make politics a reality against the congealed hierarchies of rule. That is, while hierarchy is necessary for rule, it is incompatible with politics. Thus in order for there to be politics, a space is required for a non-hierarchical form of action: the public sphere, of which councils offer an emblematic example. If citizens are to be equal in a political sense they have to be so in their singularity and uniqueness; citizenship implies the simultaneous condition of equality and individuality for each citizen. In order for individuality to be worldly, i.e., political, rather than just vital, there must be a space where individuality can become visible in a way that is never possible as a result of the processes that reproduce the conditions of life. Equality in this sense can only be realised in practice where each citizen can attain visibility and achieve uniqueness as recognised by present others. Thus a public sphere is necessary in order for formal legal equality to be completed with the lived experience of equality which is never definitively acquired in legal terms, but is enacted in deeds and words which outlive the life-cycle of particular individuals. What ideologues of totalitarianism, the end of ideology, the end of

[29] Arendt, *The Human Condition*, pp. 17–18, pp. 55–6. Also Hannah Arendt, *Between Past and Future: Eight Exercises in Political Thought*, New York: Penguin, 1961, pp. 155–6. See also Theodor W. Adorno, 'Fortschritt' ('Progress'), edited by Rolf Tiedemann, *Philosophie und Gesellschaft: Fünf Essays*, Stuttgart: Reklam, 1984, pp. 116–18. Hans Ebeling, *Das Subjekt in der Moderne: Rekonstruction der Philosophie im Zeitalter der Zerstörung*, Hamburg: Rowohlt, 1993, pp. 231–2.

[30] For a detailed account of this tradition of radical politics, see *Radical Theories*, chapter 3.

history, etc. normally fail to see is that all forms of rule, and in the last instance totalitarian rule, are predicated on the separateness of individuals – their massification in sovereign states rather than their free development in political communities.[31]

Where hierarchy flourishes, there can only be very limited forms of reciprocal visibility – and as a consequence a great deal of political inequality despite formal equal citizenship. Thus in its capacity to consolidate both hierarchy and isolation between individuals, bureaucracy is the unparalled form of the rule of the social. Isolation precludes speech, reciprocal visiblity and, indeed, politics. In this context Arendt observes that:

> Human plurality, the basic condition of both action and speech, has the twofold character of equality and distinction. If men were not equal, they could neither understand each other and those who came before them nor plan for the future and foresee the needs of those who will come after them. If men were not distinct, each human being distinguished from any other who is, was, or will be, they would need neither speech nor action to make themselves understood. Signs and sounds to communicate immediate, identical needs would be enough.[32]

The difficulties involved in realising political equality as plurality are distinct from the problems involved in remedying the inequalities resulting from differential performances in competitive spheres like labour and work. The former requires a horizontal space for voice and visibility; the latter requires a vertical chain of execution permitting relative swiftness and efficiency. This distinc-

---

[31] Returning briefly to Kafka (see footnote 15 above), formal legal equality did not prevent K's execution in *The Trial*. On the contrary, the absolute lack of a public sphere and any communication between the characters in the novel foreshadow his eventual execution. As a result of his isolation, the accused has no political representation, indeed, no one who can even attest to his existence, let alone his innocence. From this starting point he is already condemned, as it were, and completely exterminable at any time. There are of course many ways to read *The Trial*. From a political perspective, however, the story offers an unrivalled depiction of the sanction of murder through rational-legal domination. In his private embarrassment K achieves a kind of negative immortality akin to damnation. Thus the very last two lines of the novel show K. protesting against his execution ('like a dog!') while the narrator concludes that it was 'as if the shame would outlive him'. This point is also raised by Benjamin in his essay 'Kafka' in Optiz (ed.), *Walter Benjamin*, pp. 241–5. This essay is translated in the collection *Illuminations*.

[32] Arendt, *The Human Condition*, pp. 175–6.

tion between horizontally-practised forms of political equality versus vertically-directed methods of redistribution and care evokes the distinct experiences of both the time and the quality of action demanded. The absolute incommensurability of the quality of the action pertaining to their respective domains precludes any possible conflation of their associated practices. That this separation is possible is suggested by the historical role of councils in creating a public sphere in opposition to both parties and the state in periods of revolutionary upheaval.

Where the parties tend to collapse the distinction between political equality and administration, council action assumes it as a point of departure and strives to realise it in practice. Thus, albeit in historical terms only fleetingly, councils' action creates a public sphere as a political space to be occupied by different perspectives. In order for the space to remain political it has to remain open, and in order for it to remain open it has to be accessible to all citizens taking turns occupying it and then leaving it to individuals with another perspective. Analogous to the classical Greek notion of democracy as fundamentally entailing taking turns ruling and being ruled, council equality is founded on a form of participation that demands the participation of differing and even strongly opposed points of view. By contrast, party behaviour directly conflicts with council action to the extent that party strategy aims at achieving the right to rule, to remain in power and to instrumentalise whatever there is of a public sphere to this end, such that visibility becomes the exclusive privilege of the leader and the few in favour around that person. The standpoints of other parties must be defeated, and within the parties themselves differences of opinion must be curtailed in order for them to be successful in electoral competition. Indeed, the worst thing that a ruling or opposition party can do is to seem divided in public, which casts doubt on its ability to achieve power and to rule with singularity of purpose. Moreover, this discipline has to be maintained in harmony with the rhythms of the changing four- or six-year 'voting seasons', which are often determined in advance by compromises normally worked out among the different parties in joint consultation! Thus there is a season to devise electoral manoeuvering, a season to 'go to the voters', and a season to reap the fruits of successful strategy or learn the lessons of defeat: the logic and practices of reproducing the material necessities of the life-cycle crowd out and dominate the worldly action of the political.[33]

The world of politics

The paradox of anti-political political parties can perhaps be partly illuminated by reconsidering the question of boundaries raised towards the end of chapter 2 from the perspective of some of the issues raised in this chapter. In chapter 2 it was seen how questions of political sovereignty and conflict can be settled in the last instance in non-political terms which in important respects have marked similarities with theological traditions of interpretation; this is especially clear in the work of Carl Schmitt. In this chapter it has been argued in a very different vein that to the extent that political parties tend to collapse the boundaries between the political space for action and the hierarchical space delineated by an administrative chain of command, they reinforce a tendency within our tradition of thinking about politics in terms of contract and will. Thus *social* contract theory assumes the relatively unproblematic nature of transforming the horizontal contract of legally equal exchange partners into the vertical contract of political authority, i.e., of grounding political authority on the basis of non-political experiences from fields of human endeavour primarily related to the economy and the household. It has also been suggested in this chapter that such activities are non-political to the extent that they: (a) allot an important role to instrumental reason rather than a form of reason concerned with autonomy and freedom, (b) are marked by certain forms of violence inherent in processes of technical transformation rather than political discussion, and (c) are structured in accordance with the strategic behaviour of individuals and parties organised as collective wills in economic competition.[34]

Looking at both chapters with the distinction between life and world developed in this chapter in mind, it would appear that we are still far from thinking political problems through in specifically political ways. It seems that our so-called political institutions

[33] Arendt, *On Revolution*, pp. 266–8.
[34] The discussion of boundaries in chapters 2 and 3 is developed further in chapter 4, where it is argued that community is a form of political action in civil society which points beyond the instrumental and strategic considerations rooted in interest and identity.

largely rely on the theory and practice of other disciplines such as economics and administration. At the same time, we often borrow from the domains of theology and law in our approach to the state. Architects and bees can both be involved in economic activity, while theology is at least in principle related to a domain beyond the sphere of material interest. But whereas both economic and theological pursuits have spheres of practice in which political interference is regarded as an intrusion, politics as worldly human action distinct from economics, theology, administration, etc. is still in need of a space for its articulation and practice. Once again from the standpoint of civil society, this implies that existing political institutions such as parties and states are inadequate, especially insofar as they attempt to settle political questions in non-political ways by transforming the political itself into questions of interest, administration, etc. As a result, politics is transformed into a matter of efficiency, while real political questions of action and values become matters of individual conscience and theology, i.e., they lose their political significance. The recurrent attempt to sustain a public sphere represents a political struggle against this transformation. It is most evident in modern revolutionary situations, but is also, as has been suggested in this chapter, evident in daily forms of political action in contemporary civil societies. In what follows I will try to draw some tentative theoretical conclusions about the relationship between politics, the public sphere and civil society discussed in this chapter with reference to the upheavals of 1968 and the post-1968 flourishing of NSMs.

The public sphere exists between rather than on the basis of individual citizens; it cannot be 'constructed' according to models borrowed from theology, architecture, economics, etc. Since it is ontologically impossible to require individual citizens to 'stand still' and form part of a solid foundation without either reifying them or coercing and manipulating them into silence, the public sphere for the voice and visibility of incommensurably different ways of 'standing' in the modern world is necessarily plural and unstable. But like Schmitt's friend–enemy relation, it is always present, and can attain acute phases of organisational autonomy and independence from the state in both the Weberian and the competitive electoral senses. In such instances politics emerges from the shadows of other discourses and logics of practice, and distinguishes itself from mere interest representation and other

forms of institutionalised class compromise. Where the public
sphere is called into existence and sustained between individuals,
it becomes clear that political action is not the re-presentation of an
original unity in the name of everyone's imputed interest to receive
an administered 'just' share in that whole: here everyone is
presumed to have more or less similar interests, while different
perspectives become deviant ones to be dealt with in one way or
another. Rather, action in the political sense is a way of letting the
human world of the political speak in its instability and plurality
from the manifold perspectives which constitute it in constellations
which form, dissolve and re-form. The political struggle to sustain
the public sphere is an attempt to preserve the possibility of non-
determined new beginnings in distinctly human rather than
natural/cyclical terms. Thus politics entails the formation of new
constellations and the de-congealing of old hierarchies, which
means that it entails the possibility of revolution.

In the last chapter it was seen how the notion of contractual
exchange between legal equals becomes problematic from the
moment one takes the labour contract into consideration, i.e., from
the moment the law between supposedly equal citizens enables
some of them to buy and command the labour power of others. The
necessity of selling one's labour power in order to receive basic
goods in order to make life possible, and the experience of the
exploitation inherent in that struggle, has historically resulted in a
situation in which for most people the lived experience of citizenship has been the reality of social class in all its diverse facets. Class
thus became both a source of identity and the origin of a range of
daily experiences such as alienation, exploitation, powerlessness,
solidarity, struggle, hope, etc., which although rooted in an experience of class, raises issues beyond the horizon of class experience.
It is thus unsurprising that in its incipience, the workers' movement bound together the struggle for political emancipation with
the struggle for a secure life which capitalism denied practically
everyone; since 'everyone' constituted an overwhelming majority,
socialism appeared to be the answer to the political riddle of
democracy.

In its most advanced sectors, the workers' movement strove
beyond the hierarchical and administrative forms of organisation
common to all parties; workers' councils thus flourished wherever
libertarian socialism managed to assert itself. More importantly, in

its most sophisticated manifestations, council movements such as Guild Socialism demanded the articulation of issues beyond class struggle. A long chapter in the history of the lost revolutionary tradition would have to address the series of political errors and authoritarian turns in the workers' movement which led to the assault on the councils by social democratic and communist parties and unions.[35] This assault has had the long-term consequence that the workers' movement has in many ways become a conservative force for the stabilisation of capitalist production relations and the administration of social welfare in parliamentary democracy. Like all developments in the history of revolution, none are irrevocable. The history of post-war Europe, North America and beyond indicates that the role of radical contestation of what counts as political experience and how this experience might be articulated may have to a certain extent been relinquished by the workers' movement to the feminist, peace, ecologist, gay rights, regionalist, native peoples', autonomist, refugees', etc. movements, i.e., to movements which are generally referred to as NSMs, and which are at the forefront of initiatives to reconstitute and enlarge the public sphere since 1968–69.

As is well known, the years 1968–69 mark a key moment in this development. The institutional left of socialist and communist parties seemed incapable and unwilling to grasp the 'critique of everyday life' beyond material interests which workers, students, anarchists, situationists and others articulated in a variety of spontaneous forms of organisation and resistance to capitalism and the state. In successfully maintaining its grip on the 'legitimate' representation of political contestation in civil society, the institutional left forfeited any critique of the 'well-functioning capitalism' of the postwar boom years. Socialist and communist parties had no real oppositional role as long as standards of living were high; the parties became the integrated administrative adjuncts of the state necessary for administering the goods of the

---

[35] Thus syndicalists and anarchists were much more sympathetic to the council idea than were social democrats and communists and were much more likely to participate in revolutionary council action (*Radical Theories*, chapters 1 and 2). In theoretical terms, the defence of council democracy to embrace issues beyond merely workers' interests received its most sophisticated articulation in the writings of Antonio Gramsci, Anton Pannekoek, and especially G.D.H. Cole (*Radical Theories*, chapters 3 and 4).

postwar consensus: gradually increased spending power and consumer choice. Because they were neither culturally nor ideologically equipped for the more radical critique coming from students, situationists, and from anarchist and councilist quarters of the workers' movement, these parties managed to sever the cultural and ideological critique of capitalism from the struggle for material interests under the capitalist system. After the stabilisation of existing political and economic institutions after 1968–69, the mass parties of the left took integration even further by way of corporatist and other forms of co-operation with the state during the 1970s. Thereafter they were forced to watch their electoral weight steadily decline. After the fall of the Berlin Wall, they have since either disappeared or transformed themselves into reformist social democratic parties, without even the pretence of trying to enact major economic or political reform. While the economic critique of capitalism has faded into obscurity, the political, cultural and ideological critique of capitalism has to some extent been taken up by the NSMs.[36]

However, by themselves NSMs cannot substitute for the economic critique of capitalism, without which their political, cultural and ideological critique is repeatedly integrated into existing forms of interest aggregation like parliamentary democracy. Without a non-statist socialist economic organisation of issues concerned with the life process, the political content of NSM action in contemporary civil socities is all too easily incorporated into reformist channels – *just as has happened with the workers' movement*. Thus the potentially radical forms of public-sphere action which NSMs strive to create and enlarge will only be partially visible and politically significant until politics in civil society is sustained by a socialist material foundation which to the greatest possible extent solves or neutralises questions of material necessity and need. Once this has been accomplished, the public sphere and politics generally will perhaps be able to take on the

[36] Guy Debord, *La société du spectacle* (*The Society of the Spectacle*, 1967), Paris: Gallimard, 1992; Raoul Vaneigem, *Traité de savoir-vivre à l'usage des jeunes générations* (1967), Paris: Gallimard, 1992; Henri Lefebvre, *La vie quotidienne dans le monde moderne*, Paris: Gallimard, 1968; Isabelle Sommier, *La violence politique et son deuil: l'après 68 en France et en Italie*, Rennes: Presses Universitaires de Rennes, 1998. For a great introduction to the ideas of the Situationists, see Sadie Plant, *The Most Radical Gesture: The Situationist International in a Postmodern Age*, London: Routledge, 1992.

full worldly significance of which we now only glimpse significant traces.

In redefining individual experience and identity in ways both compatible and in opposition to a class-centred conception of politics, NSMs challenge what had become congealed notions of interest, representation and action. Thus with exceptions such as the reformist tendencies in the ecology movement, NSMs have been reluctant to forfeit the political content of the perspectives they articulate to the bureaucratic-administrative demands of party organisation and electoral competition. Moreover, NSMs have been very effective in showing that power is at stake in the demarcation of certain spheres like the family or work as private, and others such as voting or the state as public. Yet there is no immediate reason why ecologists should enter into dialogue with gay rights activists or why feminists must find out what is going on in regional autonomy movements, etc. Hence regardless of how vibrant NSM activity has been in re-structuring the public sphere, this space will have to be enlarged still further to challenge the state in the name of a self-governing civil society. Otherwise, political perspectives, values and energies will continue to be largely transformed into demands for meritocracy in narrowly utilitarian terms, on the one hand, or ultimately futile forms of 'identity politics', on the other. The struggle for a public sphere is the political struggle to allow a perspective to emerge as a perspective and to distinguish itself from a mere interest. If one needs to see as many other perspectives as possible in order to have vision in a political sense, i.e., if the freedom associated with the open nature of the public sphere is a freedom that requires the knowledge and experience of the presence and words of others, then no perspective can be eliminated or made invisible. This is far from saying that all points of view will be showered with praise or approval – on the contrary, such a range of diversity is bound to shed light on numerous conflicts between different values for which there is no common measurement, i.e., incommensurability between positions.[37] What it does indicate is that acts like forgiving and promising which because of previously existing boundaries have been consigned to the realms of the

[37] But since the public sphere as described in this chapter is a space for voice and visibility, there is no recourse within it to solutions offered by the experiences of administration, states of exception or violence.

private or buried amidst he ruins of the social, will be 'released' to the public sphere in ways which have not yet been fully realised by NSMs or other forms of resistance to the state and the social-bureaucratic power of parties.

4

Community as politics

The absence of community is not the failure of community
Maurice Blanchot, *The Inadmissible Community*

One of the difficulties in treating the subject of community in political terms stems from its literally utopian nature: the political community, as distinct from an ethnic, religious, artistic, etc. community, has no 'place', or site or centre. Nonetheless, the various instances of different kinds of community within civil society suggest a striving towards articulation and an aspiration towards concreteness that resist the logic of essences or origins that characterise the discourses and practices of state and nationality. Community in this sense also resists interpretation either as a mediating unit between the lifeworld and the state, on the one hand, or the context for the representation of concerns related to different interests and identities, on the other. Like the public sphere, it is better understood as a degree of intensity rather than an expression of functionalist adaptation to socio-economic and political complexity. Yet while the public sphere opens as a space for the political action of non-identical yet equal individuals, community characterises a relation between individuals which assumes concrete form as the result of joint action. Crucially, however, it assumes form without becoming reified as a thing: the form of political community continually changes, as new concerted projects are undertaken which constantly change the boundaries within which joint action takes place. This chapter seeks to demonstrate that in its most utopian and emancipatory expression, community as politics unfolds in the ongoing praxis of individuals resisting the ascribed essences of fixed interests and identities, and also resists, by extension, the institution that is currently used to mediate between conflicts arising from clashing interests and identities – the state. In different ways communities attempt to reclaim a diverse range of experiences as *political* experiences against the institutionalisation of false or 'imagined' community in the form of nationalism, populism and other contrived forms of community 'from above'. In the first two sections of this chapter I will distinguish between interest and identity struggles as two distinct forms of collective behaviour, before then going on to define and explain community as a particular form of collective political action in contemporary civil societies in the third section.[1]

Collective behaviour

Common interests

In examining the projects of different communities in civil society, it becomes clear that the modes of community are distinct from both the strategies of associations like trade unions and political parties (interest), on the one hand, and the discourses of nation and state (identity), on the other. Turning first to the behaviour and strategies of different interest groups, it is clear that in contrast to family, nation and state, people *choose* the political parties, trade unions, reading groups and other associations to which they belong. Unions, parties and other groups and associations are formed for the purpose of pursuing a particular set of interests common to a membership who nonetheless have other interests which they may pursue through other associations. Party and union members pursue their material interests according to the best possible means available to them at any given time; their activity is instrumental and strategic. The strategy of a party or union is decisively shaped even before negotiations, strikes or elections begin by the fact that the goal in a specific struggle is usually clear, and the important questions turn on the best possible means to attain the goal. This is true both of Leninist vanguards and of syndicalist unions which in theory claim to be revolutionary.

---

[1] Benedict Anderson, *Imagined Communities: Reflections on the Origins and Spread of Nationalism*, London: Verso, 1983, pp. 15–16. As in the previous chapter on the public sphere, I will develop a theoretical analysis of instances of political community, while referring to specific cases in the footnotes.

The vanguard posits a chain of representation running from the socially-exploited condition of the working class to the organisational necessity of the party for the seizure of state power, which, if successful, culminates at the head in the clique or person who best incarnates the interests of the workers protected in the workers' state. Far from being a deviation related to the peculiarly difficult conditions of Russian development, the leadership cult is implicitly inscribed within the notion of the vanguard as the organisational form best suited for the seizure of power and the protection of the interests of the working class: hierarchy and secrecy allow for quick and decisive intervention, and since in theory all members of the same class have the same or similar material needs, vertical representation does little violence to the particularity of each worker. The syndicalist strategy of placing control of the production process in the hands of the workers organised in trade unions regards the question of democracy from a somewhat different angle: instead of attempting to secure power through the strategic/military conquest of the state, syndicalists argue that the battle for democracy as self-government begins and culminates with worker control of trade and industry. This strategy seeks to attack the authority of the state from the vantage point of its economic foundation, i.e., the domination of labour by capital at the site of production. From a syndicalist perspective, revolution occurs when the workers take control of the factories and thereby hollow out the bourgeois state apparatus, which rests on capitalist control of the production process. Rather than seizure of the state, its withering away is achieved by its undermining from below. Both vanguardist and syndicalist strategies correctly intuit that the existing state is not a neutral arbitrator mediating between different interests and identities. However, rather than challenging the logic of interest as the basis of political representation, they attempt to enact a system of direct co-ordination between material interest and political form. Where the bourgeois state masks a relation of domination in the formal-legal equality of both workers and capitalists as citizens, vanguardists and syndicalists in principle strive for the greatest possible transparency between the different levels of the political hierarchy, on the one hand, and the technical expertise required for collective control of the means of production, on the other. Rather than being anti-democratic, hierarchy is the precondition of transparency between socialism conceived as class dictatorship, and the chain of command required for the

administration of production and distribution without private property or markets.[2]

Vanguardist and syndicalist opposition to the bourgeois state's
protection of the interests of property and capital is belied by a more
fundamental similarity with bourgeois practice: the strategy of
making interest the basis of the state and political representation. In
theory, the exploitative contract between capital and labour is superseded by direct control of the production process – and as an
immediate consequence, the state. But what vanguardists and syndicalists usually fail to consider is that while interests can be
represented in hierarchies of performance and technical competence,
political equality cannot. Not completely unlike liberals who tend to
justify high pay differentials and other forms of power and privilege
in terms of dubious meritocratic criteria related to competitive
success, the Bolshevik institutionalisation of interest as the basis of
power directly contributed to the highly bureaucratic and hierarchical structure of Soviet society. Merit was rewarded in the form of
higher wages, better housing and access to consumer goods for those
who distinguished themselves professionally at work or administratively in government and the military. The highest skilled workers
were given material incentives to stay in the Soviet system, while the
party and army were granted access to dacha and other material
comforts. More generally, where production and efficiency are held
to be the overarching goal of society as a whole, and where it is ideologically established that hierarchy and authoritarian management
are conducive to the attainment of that goal, the institution of bureaucratic tyranny in the pursuit of increased production can be said to be
in everyone's interests, and as such codified in positive law as the
essence of democracy.[3]

The point is that in institutions and practices related to technical

---

[2] *Radical Theories*, Introduction and chapter 1.

[3] As the term *hegemony* suggests, the relationship between capital, class and
state power is far more nuanced under advanced capitalism and parliamentary
democracy than it was under state socialism. Yet under both late capitalism and
state socialism, politics is eclipsed by the rule of interests bound up with essentially technical and mechanical processes of economic growth and capital
(private or state) accumulation. Nonetheless, the theory and practice of syndicalism should be distinguished from state socialism, in particular as regards the
libertarian forms of anarcho-syndicalism which historically have rarely pursued
vanguard tactics, as the example of the Spanish Civil War shows. See *Radical
Theories*, chapter 2.

proficiency and competitive performance, interests are formed which
are very difficult to mediate in terms other than hierarchies of representation. Since efficiency is required in all technical processes, and
efficiency is best secured through minimal discussion and maximum
speed in carrying out tasks whose endpoint has already been established, the introduction of any non-instrumental criteria is likely to
retard success. Hence where material interest is allowed to take over
as the predominant factor regulating the world of politics, bureaucratic hierarchy and party competition for control of the state become
the prevalent forms of political organisation. As a consequence, in
both state socialist and parliamentary regimes, professional politicians of either a vanguard or bureaucratic-reformist stamp assume
the role of 'seeing to the needs of the people'. It might be objected that
it is imprecise to compare socialist planners and party élites with
parliamentary career politicians. Nonetheless, the electoral competition of professional politicians in parliamentary regimes cannot be
confused with perspectival or value pluralism; as in state socialist
regimes, the dominant party or coalition of parties is entrusted with
being the most efficient guarantor of a stable material existence for the
majority. The main difference between state socialist and parliamentary regimes is that once career politicians in parliamentary regimes
have worked their way up a party hierarchy before they can be
elected, they must work within terms acceptable to capital so as not to
threaten powerful private economic interests enough to cause capital
flight. Here it might be argued that in contrast to socialist authoritarianism, the pluralism of parliamentary regimes consists in the legally
protected diversity of different opinions and values in formally
democratic societies. This diversity is reflected by the different political parties, newspapers, lifestyles, etc. that characterise modern
parliamentary democracies. The question then becomes: how is it
possible to reconcile the liberal freedoms of press, assembly and party
affiliation, on the one hand, with the bourgeois necessity of securing
the conditions for the predictable investment and accumulation of
capital, on the other? Is it simply the case that the liberal freedoms are
also self-restricting freedoms which limit their critique to lifestyle and
opinion, without calling into question the privileged relation between
capital and government?[4]

---

[4] For a cogent argument demonstrating that (1) liberal freedoms are consistently undermined by the dynamic of capital accumulation and the logic of
investment for immediate and long-term private profit, and (2) liberal freedoms

Somewhat perplexed by these questions, a number of civil society theorists follow Habermas in arguing that the freedom of expression and civic associations exists in a public sphere which is systematically insulated from the workings of the economy. Systemic complexity ensures that the instrumental and strategic criteria informing economic practice are distinct from the communicative and interaction-based logic of civil society and the lifeworld; on this reading, the economy and civil society co-exist in *autopoiesic* harmony.[5] At the theoretical level, it is the removal of the economy from civil society that makes this functionalist juxtaposition and separation of their respective logics possible.[6] Yet in this case, should not powerful economic interests as well as associations and groups in civil society have equal access to state power? They do, in a sense, and this is the problem. In parliamentary regimes, the institutionalisation of politics in terms of the representation of interests and identities is accomplished as a series of compromises between contracting parties faciliated by lawyers and politicians. However, as will be argued in section 3 of this chapter, the communicative and community-based dimension of civil society does not assume visible form as a series of compromises or contractual agreements between strategic actors. Like the individuals in the public sphere explored in chapter 3, communities in civil society are more concerned with action than with rule. However, the dynamic of community action goes by and

---

are not self-restricting but rather frustrated by the privileged relation between capital and government, see T.W. Adorno, 'Gesellschaft' ('Society') (1965), pp. 16–19, and 'Anmerkungen zum sozialen Konflikte heute' ('Remarks on social conflicts today'), (1968), pp. 181–8, in *Soziologische Schriften*, I, Frankfurt: Suhrkamp, 1979.

[5] This term is now widely used by those who emulate Habermas's attempt to make theoretical concessions to socio-political complexity by way of a partial assimilation of some of the basic tenets of Luhmann's functionalism. See Niklas Luhmann, *Soziale Systeme (Social Systems)* (1984), Frankfurt: Suhrkamp, 1987, pp. 43–4; Detlef Horster, *Niklas Luhmann*, Munich: C.H. Beck, 1997, pp. 61–2. The awkwardness of this partial assimilation within the larger framework of Habermas's theory of communicative action is discussed in more detail in the next chapter.

[6] The theoretical untenability of this concession to functionalist thinking informs the approach in the current book, which is to include the economy in civil society and to argue that the defence of the political understood in the terms outlined in chapters 3 to 5 is inseparable from the argument for a simultaneous restructuring of the economy in a guild socialist/anarcho-communist direction.

large unrecognised in a political system designed to adjudicate between zero-sum conflicts. The apparent equal access of both communities and interest groups to a political system designed for the mediation of conflicting interests thus perpetuates the spurious neutrality of the state in favour of the most powerful interests.[7] Non-strategic action is not recognised as political action, and as such acquires merely symbolic value as charity or private good will. The political dimension of community in terms of collective action, self-help organisation and conflict mediation between citizens is eclipsed by the vertical channelling of interest representation to the summit of political-administrative power. This is most obvious in institution-alised forms of corporatist negotiation between the state, business and organised labour. But it is more generally salient wherever recognition is by and large institutionalised in the representation of fixed, identifiable quantities like money which can be channelled, redistributed and administered.[8] A separate but related problem to which we now turn is raised by the issue of fixed, identifiable essences such as in-groups/out-groups, and national as well as other forms of identity which appear with the rise of the modern state.

[7] That this neutrality is spurious should be obvious from the fact that parlia-mentary democracy arose as a means of adjudicating between the conflicting interests of the politically moribund aristocracy and the politically ascendant bourgeoisie; it was thus from the outset an institution for regulating conflict rather than any expression of the 'general will'. See Koselleck, *Kritik und Krise*, chapter 1. For the impossibility of the neutrality of law within such a system, see Carl Schmitt, *Legalität und Legitimität* (*Legality and Legitimacy*, 1932), Berlin: Duncker & Humblot, 1993, pp. 14–18, p. 84.

[8] Ferdinand Tönnies, *Gemeinschaft und Gesellschaft: Grundbegriffe der reinen Soziologie* (*Community and Society*, 1887). Berlin: Karl Curtius, 1921, pp. 55–66; Georg Simmel, *Die Philosophie des Geldes* (*The Philosophy of Money*, 1900), Frankfurt: Suhrkamp, 989, pp. 304–5. The issues of status and power are in some ways more complex in that they are not channelled, redistributed and administered like money. But this does not alter the problem of the insufficient recognition in state political institutions of non-strategic and non-contractual forms of political action such as community, which, in Foucault's terms, one can think of as an instance of repressed local knowledge. The lack of legal represen-tation of community and other instances of non-monetary forms of action within the sovereign state attests to the real hierarchisation of ostensibly neutral *methods* of representative government, as well as the virtual impossibility of representing community at all. For a convincing account of how this vertical centralisation of representative power systematically excludes other possible forms of political practice, see Michel Foucault, *Il faut défendre la société*, Paris: Gallimard/Seuil, 1997, pp. 9–10, 161–2.

In chapter 2 it was seen that in the period intervening between Hegel and Weber, political theory registers a dramatic shift in thinking about the state.[9] Hegel is able to write about the state as mind-objectified, and as a community that cannot be confused with individual interest or the contractual relations of civil society. Weber has a much more sober assessment, which he expresses in the famous definition in 'Politik als Beruf' ('Politics as a Vocation'): the state is the monopoly on the use of legitimate force within a given territory. Thus whereas Rousseau argues that one must distinguish between the will of all and the General Will, and Hegel argues for the dignity of the state above competing interests, Weber is forced to concede that there is no obvious principle above power and interest to legitimise the modern state, such that it becomes practically impossible to distinguish between legality and legitimacy: it is the mere belief in the sanctity of law that gives the state its legitimacy as more than a machine for settling different power, interest and identity struggles.[10] It was also seen that in Schmitt's early writings like *Politische Theologie* (*Political Theology*) (1922), he demonstrates that there is in fact no worldly principle to legitimate the state, which is why he who settles a state of exception is sovereign, and sovereignty is ultimately derived from theological arguments. In later writings such as *Die geistesgeschichtliche Lage des Heutigen Parlamentarismus* (*The Crisis of Parliamentary Democracy*) (1923) and especially *Legalität und Legitimität* (*Legality and Legitimacy*) (1932), Schmitt does not so much

[9] As discussed in chapter 2, in addition to Marx's critique of Hegel, this intervening factor is Nietzsche's genealogical critique of rights, power and the state. Weber's notion of legal-rational domination is inspired by Nietzsche's *Genealogy of Morals*, in which Nietzsche convincingly argues that legality and other forms of ostensibly neutral or objective discourses are in fact legitimations of domination. Weber underpins this analysis with a sociological investigation of the rise of demagogues and plebiscites within modern parliamentary democracies. See Weber, 'Parlamentarisierung und Demokratisierung' (1918), in *Schriften zur Sozialgeschichte und Politik*, Stuttgart: Reclam, 1997, pp. 212–14.

[10] Most liberals do not have Rousseau's or Hegel's problem of trying to generate a principle beyond interest or power in order to legitimise the state. They typically argue that either (a) the state is indeed there to mediate between different competing iterests, and thus needs no further justification, or (b) the competition of different interests leads to the aggregate good or utility of all, i.e., generates its own good. The first argument has been effectively discredited by Rousseau, Hegel, Marx, Weber and Schmitt, while history has effectively discredited the second argument. Liberal attempts to think beyond (a) to (b) tend to either reproduce problems which already appear in Kant (Rawls), or founder between liberalism and Hegel (Croce).

renounce his views on the state and theology as attempt to formulate ways of re-legitimising the executive of the state once it has become clear that the legislature is mired in material disputes. Weber and Schmitt are fundamentally important in explaining why the legitimacy of the modern state rests on the fiction of a re-formulated General Will or general interest, in whose manifest absence parties and politicians are compelled to embrace either populist tactics like the plebiscite, or ideological manipulation like national identity, in an attempt to solve the ensuing legitimation crisis from above.[11] Thus while chapter 2 attempts to provide a critique of the violent and theological implications of the doctrine of sovereignty, this chapter proceeds to focus on the manifest problems in attempting to solve the problem of the legitimacy of the state through different appeals to identity. After showing that neither state sovereignty nor ideologically manipulated forms of interest can provide a *political* solution to the question of how to reconcile freedom and authority, it will now be argued that contrived forms of identity are also unconvincing in this regard. Thereafter it will be argued in section 3 of this chapter that in addition to the public sphere, instances of community in civil society do suggest a political solution to the question of human freedom. It will then be possible to examine the idea of recognition as the third dimension of the political in civil society in the last chapter of this book.[12]

Unity and identity

Hegel's refusal to ground the state in interest or any other mode of individualism he associates with civil society is based on the premise that the state cannot have a contractual foundation. It is

[11] Somewhat surprisingly, given the clarity of their analyses, Weber and Schmitt are inclined to regard national identity and national power interests as sources of legitimacy for the state. See Weber, 'Parlamentarisierung und Demokratisierung', pp. 212–13; Schmitt, *Die geistesgeschichtliche Lage des heutigen Parlamentarismus*, pp. 88–9, *Legalität und Legitimität*, pp. 90–1.

[12] It might seem as if the argument is assuming a Hegelian structure, i.e., one where individual action in the public sphere (thesis) is contrasted with collective action in communities (anithesis), which is resolved in the higher unity of recognition that is both individual and communicative-communal (synthesis). This is not the case, since the idea of the stuggle for recognition defended in this book is not Hegelian, as will be seen in the next chapter. Moreover, in my usage the political, as enacted as a relation between the public sphere, community and recognition, is best understood as a constellation of interconnecting instances of political action, rather than a series of dialectical negations.

not only that the institution of contract presupposes the state for its validity, which is why contract is derived from the state rather than the other way round, but more importantly, Hegel is convinced that beyond mere security, individuals must recognise the bases of their own *freedom* in the institutions of the modern state. Otherwise, the citizen will have an instrumental relationship with the state at best or an antagonistic one at worst, which is to say an instrumental or antagonistic relationship will prevail among citizens. Anticipating contemporary political problems, Hegel intuits that if the aim of the state becomes security, politics will degenerate into competing claims to make the people secure. Hence where security is won through the system of needs (the economy), police and corporation (welfare and order) in civil society, the state exists in and for itself as objectivity of freedom; it has no end, but is an end in itself.[13] Thus for Hegel material stability is not the same as political freedom, which is why life in civil society cannot be cofused with the aims of the state. As was seen in chapters 1 and 2 however, Marx and Nietzsche are able to put forward strong enough arguments against Hegel to make the diagnoses of Weber, Schmitt and Benjamin seem almost irrefutable. In terms of actual political institutions, the theoretical failure of the Hegelian defence of the state does not absolve actual political power of the need to justify its forms of domination in a Hegelian manner, i.e., as a thing supposedly beyond contract and interest: the state has to seem to stand above these in order for it to be able to claim to arbitrate in a neutral way in the institution of law, and at the same time incarnate principles beyond private security and ambition. But if laws are made by the people (or more precisely by their representatives), and the people are divided along class and other lines, law

---

[13] The flaw in Hegel's argument spotted by Marx is that Hegel is wrong to suppose that the contractual element of civil law can happily co-exist with the universal and non-interest-based postulates of public law. To make this argument, Hegel needs the idea of a movement of spirit which cancels and preserves the contractual moment of civil society in the political community of the state. It is the manifest failure of this to happen in practice which prompts Marx to quip that the separation of the state and civil society means that the constitution rules without really ruling: inequality in civil life undermines political equality at every turn. This allows people to exploit each other via contract, while the state enjoys a monopoly on the legitimate practice of community. See Marx, 'Introduction' to *Zur Kritik der Hegelschen Rechtsphilosophie* (1843), in Iring Fetscher (ed.), *Karl Marx und Friedrich Engels: Studienausgabe, Vol. 1*, Frankfurt: Fischer, 1990, pp. 21–33.

cannot be neutral but is rather a reflection of interest. Thus in terms of its legitimacy, there must be unifying forces beyond law which make the state both neutral and the source of popular unity beyond material and other forms of conflict. These forces must be seen to be principles common to all citizens in a way that transcends their private aims, and something with which they can unconditionally identify in non-instrumental terms. As frequently occurs, this unity can be fabricated from above, when politicians successfully appeal to something natural, timeless and original, such as the imagined community of the nation. It can also be fabricated when citizens in civil society either define themselves or allow themselves to be defined as subjects with fixed identities which mean they can be categorised, labelled and eventually cared for or cured. In the first instance politics as perspectival pluralism is eclipsed by the pre-given requirement of having to continually construct and reconstruct national unity (constant mobilisation), while in the second instance politics as free, non-instrumental praxis is dissipated into passive forms of spectatorship by the ideology of plural 'lifestyles' (consumption). These two ideas will now be briefly looked at in turn.[14]

An analysis of the concept of sovereignty ends in an ambigu-

[14] Ideologies of common origin, identity and natural belonging share certain presuppositions with the pursuit of collective interests. In both cases, there is a pre-given goal towards which all behaviour and energy is directed. The pursuit of a common set of interests often takes the form of a set of strategies and compromises which must be continually renewed from the outset in the next round of negotiations. This is exemplified in the annual discussions of the autumn *rentrée* in France, in which each year the representatives of capital, labour and the state poise for a series of strikes and subsequent compromises which inevitably finish with a return to work, university, etc., on slightly modified terms. All sides in the disputes usually know in advance more or less what claims will be made by their opponents, after which a series of predictable compromises is worked out by the political parties in power. The process resumes year after year with remarkably few differences. While struggles of this nature are intrinsically limited in political scope by being defined by pre-given ends, discourses of common identity and unity are intrinsically limited in political scope by being circumscribed by the ideology of pre-given common origins. The instrumental rationality of adjusting means to ends in the first instance is paralleled by the necessity of a return to an origin in the second; in both cases, it is a question of reaching a fixed point around which everything moves or to which all things have to gravitate. Following the discussion in the last chapter, one could say that both instrumental rationality and 'origins rationality' are predicated on empty versions of time and the eternal return of the same, while political time is more akin to Benjamin's 'nowtime' (*Jetztzeit*) in the 'Theses on

ous cul-de-sac. The source of the political legitimacy of the state
is the will of the people; but where does the legitimacy of the will
of the people come from – the state? It was seen in previous chapters that in the absence of a convincing political way out of this
dilemma, apologists of the state have had to resort to abstractions
of a metaphysical (general will/objective spirit), historically
fictive (spontaneous and collective exit from the state of nature)
and even theological (sovereignty) character in an attempt to
argue for state legitimacy.[15] Since these arguments fail, states
continually fall back on the principle of the nation as a community of fate or organic unity, in order to try to uphold a principle
of allegiance beyond private interest which might act as the
cement necessary to hold together people who have conflicting
interests within the territory of the state. This contrived unity is
necessary in order for the state to tax and conscript people in an
orderly and predictable way. In the case of states or empires with
expansionist ambitions, a rationalised system of tax law, contract
and conscription is also needed in order to fund and staff military
and other colonial ventures abroad. In return for the payment of
taxes and the eventual willingness to go to war, the state (i.e., the
political parties representing social interests and the executive)
must normally be able to guarantee an at least tolerable standard
of living for those legally living within its territory, and must also
be able to keep the peace in either an authoritarian or a more or

---

the Philosophy of History'. This argument will be developed further in this chapter
in the discussion of community in the third section. For a refutation of 'origins
rationality', see Theodor W. Adorno, 'Kritik der Ursprungsphilosophie (1956)', in
Philosophie und Gesellschaft: Fürf Essays, edited by Rolf Tiedemann, Stuttgart:
Reclam, 1984, pp. 57–9.

[15] Seyla Benhabib, 'Demokratie und Differenz', in Micha Brumlik and
Hauke Brunkhorst (eds), *Gemeinschaft und Gerechtigkeit*, Frankfurt: Fischer,
1995, pp. 103–5. Thus in arguing that 'he is sovereign who decides over the
state of exception' in *Politische Theorie*, Schmitt fails in his attempt to give a
precise definition of the political in non-technical terms: the determinate
necessity of deciding a dispute without precedent merely requires that a
sovereign be strategically placed to make a decision to keep the machinery of
government in motion when a stalemate between the parties threatens to slow
things down. That this theologically-inspired form of decisionism is easily
accommodated within a more explicitly technical conception of government is
reflected in Schmitt's later writings such as *Legalität und Legitimität*. See Chris
Thornhill's chapter on Schmitt in *The Theory of Politics in Modern Germany*,
Cambridge: Polity, 1999.

less spontaneously accepted way.[16]

Since theoretical justifications of sovereignty fail, and because the composition of the nation under modern conditions is in constant flux due to population migrations, the influx of minorities, the changing tides of the world economy, etc., the state is always in a precarious position needing shoring up. In order to retain its legitimacy, the state must both control the population living within its territory and keep it in a state of constant mobilisation. It must be seen to be solving problems that constantly threaten to undermine the unity, lifestyle and culture of the people as a unified nation, and as such must also invoke the co-operation and participation of the 'national community' in attacking these threats. Here the state can be seen to be rising above private interests in order to help attack problems which potentially threaten everyone, regardless of their class or status: international drug trade, epidemics, food poisoning, various forms of fundamentalism, terrorists and external enemies of one kind or another, etc. Like the bourgeoisie described by Marx and Engels in the *Communist Manifesto* that must revolutionise the means of production in order for the gigantic apparatus of production to be constantly moving forward, the state must manage the contradictory imperative of ensuring both the mobilisation and the passivity of its population, in order to be the police and guardian protector against internal and external threats. Here the holes in the liberal version of the state of nature argument are filled by the exclusionist implications of nation: if trade and the exchange of opinion between private individuals endowed with natural rights really did lead to the aggregate good and welfare of all, would the state not be superfluous? Or is it the case that in the founding act of the democratic republic or constitutional monarchy that defined the co-founding 'we' against the non-participating and external 'them', elements of the latter managed to establish themselves within our

---

[16] Thus Cole is right to maintain that the state is not a community, but rather a territorally-based association ignoring the differences between citizens and forcibly including all those who reside within its jurisdiction. See G.D.H. Cole, *Social Theory* (1920), London: Methuen, 1970, p. 95. For a discussion on the distinction between community and state informed by Heidegger's critique of reification and Bataille's notion that the individual is far more capable of appreciating the sense of his or her existence within the framework of community action, see Jean-Luc Nancy, *La communauté desoeuvrée* (1986), Paris: Christian Bourgeois, 1990.

midst, and these must be vigilantly controlled and eventually eliminated by the surveillance and security forces of the state?[17]
Depending on the context, the state's ability to simultaneously
mobilise and control is to varying degrees accomplished by continually renewing the possibility of threat and uncertainty, on the one
hand, and minimising the acuteness of historical memory and the effi-
cacity of forms of local knowledge and community in civil society, on
the other. This contradictory tension between state and civil society
clearly emerges in some of the theoretical analyses of the newly
created states in Eastern Europe. Here the uncertainty generated in
the rapid transition from state socialism to capitalism has thrown up
a series of paradigm cases of attempts by states to manipulate
communities for military and ideological purposes. Gvozden Flego
emphasises how media hysteria and economic problems make any
critical distance between daily events and their political exploitation
by élites almost impossible in contemporary Eastern Europe: people
are invited to identify themselves with 'the changes' or be left out of
the newly emerging post-communist civil society. While previously
problems could be attributed to Russian interference with national
traditions, setbacks and delays in the current transition stage are now
explained as the work of mysterious 'foreign elements' which must be
monitored. In connection with similar instances of mobilisation from
above, Slavoj Zizek remarks that anti-semitism and other forms of
prejudice have recently been exploited with particular skill where
there are actually very few Jews or other scapegoated minorities:
unseen enemies can be portrayed as especially dangerous because of
their hidden identities and power resources.[18] The recent examples
from Eastern Europe are more obvious and clear forms of a more
general pattern. The configuration of competing private interests,
state adjudication between conflicts of interest, and national identity
raises the question of hegemony, and suggests that private interests

---

[17] Helmut Plessner, *Die verspätete Nation: Über die Verführbarkeit des bürger-
lichen Geistes* (1959), Stuttgart: W. Kohlhammer, 1969, chapter 3; Alex
Demirovic, *Demokratie und Herrschaft: Aspekte kritischer Gesellschaftstheorie*,
Münster: Westfälisches Dampfboot, 1997, pp. 95–7.
[18] Gvozden Flego, 'Gemeinschaften ohne Gesellschaft? Zur Problematik des
"Postsozialismus"', in Brumlik and Brunkhorst (eds), *Gemeinschaft und
Gerechtigkeit*, pp. 65–71; Slavoj Zizek, 'Geniesse Deine Nation wie Dich selbst!
Der Andere und das Böse – vomßegehren des ethnischen "Dings"', in Joseph
Vogl (ed.), *Gemeinschaften: Positionen zu einer Philosophie des Politischen*,
Frankfurt: Suhrkamp, 1994, pp. 139–41.

cannot appear as universal interests without seeming to be national-popular. Further, the image of the national-popular must be constantly overhauled and re-established to adapt to changing international economic conditions.[19] In order for this steady manipulation and co-ordination to occur without it seeming to be the work of anyone in particular, one might say that power circulates in ways which transgress the boundaries between state and civil society in anonymous channels without obvious subjects, and at the same time, that projects of domination and control are undertaken by specific, strategically concerned interests. Keeping in mind that each national context has absolutely unique characteristics, the general pattern suggests that rather than an economic base giving rise to a political, ideological, legal and aesthetic superstructure, there is more likely to be a historic bloc between landowning, financial and manufacturing interests with powerful positions in local government, executive and legislature. This unstable alliance of forces is mediated by political parties with organisational ties with family, media, church, university and other institutions in civil society. Because of the omnipresent possibility of capital flight and the imminent economic collapse that this would entail, economic interests within the bloc are in a position to mobilise the workforce with the constant fear of redundancy. Amidst this climate of threat and fear, the government component of the bloc is often well positioned to conjure up the spectre of various unhealthy and foreign elements which sabotage the national production effort and threaten the economic stability necessary to sustain the ethnic and cultural survival of the nation. In this way a civil society riven by material conflict can be ideologically re-unified as a result of the threat of potential economic or cultural extinction. But since the power of the individual forces within a given historic bloc constantly changes in relation to the flux in international political economy and other factors, the recomposition and reconstruction of unity must be achieved on a daily basis.[20]

Constant mobilisation contributes to the maintenance of the

---

[19] As for instance in the pathetic example of New Labour's 'Cool Britannia' campaign.

[20] Foucault, *Il faut défendre la société*, pp. 28–40. In terms of a theoretical understanding of power, it thus appears that Gramsci's notions of hegemony, passive revolution and historic bloc, i.e., a class and materialist perspective, would be well complemented by Foucault's structuralist and genealogical analyses. For a synthesis of their respective approaches, see Arianna Bove, 'Gramsci and Foucault', D.Phil at the University of Sussex, forthcoming.

plebiscitary version of democracy which currently prevails in most parliamentary states. In plebiscites the people are called upon to say yes or no to a party slogan; the period of government campaigning leading up to the yes/no vote prepares the voters for this exercise in forming the people's will in a determinate direction. In relation to the discussion of the public sphere in chapter 3, this tactic represents an almost complete inversion of the Kantian ideal of allowing ethical perspectives and issues of judgement to modify law. The proposed unity of state and nation is forged in an effort to manufacture a direct bond between the government and the people through a direct appeal seeking to extract the essence of the will of the latter with a clear 'yes' or 'no'. Yet even in 'normal' elections people are also voting yes or no to the arrival in power of parties or coalitions of parties. Within this framework self-government in civil society is not an option or even a possibility, since the institutional matrix for transforming the public sphere into legitimation fodder already posits an implicit unity of state and civil society rooted in the nation and national interest. In order for a yes/no plebiscite or, in normal electoral instances, a yes/no vote for different parties/party coalitions to have been legitimate in the first place, the unity of the subject-object of political life (state, nation, nation-state, party or the people) is assumed and ideologically reaffirmed: the strait-jacket of approval or non-approval takes for granted that *representative government* is only possible where the government reproduces an essential pre-given unity of the terms in question (people–leaders, voters–government, civil society–state).[21] Hence the nation is as much of a metaphysical sleight-of-hand as the state. Where the state posits the unity of citizen and state in the concept of representation, the nation posits the unity of the individual and the people in ideas like the spirit of the people and national character which can also be symbolically represented; in different ways, both turn on the philosophical idealist unity of subject and object with its obvious metaphysical implications.[22]

While the discourses and practices of national unity turn on the possibility of returning to a hypothetical point of origin which

[21] Roberto Esposito, *Communitas: Origine e destino della comunità*, Turin: Einaudi, 1998, pp. xvii–xviii, 9–18; Giorgio Agamben, *La comunità che viene*, Turin: Einaudi, 1990, pp. 42–3; Demirovic, *Demokratie und Herrschaft*, pp. 81–2, p. 244; Nancy, *La communauté desoeuvrée*, pp. 256–7.

[22] That this kind of thinking is also possible within a Marxist framework is well illustrated by Georg Lukács's *Geschichte und Klassenbewusstsein* (*History and Class Consciousness*, 1923), Cambridge, Mass., MIT Press, 1971.

stretches into the common destiny of the future, the defence of
political or other forms of identity is often expressed as the defence
of an essence which must be continually reaffirmed or abandoned
for a new identity, but which does not fundamentally change in
relation to time, experience or political action. To this extent political identities are articulated in a manner similar to claims about
national origin. Group members attempt to define themselves in
the exclusive terms of us/them categories in the search for the
confirmation of a pre-established 'we'. Moreover, the categorisa-
tion of a given struggle as feminist, black, gay, etc. makes it
possible to strip it of its politically active character, and transform
the struggle into a category of economic interest (the right to
compete on an equal basis and accept the unequal outcomes of
competition) or lifestyle (the right to non-interference in private
forms of consumption and leisure in return for compliance) which
can normally be accommodated within the structures of interest
bargaining of the parliamentary state. This is not to say that feminist, black, gay and other struggles are not important or have not
achieved important strategic victories for their memberships. It is
rather to say that these struggles become politically relevant
precisely when they shed their character as identity struggles. Like
'the nation' or 'the people', identities can be integrated into the
political system of power, money and interest representation, at
which point they lose the *specificity* of their perspective, and at
which point they can be dealt with administratively like any other
interest group.[23]

In chapter 1 it is argued that Marx is correct in 'Zur
Judenfrage' ('On the Jewish Question') (1843) to claim that the
freedom to practise Judaism is not freedom from Judaism, i.e.,
freedom from the material, cultural and ideological conditions
which give rise to institutional religions. Obviously Marx does
not oppose Judaism for racist reasons. Instead, he criticises the
absence of politics which a concept of freedom rooted primarily
in religious toleration implies. If the state can free itself of religion
by making it a private matter, there is no state religion, but rather

---

[23] A case in point is the Italian feminist movement which, after the tremendous victories on issues of equal pay, maternity leave, divorce and abortion in
the 1960s and 1970s, has assumed a very minor role in contemporary Italian
civil society. Bianca Becalli, 'The Modern Women's Movement in Italy', *New Left
Review*, No. 204 (1994), pp. 86–112.

the freedom to practise religious prejudice in civil society. The state is then neutral with regard to religion, and thereby attains a 'religious' (ideological) character of a different kind: that of sheer neutrality – legality with no particular content rising above particular interests. Here is Marx's real concern: if the state is seen to be neutral with regard to religion, it can also distance itself from other particular interests, such as those of capital. The more the state can in appearance distance itself from particular interests, the more the state seems objective, and the more private interests can govern in reality. Similarly, the 'official' toleration of different ethnic, racial, gender and other differences is a strategically prudent way for the state to boast neutrality with regard to category, and at the same time claim impartiality with regard to the processes which pit individuals in and between various category groups against each other as competitors.[24] This is not a critique of NSMs so much as an observation of their limitations when construed primarily as identity struggles. It is also to suggest that NSMs are most political when they go beyond identity struggles to engage in more inclusive forms of action like community which belong to no identity or category: the specificity of a particular issue is achieved in the course of concrete practice rather than as the confirmation of pre-given interest or attribute, as will be seen in the last section of this chapter.[25]

The question of identity struggles and the transformatory potential of NSMs in civil society has historical precedents in the struggle for socialism. Before its legal incorporation into the official bargaining structures of parliamentary democracy, socialism was also a social movement. Where it could organise beyond economic-corporative issues of working-class interest and identity to pose

---

[24] Theodor W. Adorno, 'They, the People', in *Minima Moralia: Reflexionen aus dem beschädigten Leben* (1951, written in 1944–47), Frankfurt: Suhrkamp, 1997, p. 25.

[25] This certainly seems to be true of the Zapatista movement in Chiapas. But it also characterises such diverse examples of community as the squatters' movement in Turin and other Italian cities as well as the action of the social centres (*centri sociali*) throughout Italy. There has also been a recent surge of movements for more local participatory democracy with important implications for the idea of political community in a number of European cities. On the particular case of Hamburg, see Max Miller, 'Bürgerarenen und demokratischer Prozeß', in Giegel (ed.), *Konflikt in modernen Gesellschaften*, Frankfurt: Suhrkamp, 1998, pp. 293–313.

larger questions about culture, politics, power and the state, social-ist movements have been able to transform the boundaries between state and civil society. With the benefit of both the experience of political action since 1968 and the critique of parties, power and state socialism which has developed thereafter, NSMs are now in a position to raise the possibility of moving beyond economic-corpo-rative and lifestyle issues, without this leading to a military-strategic conception of politics as seizing state power or instituting party rule. This will not be enacted as an identity strug-gle, however, since identities run up against some of the same problems as natural rights arguments. If we all have natural rights, but in a concrete instance my conception of rights clashes with yours, we need the state to adjudicate between our claims. We are no longer non-identical equals in a political community, but rather mutually opposed parties in need of protection from each other by the state. The same applies to conflicting identities, which is why arguments for natural rights and identities will produce arguments for the state as the supposedly neutral guarantor of security, rather than arguments for political action as the enactment of freedom in civil society. This raises a central point about the constellation of community, politics and freedom. Freedom is not guaranteed in the form of security or identity when, like welfare, they are provided and protected by the state: Hegel is correct to maintain that freedom and security are not the same. Freedom has a political dimension which is actively practised both in the public sphere and as community.

Community as politics

The argument being made in this book on the basis of distinctions between life/world, behaviour/action and social/political is not that there is less social oppression than political oppression, or that social oppression is somehow less important than other forms of domination. It is rather that there are three principal forms of collective, non-instrumental action in civil society which are not dependent on notions of origin, goal or identity, and that these are enacted as distinct forms of praxis as politics. Politics is thus distinct from economics, administration and other institutions and practices with which the political is confused in ways which obscure the link between politics and human freedom. The analysis thus far also points towards the idea that politics in this sense is not conferred in the manner of welfare or rights, nor exhausted in the concept of communicative action: politics is realised as a process, in which no strict separation of means/ends or form/content is possible. The first two sections of this chapter attempt to distinguish between three prevalent ways in which the ideal of democratic politics is either confused with issues related to security, on the one hand, or ideologically manipulated in various discourses and practices in an attempt to consolidate the legitimacy of the state, on the other. These three tendencies can be summarised as (1) the conflation of material stability with freedom, (2) the attempt to fabricate national unity as a renewable reservoir of 'common sense' and common cause, and (3) the attempt to defend politically relevant forms of identity on the part of oppressed groups as an attempt to generate solidarity and resistance to social oppression. It is also argued that the parameters defining the pursuit of these aims are largely set in advance by adjusting strategic means to the attainment of already established ends. Following on from the discussion of the public sphere in the last chapter, it is suggested that NSMs in civil society exhibit a range of different forms of praxis that increase in political intensity as they move away from identity struggles towards more inclusive forms of democratic politics such as community, which in turn pose the question of their self-abolition as NSMs. This last strand of the argument will now be developed in more detail. It begins with the seemingly contradictory idea that rather than the strategic aims of particular groups, associations or categories of individuals, it is the inclusiveness of community in terms of its open character that is actually concrete.[26] This will be illustrated by looking at the respective conceptions of time underlying the instrumental rationality employed in mediating conflicts between particular groups, associations and categories of individuals, on the one hand, and the conception of time which

---

[26] In this sense community is not a means to an end or the result of a compromise, but rather opens up a common world between people. See Tönnies, *Gemeinschaft und Gesellschaft*, pp. 19–22. Tönnies stresses that there is an affinity between language, which is not invented like a machine or tool by anyone nor belongs to any particular group or interest, and the practice of community. Similar views are expressed in Rainer Forst, *Kontexte der Gerechtigkeit: Politische Philosophie jenseits von Liberalismus und Kommunitarismus*, Frankfurt: Suhrkamp, 1996, pp. 181–90, Esposito, *Communitas*, pp. 100–3, and Francesco Remoti, *Contro l'identità*, Bari: Laterza, 1996, pp. 61–2.

emerges in the course of the formation of political communities, on the other.

Earlier in this chapter it is argued that a predictable form of instrumental rationality is used by both sides in various zero-sum conflicts, such that a compromise between the opposing sides is already assumed at the beginning as the eventual outcome. Inscribed within this process is a version of the empty time discussed in chapter 2 in relation to the production and fetishism of commodities. In most socio-economic conflicts, but also in ostensibly more political conflicts, it is based on the model of an exchange of equivalents. Each side in the contractual negotiations purports to give something equivalent to that which it receives, and the end result is a cancelling of initial positions for an agreed-upon compromise position. The subsequent resuming of negotiations with new initial starting points which again are modified in apparently new outcome positions can carry on indefinitely, as long as the dynamic fuelling this modified exchange process is maintained and renewed. But the nature of the transaction is not an exchange of equivalents, which in principle would leave both sides in their initial positions (if something truly equivalent is exchanged, then nothing changes). Instead, the continual return of the same in new guise is perpetuated in the repetitive cycle of a supposed exchange of equivalents which in reality leaves both sides unsatisfied: the attainment of the goal of a compromise is reached with the simultaneous realisation that each side must then repeat the defence of its strategic position under the new terms of exchange. Rather than being an affirmation of new values or the possibility of new beginnings, these negotiations have a goal that would virtually disappear without the opposition of the opponent. Thus each side actually needs the opponent as the negative image of its own identity. Without each side's opposition, there would not be an autonomous basis for the affirmation of the respective positions involved. Hence there can be no real resolution to such conflicts within the exchange-based model of mediation, but only a change in the terms in which the mediated negativity is cast; the temporary satisfaction of compromise goals silences critical judgement about the movement of the process as a whole. To the extent that each of the new outcome positions is merely a re-enacted staging of the initial position as if nothing had changed, 'exchange conflicts' unfold according to the logic of empty time. This empty time assumes an almost unalterable form reminiscent of Hegel's notion of a 'second nature' which is foreign to human intentions and barely recognisable as the outcome of human social and economic behaviour.[27]

Such forms of mediated negativity are determined by means-ends considerations of strategy, which in practice implies that they reach a goal (compromise as an exchange of ostensible equivalents), but rarely generate meaning or sense. The outcomes of the exchanges are largely predictable because they are usually bound to either material interests linked to the life-cycle and its reproduction, or the confirmation of identities which are known in advance such as those based on gender, race, religion or ethnicity. The intrumental rationality in achieving aims connected with the life-cycle or identity struggles can in most cases be categorised as a success or failure with regard to the attainment of the goal in question. By contrast, the sense of community action which bridges gender, race and religious differences cannot be classified in terms of success or failure, but is rather interpreted from the plurality of perspectives of both those directly involved in community politics at a particular moment, and those who later attempt to historically read meaning out of the specific context they seek to understand. Because they are not directed towards any goal in particular but assume concrete form over time, the sense or meaning of individual events can only be reconstructed historically through critical judgement and interpretation. Yet this reconstruction can never reach any definitive conclusions, since communities decline or are renewed in ways that alter the meaning of the past, and keep the meaning of both the past and the future free and undetermined. They are undetermined in the concrete sense of their being subject only to creative human intervention and the unforeseen outcomes of non-instrumental collective action. The possibility of there being sense rather than merely a goal to an action thus turns on keeping the future open to different possible courses, which in turn depends on enacting freedom as individual self-creation and

[27] Thus equivalence is achieved by a return to parity, as, for example, in the exchange of formal-legal equivalents such as labour power for a wage. See Theodor W. Adorno, 'Fortschritt' ('Progress, 1962'), in *Stichworte: Kritische Modelle 2*, Frankfurt: Suhrkamp, 1969, pp. 48–9. As was seen in chapters 2 and 3, Benjamin and Arendt suggest that revolutions have historically demonstrated that the freedom to break out of the eternal return of empty time is political.

collective self-government in continually forming and re-forming political communities at local, city, regional and international levels. Thus community as action rather than association (party, interest, identity) is a form of enacting politics which subverts strategic and instrumental considerations by preserving the open nature of the future. As such, the political practice of community enters into conflict with the imperative of capital to secure the conditions of its own accumulation. Capital must constantly create the economic, political, ideological and cultural conditions of future growth and accumulation of an eternally recurring today. It seeks to impose the exchange logic of success vs. failure over the political faculty of judgement and plurality of perspective, which is exercised in communities in the open horizon of possible futures in anticipation of the sense of the past.[28]

In order for the logic of capital to be able to maintain its hegemony, it must impose its logic on all spheres of human activity, and in particular in the place where humans are potentially most free to create new beginnings through concerted action – in politics. To the extent that the logic of capital succeeds in articulating itself beyond the economy to transform the public sphere, community and struggles for recognition in civil society into forms of interest and identity which can be administered by the state, capital manages to assert the seeming inevitability of empty time. To the extent that the different forms of action in civil society challenge capital and the categories of interest, reification and the time of commodity production, politics creates spaces to maintain the open nature of the future and the possible reinterpretation of the past as more than mere fact.[29] This is to posit a state of exception arising from the pretended sovereign permanence of existing legal

[28] The logic of accumulation and private capital investment fetishises technology, progress, being up-to-date, etc., in short today. If Montesquieu is correct to argue that the essence of despotism is fear, then one might add that it is the trust made posible through community which breaks down fear and shows that the despotism of the eternal return of a commodified now is not inevitable. This point is well illustrated by Benjamin's 'Theses on the Philosophy of History'.

[29] Antonio Gramsci, *Note sul Machiavelli e sullo stato moderno*, Rome: Editori Riuniti, 1979, pp. 13–4, 36–7, 161–7, 199–203, and Gramsci, *Il materialismo storico*, Rome: Editori Riuniti, 1979, pp. 47–8. Gramsci's concepts of the historic bloc, war of position and hegemony indicate that an accurate analysis of politics can never pose any rigid distinction between state and civil society or between base and superstructure. Both of these works are part of the *Prison Notebooks*, which have recently been translated into English by Columbia University Press.

and political state institutions, on the one hand, and alternative forms of enacting politics in civil society, on the other. The former tend to perpetuate the logic of capital indefinitely into the future by recognising interest, identity and other forms of zero-sum conflict rooted in exchange time as the only legitimate forms of politics. In different ways the latter reject the liberal belief that the legitimacy of the state can be secured by transforming the horizontal contract of exchange partners into a vertical contract between citizens and political authority. In addition to the public sphere considered in the last chapter and the phenomenon of recognition to be analysed in chapter 5, community as politics responds to the state of exception with different forms of permanent revolution. This permanent revolution consists in enacting forms of trust and solidarity which question the institution of contract as the best possible way of ensuring co-operation, and which highlight boundaries between people in terms of mutual suspicion and fear which contract both presupposes and reinforces. Communities raise the possibility of changing those boundaries by staging a continual set of ruptures with the various contractual frameworks within which the sovereign state recognises strategic behaviour as the only legitimate form of collective agency.[30]

Whether derived from a metaphysical-theological origin or the fictitious first contract dear to theorists in the tradition of Kant and Rousseau, sovereignty can absorb all challenges to its authority made in terms of power, interest or identity. A revolutionary party cannot challenge the authority of the state since, like the general strike in Sorel's conception, it represents a rival sovereign power: it will either be destroyed or it will itself become sovereign, in which case sovereignty has merely changed hands. Nor can sovereignty be contested through a compromise secured through contract, since valid contracts presuppose a sovereign state and, in recognising a contract, the state is also recognising itself as the sole source of political authority. NSMs run up against the boundary of their transformatory potential at that point where they manage to achieve aims recognised by the state as legitimate. Insofar as these

---

[30] Foucault, *Il faut défendre la société*, pp. 58–61. Thus in addition to Benjamin's distinction between legal measures establishing the legitimacy of the law and those maintaining it in 'On the Critique of Violence', one can also distinguish between boundary-maintaining and boundary-undermining political action.

claims are transformed into legislation, NSMs are in effect conceding to and abetting a process in which strategic claims constitute the essence of the political, in which case the state becomes a necessity. NSMs then recognise themselves in the state, and the state recognises itself in NSMs: the horizontal contract between exchange partners in effect becomes a vertical contract between citizens and the state. *Insofar as it manages to transform a horizontal contract into a vertical one, the state succeeds in suppressing politics in civil society by politicising the social.* Legally dependent on the state for recognition, the citizens who animate NSMs are also dependent on the state for making sense of their own action, which comes back to them in virtually unrecognisable form as a mode of exchange. To raise the possibility for NSMs to break out of exchange time, however, is to pose the question of free, non-contractual and non-strategic relations amongst people within and between NSMs. This is to pose the question of community and alternative forms of recognition.

By creating a shared history and preserving the past through language and memory, community indicates ways out of the necessity of having to either wait for the end of history in order for the meaning of a particular moment to reveal itself, or being forced to affirm the inevitability of the political forms of the present as the only standard of validation for the truth or falsity of an ideal. The participants in a community which emerges in the process of joint action can identify themselves with their action and recognise it as theirs, though without having to individually commit themselves to fixed identities or interests as a result. In this context, identification is not the same as identity: it is the recognition of one's participation in a project that belongs to no generic interest, group or category, but which is realised through action and preserved in memory – neither of which can be exchanged or represented. In contrast to the modes of contract and negotiated compromise that have a fixed endpoint, the concreteness of community is not that it 'is', in the manner of a thing, but rather that community emerges in the process of communal action in a 'now'. Citizens do not become members of a political community on the basis of who they are in terms of social categories. A political community takes shape as an identification of particular actors with a process that goes through constant mutation, and then continues into the future within a new frame of reference. What is shared is not an identity, but rather a boundary between the memory of that which has been undertaken, and the horizon of possible futures which opens against the blindness of empty time. The sense of a collective action which is not undertaken for strategic purposes but as a *project* reveals itself when that action has taken a certain course. From this moment on, various possible meanings can be discerned from the different perspectives of those in civil society who have been involved, think about what has loosely crystallised in the process, and consider how action might assume different concrete form in new projects.[31]

Unlike an origin, goal or an end which is fixed and which dictates the range of 'rational' means to attain it, the boundary separating a 'now' between the members of a political community and the open horizon of possible futures is common without being the same for each of those individuals. It is open in that the possibility of imminent action is omnipresent, and the range of new projects is virtually limitless – it is rarely a question of finding the appropriate means for pre-given ends. The boundary is also common in a way that has little to do with belonging in the sense that one might belong to a party or association which subsumes individuals under broad sociological categories. It is not a position that is shared, which is why individuals distinguish themselves in non-competitive terms in communities: since each person is unique, and no two people can stand in the same place or have an identical perspective, no two people can share the same *view*. The impossibility of representing community is thus the corollary of the fact that representation is only possible where people have the same interests or identities, i.e., where what is particular about a perspective is not distorted in the process of vertical channelling to a politico-administrative centre. Thus while an interest or identity can be represented in numbers such as vote totals, the non-identical equals of a community are neither equivalent nor replaceable as systemic inputs, i.e., they are not simply purveyors of information to the 'political system'.[32] By illustrating the distinction between goal-oriented strategy in time and sense generating action as history, communities indicate the irreducibility of human relationships to instrumental and technical considerations. In sounding out

---

[31] A.P. Cohen, *The Symbolic Construction of Community*, London: Routledge, 1985, pp. 32–8.

[32] Gerard Raulet, 'Die Modernität der Gemeinschaft', in Brumlik and Brunkhorst (eds), *Gemeinschaft und Gerechtigkeit*, pp. 85–9.

the possible points of transition from exchange time to the undetermined time of the political, the practice of community suggests that
their implicit critique of social and political relations is a political-
epistemological critique of how social and political relations are
studied and 'known'.

Communities forfeit recognition from the state by not entering
into the vertical contract borrowed from exchange-based negotiation. Thus they indicate that instrumental strategies and zero-sum
outcomes are in no sense inevitable, even though they are the most
'effective' within the existing boundaries between state and civil
society. To be effective in this context is to perpetuate the dynamic
of zero-sum struggles and the reduction of rationality to means-
ends calculation. Yet where such power struggles are mired in an
almost motionless negation of the opponent's initial negation,
communities signal the freedom to affirm values without the necessity to negate an opposing position. A community's self-over-
coming is thus enacted not at the expense of another community or
in terms of a concession from the state in return for integration or
compliance, but rather in terms of its own autonomous acknowl-
edgement that a given collective project has taken its course, and
that new projects with the same or new members can now be
undertaken. The political-epistemological implication is that the
relativistic consequences of collapsing the distinction between
instrumental strategic action and reason can be avoided without
having to embrace some version of historicism. To the extent that
they have no fixed starting points or endpoints and yet allow citizens across different backgrounds to recognise a breaking down of
fear and mutual suspicion between them, communities show that
neither a *telos* nor subject-object of history is the necessary precondition for non-instrumental meaningful action. If in terms of ideal
types contract can be thought of as an intermediate boundary
between the friend/enemy dichotomy and community, communities demonstrate how collective projects make existing boundaries
between friend–enemy, contract and community visible. Moreover,
the emergence of this visibility is only possible through the political action which reveals at what point contractual relations
between people in civil society can be superseded by more communal ones, which signifies that knowing where such boundaries lie is
only clear through political action. Important in this regard is that
this overcoming of contractual relations between members of a

community expresses something about the quality of an action or relation which makes the supersession of contract possible; to raise the possibility of experiencing an action in qualitative terms rather than its effectivesness/success or failure is to point towards a political epistemology of perspective. The appreciation of the quality of an action is a matter of judgement, which can only be cultivated through experience and through acquaintance with other perspectives on the same issue.[33]

The permanent conflict between boundary-constituting strategy and boundary-discovering action frustrates any instrumental approach to either understanding or enacting politics. Whereas instrumental behaviour is constrained by the necessity of adapting the appropriate means to a pre-given end, communities take shape in the course of and at the end of projects which themselves evolve in the process of their unfolding. Like the opening of public spaces in revolutionary situations looked at in the last chapter, communities form spontaneously on the basis of individual commitments which open up new perspectives in highly unpredictable ways. It is not a question of adjusting means to ends, but rather of participating in and observing the changing constellation of perspectives which are opened up by political action. Like the public sphere, a community is not formed for a purpose, and as such there are no means with which a collective subject might 'make' a community. By making purely instrumental behaviour impossible, communities dissolve the means-ends dichotomy in a form of politics which is an end in itself; the form a community assumes is the content of community – free development and self-government. This constitutes a contestation of sovereign power which does not itself seek sovereignty, but rather affirms the possible transition to a different experience of time than the sovereign time of negation, exchange and eternal recurrence. Insofar as it is not an end in itself but rather the means to security, the protection of valid contract and interest mediation, the state functions in the manner of the ultimate medium of exchange, money. Money does not represent any non-

---

[33] If one reconsiders the friend/enemy relation as one possible attempt to distil the essence of the political, one might regard the legal institution of contract as an intermediate boundary between friend/enemy and community. This highlights the reductioism inherent in Schmitt's formulation: it is equally plausible that the political will take shape as community rather than a friend/enemy conflict.

negotiable value, but under capitalism simply changes form as capital and property. Where the state attempts to provide the citizens of civil society with the categories of interest, power and exchange to make sense of their individual political experience, communities respond with incomprehension and non-participation. In attempting to make sense of political experience on their own terms, members of communities ask a different set of questions, such as where are the boundaries between a coup d'état and a revolution, and what are the differences between empty time, more leisure time under capitalism and an altogether different kind of time?

Incomprehension and non-participation in state attempts to enlist community support generally result in the non-recognition of community as politics, and state recourse to (a) material concessions to the best-organised interests in civil society and (b) nationalist rhetoric addressed to everyone living within the sovereign territory. From the community perspective it makes little sense to argue that such a system of interest mediation is prone to corruption. As a modified form of contract and capital-driven exchange, it is simply corrupt in ways which go beyond the fact that at present votes and political support are 'bought'. Within this system, democracy is said to be protected by the separation of civil laws governing contract, exchange, property, etc. from non-commodified and non-saleable political rights and freedoms such as privacy, equality before the law, freedom of press, assembly and universal suffrage. But to the extent that political action in civil society is only recognised at state-level political institutions within the instrumental categories of power, contract, exchange and the time proper to production, politics, political time and political freedom are suppressed. In terms of Blanchot's remark at the beginning of this chapter, by not entering into the exchange logic of success and failure, politics is absent. It is argued in this chapter that the separation between state and civil society mediated by the transformation of the horizontal contract between exchange partners into the political contract between citizens and the state suppresses the political, while politicising the social. It is also suggested that the presence of the absence of community haunts sovereign power with the omnipresent possibility of a permanent political revolution based on the unfolding of various forms of *recognition*.

5

Civil society and recognition

To affirm that the passage from one content or being to another can only occur without violence if the truth taught by the master resides forever with the pupil, is to extrapolate beyond the Socratic method of bringing out the latent ideas that they already possess. The idea of the infinity in me, implying a content bursting the confines of its container, breaks with Socratic prejudices without breaking with rationality, since the idea of infinity, far from harming the mind, is the very condition of non-violence and the basis of ethics. The 'other' as another person does not pose itself as a scandal which sets off a dialectic of conflict between two subjects, but is rather our first lesson.

Emmanuel Lévinas, *Totality and Infinity*

Building on the arguments of preceding chapters, this chapter attempts to demonstrate the importance of the idea of *recognition* for an understanding of political action in contemporary civil societies. In chapter 2 it was seen how the formal equality which bestows the same legal status on all individuals despite their radically different standpoints is not enough, when taken by itself, to ensure the establishment of non-plebiscitary and non-theological political institutions. This is true especially if one wants to retain a *political* perspective on the question of institutions, i.e., if the incommensurability of different value positions is not to be reduced to a technical procedure of redistribution or merely voting in a yes/no manner for parties vying for control of the state. What is actually meant by the word politics and *the political* should now start to become clear following the critique of sovereignty and state violence in chapter 2, and the discussion of the public sphere and community in chapters 3 and 4. In the context of civil society and the question of the different types of democracy possible, politics means in part exploring forms of praxis which push beyond the boundaries of formal-legal equality, to test the potential political forms of self-government amongst non-identical but equal citizens. Previous chapters have sought to demonstrate that such forms are suggested both by attempts to sustain a public sphere for a plurality of perspectives and political energies, and by the lived experience of community as a non-technical, non-instrumental practice of undertaking common projects in a process of continual evolution and development. In both cases, the dynamic of political action continually shatters reified unities and 'natural' identities such as state and nation. This happens in a number of ways, all of which indicate that the word political suggests a *relationship* between citizens rather than a thing, essence or assigned identity; it also suggests a space in which this relationship can continually change. Thus throughout the book it has been emphasised how the friend–enemy model is suggestive of the political, insofar as it denotes the quality of an interaction rather than a functional sphere or sociological identity category such as social class, gender, race, religion, ethnicity, etc. But as will by now have become clear, in the present study the public sphere, community and recognition are argued to be far more appropriate as frameworks of analysis for civil society and contemporary politics than the reductionist implications of the friend-enemy couple, and it is to the relation and process of recognition that we now turn.[1] As indicated in the Introduction and in keeping with the approach followed throughout the book, the study of civil society is pursued by way of a careful reading of modern critical political theory. In this chapter, this primarily means Kant, Hegel and Feuerbach. A careful obser-

---

[1] It should perhaps be repeated that the complexity of Schmitt's thinking about the political is not exhausted in the friend/enemy couplet. This is especially clear in works such as *Die geistesgeschichtliche Lage des heutigen Parlamentarismus* (*The Crisis of Parliamentary Democracy*) and *Legalität und Legitimität* (*Legality and Legitimacy*), where Schmitt argues in a highly Weberian vein that in the twentieth century parliamentary democracy reveals itself to be increasingly incapable of generating a political élite able to prevent the transformation of the legislature into a forum for the expression and compromise of almost exclusively material interests. In fact, far from being a reactionary text foreshadowing Schmitt's temporary compromise with National Socialism, the book reads very much in places like Habermas's *Strukturwandel der Öffentlichkeit* (*Structural Transformation of the Public Sphere*).

vation of contemporary politics suggests that a correct understanding of both the analytical power of the concept of civil society and its transformatory potential now, is contained in the writings of those thinkers who most presciently diagnose the emergence of civil society in its incipient stages. The political-philosophical insight of the aforementioned thinkers is an indispensable complement to contemporary sociological theory and methodology for a correct understanding of civil society and contemporary politics. A close reading of their texts in conjunction with a careful observation of empirical evidence has guided the entire text of the present study.

There are two main versions of recognition in contemporary political theory and philosophy which will be examined in the first two sections of this chapter. These preliminary sections will be followed by a subsequent discussion of the possibility of an alternative and more convincing conception of the political significance of recognition for civil society than that offered by the other two approaches. The first argument draws heavily on the young Hegel's vision of recognition as the result of a series of stages. In general, defenders of this position maintain that these stages do not assume the already given or assumed anthropological universality of a static natural law-inspired conception of human nature. Recognition is instead the end result of a process in which oppposed positions move towards reconciliation after a series of confrontations. The model at the base of this approach is the master-slave dialectic in Hegel's *Phenomenology of Spirit* of 1807.[2] The second, contrasting position which will be analysed in this chapter, is an attempted refutation of the Hegelian-inspired attempt to construe recognition as reconciliation, i.e., as the 'coming home' or returning of the subject to itself after having

---

[2] This position is forcefully argued in Axel Honneth, *Kampf um Anerkennung: Zur moralischen Grammatik sozialer Konflikte* (*The Struggle for Recognition*), Frankfurt: Suhrkamp, 1992, pp. 23–4; Ludwig Siep, *Anerkennung als Prinzip der praktischen Philosophie: Untersuchungen zu Hegels Jenaer Philosophie des Geistes*, Munich: Verlag Karl Alber, 1979, pp. 115–16; Robert R. Williams, *Recognition: Fichte and Hegel on the Other*, Albany: State University of New York at Albany Press, 1994, p. 80; and Andreas Wildt, *Autonomie und Anerkennung: Hegels Moralitätskritik im Lichte seiner Fichte Rezeption*, Stuttgart: Klett-Cotta, 1982, pp. 334–70. All of these books stress in varying ways the importance of Hegel's early theological writings and especially the writings of the Jena period (1805/6) as being necessary for a correct understanding of the far better-known *Phenomenology*.

experienced and seen itself as an estranged other. Critics of the Hegelian position argue that it entails an imperious re-appropriation or re-assimilation of otherness, i.e., ultimately, a conquest of otherness. Otherness and difference are thus seen and known as emanating from within the self and become, after the experience of struggle, neither 'other' nor estranged. Against this view of recognition, there has emerged an ethically-inspired conception of recognition. This latter position insists that the process towards recognition cannot be logically derived from categories of experience or universal anthropological notions about law or the nature of human beings, but must be experienced itself as radical otherness. Against Hegel, however, defenders of the second position also insist on leaving radical otherness intact in its integrity as the radically other. They refuse to make 'the Hegelian move' toward final reconciliation as a re-appropriation of that which was originally subject, and which has only temporarily been estranged. This second position initially emerges implicitly in the writings of what could be termed the 'ethical theology' of thinkers like Jacques Maritain and Martin Buber, and has been more recently defended by Emmanuel Lévinas and his followers.[3] In what follows it will be argued that recognition is indeed a vital concept for understanding civil society today. Nonetheless, both the conceptions of recognition derived from the writings of the young Hegel as well as the radical ethics of people like Buber and Lévinas are flawed. While it is true that there is an undoubtedly authoritarian element in attempting to construe recognition as re-appropriation of otherness, it is also mistaken to construe recognition as exaltation of absolute otherness. Both positions miss what is at stake in recognition struggles in contemporary civil societies. They will be analysed in turn in the first two sections of this chapter, before proceding to an alternative perspective on recognition in the third.

The first position to be examined below starts with the concession that the theory of the Hegel of *The Philosophy of Right* is in some ways mistaken. As an idealised version of the (collective)

---

[3] Jacques Maritain, 'Natural Law and Moral Law' in Will Herberg (ed.), *Four Existentialist Philosophers*, New York: Doubleday, 1958, pp. 80–96; Martin Buber, *Ich und Du (I and Thou)*, Cologne: Jacob Hegner, 1962, p. 9 and the epilogue to Buber's *Paths in Utopia*, New York: Macmillan, 1949, pp. 139–49; Emmanuel Lévinas, *Totalité et infini: essai sur extériorité* (*Totality and Infinity*), Paris: Martinus Nijhoff, 1971, p. 186.

subject's re-appropriation of its temporarily estranged self, Hegel's mature conception of the state could in practice lend itself to plebiscitary manipulation. The first position to be examined in this chapter nonetheless maintains that the mature Hegel can be corrected in theoretical terms by mediating the moment of struggle as represented by figures like Marx, Nietzsche and Sorel, with the moment of consensus, as represented by Kant, Mead and Habermas. This is accomplished by way of a return to the concept of recognition in the young Hegel. For theorists of the first position, the correction of the mature Hegel through a careful reinterpretation of the *Phenomenology* and the Jena writings leads to a defence of the institution of *law*. For 'the legal theorists of recognition', law need neither be reducible to a compromise between classes and other interests, on the one hand, nor exalted independently of actual struggles as a categorical imperative, on the other. In various ways they argue that law is the institutionalisation of the various moments of the recognition process, which includes love, contract and citizenship.[4]

It will be argued below that the attempt to wrest a theory of recognition from the writings of the young Hegel is not tenable for reasons brought forward in the critique of sovereignty in chapter 2, i.e., because it presupposes a sovereign rather than a pluralist state, and as such offers a modified version of the same state that is defended by Weber and Schmitt. This argument will be made by showing that in practice recognition of this kind means a defence of different forms of identity politics, which in its turn means the defence of a strong, sovereign state adjudicating a competition between status-seeking citizens. As shown in chapter 2, this conception carries quite authoritarian implications. At the same time, the radical ethical approach, despite offering many important insights into the flaws of statist and legalistic approaches to recognition, is almost impossible to envisage in political terms. It renounces the political dimension of the public sphere, community

---

[4] Honneth, *Kampf um Anerkennung*, p. 8. For a critical but balanced assessment of Honneth's position see Klaus Roth, 'Neue Entwicklungen der kritischen Theorie', *Leviathan*, 3 (1994), pp. 439–41. Some of these implicit criticisms do not fully take into account Honneth's revision of his own position, in which he does seem to concede that recognition as politics will only be possible once labour and the labour process come under some form of collective control. See Honneth, 'Die soziale Dynamik von Mißachtung: Zur Ortsbestimmung einer kritischen Gesellschaftstheorie', *Leviathan*, 1 (1994), pp. 90–1.

and recognition, and consigns radical ethics to an ultimately other-worldly realm of religious isolation from civil society. This chapter will attempt to explain political action in contemporary civil societies by moving beyond both a legalistic approach to the question of recognition (in the writings of Honneth and Habermas) and a theological-ethical approach (in the writings of Buber and Levinas), to analyse the concept of recognition in terms of a relation, a project and a political space in contemporary civil societies.

Recognition as law – law as recognition

The concept of recognition first attains a prominent position in political theory with post-Kantian idealist philosopher Johann Gottlieb Fichte. Even prior to Hegel, Fichte thought it was necessary to think of freedom not in the abstract terms suggested by universal moral laws which never assume concrete form in political institutions, but instead, in the institutions and 'lifeforms' of a community, i.e., in the rules, duties and obligations that make a political community possible. Thus Fichte argues that there is a mediated unity between idealist philosophy, social and political institutions, and the historical evolution of a community; all of these elements later find expression in his concept of the nation. He argues further that it is wrong to posit a noumenal or objective world independent of human experience. Instead, there exists a unity of subject and object in self-consciousness, where *self-consciousness* develops from *mere consciousness* in a series of steps towards self-consciousness. In reaching self-consciousness, consciousness has to recognise that which is external to itself, and only in this way sets in motion the process through which the self can emerge as something distinct from other selves. The key idea in Fichte which Hegel takes up, is that it is only through the recognition of other selves that each individual self can reach consciousness of itself in self-consciousness. That is, for Fichte there is an intersubjective basis to knowledge, experience, and hence to freedom as well.[5]

It is thus by way of Fichte that Hegel comes to the central ques-

---

[5] Johann Gottlieb Fichte, *Ausgewählte politische Schriften*, edited by Zwi Batscha and Richard Saage, Frankfurt: Suhrkamp, 1977, pp. 344–5; Siep, *Anerkennung als Prinzip der praktischen Philosophie*, pp. 24–5; Wildt, *Autonomie und Anerkennung*, pp. 206–8.

tion of his social and political thought prior to *The Philosophy of Right:* how and under what conditions can I view other selves not as impediments to my freedom from whom I need protection, but rather as the very condition of my freedom itself? Hegel sets about answering this question by evaluating the philosophies of Hobbes, Kant and Fichte and developing a critique of different theories of natural law, which Hegel considers inadequate if taken as the only measure of ethical life. In his early writings he maintains that natural law represents universality in a merely abstract sense. This evaluation prefigures the argument in his later writings in which morality can only be real insofar as it is one moment of ethical life in its totality.[6]

Prior to the theory of ethical life fully developed in *The Philosophy of Right* (1821) and the struggle for recognition outlined in the *Phenomenology* (1807), Hegel conceives of recognition in quasi-religious terms as a matter of destiny. He owes his understanding of conflict and its possible forms of resolution to both his study of theology and his reading of Greek tragedy. In his Jena writings (1805–6), he is concerned to incorporate some of the romantic themes in the writings of Schiller and Hölderlin as part of his critique of Kant without, however, losing sight of the fact that Kant is correct in seeking to ground morality and freedom in reason rather than in terms of self-interest or individualism. Since both law and contract are still expressions of calculation and interest for Hegel at this stage, these can not serve as the basis for reconciling the criminal and the community in a non-punitive way. In these pre-1807 writings he reasons that reconciliation can only take place on the basis of the experience of our common destiny as members of the same community – despite whatever accidental conflicts might temporarily divide that community. From the moment that we experience our destiny as being also common to the other members of a given community, we become capable of regarding the criminal not in abstract or general terms as a violator of the law or as someone distant from our reality, but instead, as someone with a particular history and individuality who, despite the contravention he or she has committed, is still capable of being part of the community they have attempted to undermine. Here the

---

[6] Wildt, *Autonomie und Anerkennung*, pp. 336–7; Ludwig Siep, 'Der Kampf um Anerkennung: Zu Hegels Auseinandersetzung mit Hobbes in den Jenaer Schriften', *Hegel-Studien*, 9 (1974), p. 175.

idea of destiny serves Hegel as a bridge between modern German culture and that of ancient Greece where, according to Hegel, life was conceived of and lived as a unified whole. This whole was comprised of moments which could become separated in the course of activities, and institutions which separated the faculty of reason from the life of the senses, political authority from the obligations of family life and friendship, etc. But it is nonetheless the life of the community as a whole in Greek life which for Hegel bestows meaning on the unique aspects of particular individuals' lives. The community restores the unity of reason and sensuality as well as the unity of freedom and authority, without which there can be no meaningful sense of overall purpose in an individual's life.[7]

Just as friend and enemy will not be reconciled by natural or positive law, for the young Hegel reconciliation between victim and criminal are only possible where they are united in something greater than legal equality, i.e., in a community where friendship, trust and forgiving are a way of life. But Hegel rejects Jesus's solution to the issue of conflict, which for Hegel seems to consist in renouncing property and law in the name of unconditional love. This amounts to a sermon rather than politics, and would in practice condemn actual subjects in concrete situations to resort either to cunning and force, or to withdraw into passivity. Since both passivity and brutality are bad answers to the insufficiency of law to reconcile, Hegel argues that individuals must experience their common destiny not in the passive sense of fate, but in the *political* sense as a struggle for recognition in which they are all participants. The fact that all members of this community are actively involved in this struggle signalled to the young Hegel the possibility of genuine universality which does not reduce the universal to the codes of law or self-interest and which, beyond the conception of law as a system providing rules for mutual non-interference, actually moves towards a positive conception of freedom in which people require each other for the fullness of their respective subjectivities. In working out his positive theory of freedom, Hegel takes Fichte's epistemological critique of Kant's notion of the isolated transcendental subject, and gives it a social and political ontological basis. The various moments in the successive stages of struggle between individual subjectivities for recognition unite divergent

    [7] G.W.F. Hegel, *Frühe Schriften*, Frankfurt: Suhrkamp, 1994 (3rd edn), pp. 336–45; Wildt, *Autonomie und Anerkennung*, pp. 192–3.

perspectives in their mutually-conditioned institutionalisation of freedom. Conceived in these terms, freedom consists not in the renunciation of self for the sake of social harmony, but rather in the ongoing negotiation through institutions – family, work, property, law, the state – about the different possible forms of democracy.[8]

Hegel thus acknowledges that struggle is an ineluctable element of life in a political community. However, it is crucially important in terms of the attempted redefinition of politics and the role of recognition in civil society undertaken in the present book, that for Hegel it is not mainly a struggle over material interests. It is concerned instead with the clash between different values, forms of life and ways of existence.[9] Here Hegel differs decisively from Hobbes, for whom conflict can be avoided through the mechanism of the social contract. This is not an option for Hegel, for whom conflict is inevitable, and, insofar as it is conducive to pluralism, is a positive factor in political life – *given the right mediating institutions*. For Hegel conflict need not lead to death, as in Hobbes, but to recognition of difference which confirms the respective positions of each. Hegel argues that it is naive to think that individuals can live in the same commnunity simply by not infringing on each other's freedom. For Hegel each person represents a kind of totality. They carry within them impulses, values and ideas which distinguish them from others and which are fundamental to their self-understanding. These they cannot give up without ceasing to be themselves. This is true to such a degree, that when confronted with opposed impulses, values and ideas in others, the individual at first finds him or herself confronted with something that is alien, strange and life-threatening. The mediation of these differences cannot occur as the result of some transcendental unity of isolated subjects which occurs independently of experience. It must occur instead as a

---

[8] Wildt, *Autonomie und Anerkennung*, pp. 193–4; Jürgen Habermas, *Technik und Wissenschaft als Ideologie* (*Science as Ideology*), Frankfurt, Suhrkamp, 1968, p. 17.

[9] Indeed, in this sense Hegel is extremely modern and indispensable for understanding civil society today. Hegel, *Die Phänomenologie des Geistes* (*The Phenomenology of Spirit*, 1807), Stuttgart: Reclam, 1987, pp. 140–9. For an excellent analysis of the strugle for recognition both in *Phenomenology* and in the preceding Jena *Realphilosophie* writings, as well as an incisive look at Hegel's reception of Kant and Fichte, see Williams, *Recognition: Fichte and Hegel on the Other*, p. 209.

radical confrontation with the concrete experience of the otherness of different selves, which, in a contemporary context,
happens every day in the different institutions of civil society.[10]
For Hobbes this situation results either in the war of all against
all, or the contractual agreement of all not to go to war against
each other by bestowing all power upon the state. For the young
Hegel the choice is not that between civil war or state-insured
self-isolation. For Hegel it is clear that subjects cannot be themselves without other subjects, without, that is, recognising that
they are individually different by being confronted in potentially
life-and-death struggles such as that between the master and
slave. The outcome is not withdrawal and compromise, as in
Hobbes, but mediated intersubjectivity through various forms of
communicative interaction such as speech and work.[11]

In the *Phenomenology*, Hegel indicates that slave cannot exist
without master and vice versa, so that their mutual recognition
will move them both away from their initial positions – they will
be neither master nor slave in the post-struggle situation if recognition indeed takes place. This he seeks to demonstrate with the
exposition of the differences in the movement or stages of
consciousness between 'in itself', 'for itself', and 'in and for itself',
which he explains with his conception of spirit. This is surprisingly unproblematic for Hegel, because, he affirms, real
self-consciousness is always only self-consciousness in its status
as *recognised* self-consciousness, i.e., recognised as a moment of
itself in otherness. In his terms it is not merely isolated consciousness (in itself), but recognised (in and for itself, conscious of itself)
self-consciousness. What restores the concreteness to his discussion is his notion of spirit, which, in his usage, is not what we
might normally understand it to be. Spirit is neither ethereal nor
other-worldly; it exists between subjects and mediates their
perspectives not in simple unity, but by preserving the moment
of truth in their respective experiences even in the mediated
outcome position. In so doing each sees the truth and the

---

[10] Thus the choice is not between transcendent reconciliation versus friend-
enemy or ontological solipsism, as Sartre would have it in *L'être et le néant:
essai d'ontologie phénoménologique* (*Being and Nothingness*), Paris: Gallimard,
1943.

[11] Ludwig Siep, *Hegels Fichtekritik und die Wissenschaftslehre von 1804*,
Freiburg and Munich: Karl Albert Verlag, 1970, pp. 96–8.

validity of the other, and they both concretely experience Hegel's dictum that 'the truth is in the whole'.[12]

The preservation of the moment of truth in the respective experiences of individual consciousnesses moving to self-consciousness (and from there to reason and spirit as absolute knowledge[13]) is enacted in ethical life (*Sittlichkeit*). In the early writing this occurs through the medium of spirit, whereas in the later writings the *telos* of the movement towards recognition culminates in the state. The Jena writings, and to a slightly lesser extent *Phenomenology*, place great emphasis on speech and memory as the media through which the recognition of mutual rights and obligations between individual subjects becomes realised in the *Sitten* or *moeurs* of a community. The stages in the movement towards absolute knowledge and true universality are marked by a succession of forms. These forms are the phenomenological appearance of social and political life, not, however as objects, things or static essences, but instead, institutions such as the state and civil society evolve historically as the lived and ongoing negotiation of individuals struggling for recognition and freedom. If Hegel refers to the process as a whole as a phenomenology of spirit, what he means is that there is a series of stages in which the forms of recognition change in a constant movement of collective creation and re-appropriation of that which is created, i.e., that which has become visible is assimilated to mind, and the process ensues further when minds exchange and interact on the basis of what they have experienced.

---

[12] Hegel, *Die Phänomenologie des Geistes*, p. 22, p. 325. My interpretation of Hegel's early writings offered in this chapter is that the term recognition implies not only that divergent positions are mediated, but that it also means that the institutional form which the mediated position assumes may appear alienated or strange to the participants who together have brought it into existence, and this is indeed what happens when law and the state appear to the citizens of civil society as external, objective and unquestionably authoritative. Just as there are no laws of supply and demand (or economic laws, full stop) because humans choose to enact specific forms of economic life, political institutions are also the result of creative human intervention in history. If this is true, citizens can create political institutions in which both the initial and final positions of erstwhile political allies and opponents are recognisable in ever-changing constellations, or politics can assume the form of mysteriously opaque and oppressive relations, as they do in Kafka's *The Trial*. For Hegel *philosophy* makes recognition possible by explaining the movement of the historical process in its ethical totality. For citizens in civil society, however, it is only through *politics* that individual and group recognition becomes real and actual.

[13] Hegel, *Die Phänomenologie des Geistes*, p. 474.

Contemporary theoretical perspectives on Hegel and the concept of
recognition in varying ways submit that it is in *law* (as distinct from
the state, with its police, military and bureaucratic apparatuses) that
we can see the various forms of struggle for recognition in civil
society mapped out as a kind of topography of the socio-political;
thus law provides us with a kind of hermeneutic key for interpreting social and political conflict as well as its mediation. This sort of
approach to the law and reinterpreting the young Hegel has been
undertaken by Axel Honneth in *Kampf um Anerkennung* (*The
Struggle for Recognition*) and in a somewhat different way by Jürgen
Habermas in *Faktizität und Geltung* (*Between Facts and Norms*).

Honneth notes that by taking the term 'ethical life' as including
but also transcending morality, Hegel wants to show that neither
the legal system nor moral norms by themselves can legitimate the
practical outcomes of recognition struggles. Hegel is correct to
observe that both social contract and natural law approaches to
mediating difference fail to see that the moment of struggle and
reciprocal negation between individuals is based on more than
simply fear or interest. Thus Honneth maintains that Hegel can be
interpreted as rightly refusing to universalise the contractual
moment of social interaction, and seeing contractual forms of
agreement as being embedded in a wider system of communicative
action including love, work and normativity. According to
Honneth, however, Hegel's attempt ultimately fails to fully appreciate the communicative dimension to love, work and other facets
of social and political life in civil society. This is because Hegel's is
a philosophy of consciousness, such that the stages involved in the
knowledge and recognition processes culminate in the return of
consciousness to itself. Consciousness is now immeasurably
enriched and many-sided after the encounter with other consciousnesses. However, the fact that it is a return journey to an 'in and for
itself' in *consciousness*, prompts Honneth to argue that the writings
of the young Hegel alone will not suffice to answer the Hegelian
question: under what conditions might I see the conditions of my
liberty in others?[14]

Honneth argues that this solipsistic dimension in Hegel's thinking can be corrected by supplementing the basic Hegelian structure
with the insights of Mead (symbolic interactionism), Marx (class

[14] Honneth, *Kampf um Anerkennung*, pp. 103–4.

struggle), Sorel (ethical intransigence) and Sartre (existential phemomenology). He attempts to do this by retaining the original Hegelian structure, which, following Hegel's critique of Fichte, maintains that (1) there is a structure to self-consciousness which makes the movement from consciousness to self-consciousness possible, and (2) the process which begins with isolated consciousness and moves towards the recognition of other consciousnesses also has a structure. If for the young Hegel the stages which structure this phenomenological process constitute spirit assuming form in institutions, for Honneth the process results in ever-more richly articulated forms of recognition which are codified in law. Law mirrors the various struggles in society and confers esteem on all the participants.[15] Rather than merely stipulating the 'rules of the game', in this formulation law has a normative and communicative function which charts and then makes visible the various conflicts which divide civil society. Through law, various conflicts involving the struggle to defend a particular way of life and its values, as in the case of feminism, gay rights, green politics and other NSMs, acquire a moral validity going beyond the logic of interest mediation. In attempting to enlarge the socio-political space for visibility and action, NSMs suggest the possibility of potentially quite radical socio-political change. Moreover, by positing the reality of political praxis which follows neither technical nor narrowly strategic logics, these movements are fundamentally distinct from zero-sum conflicts and their forms of adjudication.[16]

Honneth argues that insofar as NSMs and other recognition struggles attempt to transform and enlarge the existing socio-political space of visibility and thereby elude zero-sum/friend-enemy adjudication, they directly indicate the inadequacy of forms of conflict mediation based on technical or administrative expertise

---

[15] Honneth, *Kampf um Anerkennung*, p. 8.

[16] Honneth, *Kampf um Anerkennung*, pp. 148–9, 203–5, 259. On the theoretical and practical significance of NSMs for the politics of recognition, see Alberto Melucci, *L'invenzione del presente: movimenti sociali nelle società complesse* (*Nomads of the Present*), Bologna: Il Mulino, 1991, pp. 109–32, 168–71; Alain Touraine, *Le voix et le regard: Sociologie des mouvements sociaux* (*The Voice and the Eye*), Paris: Seuil, 1973 p. 42; Alan Scott, *Ideology and the New Social Movements*, London: Routledge, 1990, pp. 9–10, and Sidney Tarrow, *Power in Movement: Social Movements, Collective Action and Politics*, Cambridge: CUP, 1994, pp. 193–8. By now the literature on NSMs has become vast, but a very fine attempt at synthesis with important theoretical implications is made by Neil Stammers in 'New Social Movements and Human Rights', forthcoming.

alone. Questions concerning incommensurable values and ways of life are not primarily about adjusting the economy or increasing security measures. They are more concerned with making struggles visible and recognisable which are normally obscured by potentially totalising ideological constructs such as 'the general will', 'the body politic', 'popular sovereignty', 'the people', etc., i.e., by abstractions that group different people who are living radically different realities under an identical category. This kind of asymmetry causes symbolic as well as violent conflict in cases where the institutions of political representation and conflict mediation tend to collapse difference and asymmetry into homogeneity (vote totals) on the basis of categories of identity (citizenship) or unity (sovereignty). Where division and difference are not recognised, what exists is not politics but the administration of the universally accepted (imposed) 'common good' or the elimination of the enemy. It was argued in chapter 2 that both of these are best provided for by a bureaucratic chain of command rather than a political community of non-identical equals. In order for citizens to be both non-identical and equal, there must be political institutions and a space of appearances in which non-identical equality can be recognised. After the discussion in chapter 2, it seems clear that neither a bureaucratic chain of command nor the instrumental-strategic dimension of competitive party struggle for control of the state will allow such a space to open. According to Honneth, it is possible to discern the emergence of a legally guaranteed 'post-traditional ethical life' in contemporary civil societies which presupposes and enlarges the political space of recognition struggles. However, this idea is never concretely spelled out in Honneth's work, and as a consequence it is impossible to know what forms of recognition he has in mind that are distinct from those codified in current legal and political practice. More importantly, however, is that he also never explains how the mediating and communicative aspects of law can be separated from the coercive element of bureaucracy, police and army within a framework retaining a capitalist economic system and state sovereignty.[17] The vagueness of Honneth's concept of post-traditional ethical life retaining the centrality of the traditional state is paralleled in

---

[17] Honneth, *Kampf um Anerkennung*, pp. 143–4, 178–80, pp. 281–3; Habermas, *Theorie des kommunikativen Handelns* (*Theory of Communicative Action*, 2 vols), Frankfurt: Suhrkamp, 1981, Volume 1, pp. 113–15, 485–6, 518.

Habermas's theory of communicative action.

A common thread running through Habermas's entire trajectory right up until the recent *Faktizität und Geltung* (*Between Facts and Norms*) (1992) is already present in *Strukturwandel der Öffentlichkeit* (*The Structural Transformation of the Public Sphere*) (1962) and *Technik und Wissenschaft als Ideologie* (*Science as Ideology*) (1968). In the 1968 work he argues with reference to the young Hegel that human emancipation from the drudgery of toil is not synonymous with the end of domination and oppression.[18] Thus even if it were possible within a capitalist economic framework to provide a stable material fondation for freedom of assembly, expression, etc., enabling all citizens regardless of their class position to lead full political lives, for Habermas this by itself would not be sufficient to guarantee a democratic political process. Contrary to both liberal notions about the sufficiency of negative freedom and Marxist notions about the superfluousness of politics in a post-capitalist society, Habermas remains committed to a participatory and communicative dimension to the political value of freedom and the question of how to mediate conflict. Like Honneth, he asserts that this is possible through the institution of law, though with the very important proviso that the citizens of the polity must be able to recognise themselves as the authors of those laws that govern their life together in a political community. This ability of citizens to recognise themselves as the authors of the laws that govern them is only possible in its turn on the basis of a 'radical democracy' anchored specifically in the communicative network of the public sphere, and in civil society generally.[19] Habermas borrows from the young Hegel's critique of Kant to argue for the move from practical reason to communicative reason and praxis. In contrast to the atomistic and narrowly legalistic premises in the political ideas of the former, communicative reason holds out the promise of the broadest possible, i.e., anthropological, significance of law as the basis of an instance of 'this-worldly transcendence'.[20]

According to this line of reasoning, the moment of legally codified consensus is 'post-metaphysical' even though it is also transcendent.

---

[18] Jürgen Habermas, *Technik und Wissenschaft als Ideologie*, Frankfurt: Suhrkamp, 1968, p. 47.

[19] Habermas, *Faktizität und Geltung*, pp. 51–2.

[20] See Habermas, *Faktizität und Geltung*, p. 19, where he explains his argument in terms of 'dieser innerweltlichen Transzendenz'.

The implication is that there is a moment of truth in liberalism that simultaneously points beyond liberalism, and it is to be found in the communicative rather than the merely functional or punitive structure of legal rationality. In Habermas's formulation, liberal freedoms such as those of expression, assembly and political participation can really work towards making political power both truly recognisable as the work of the collective citizenry and accountable to that assembly. For Habermas this is precisely what occurs when communication is anchored in civil society as the basis of a network of autonomous public spheres.[21] However, Habermas is also adamant that the very political system which excludes domination-free communication and which by his own admission is run by quasi-corporatist economic interests and administrative power must rule. Since money and power have insulated themselves against any pluralist and democratic impulses from civil society the capitalist economy is no longer a solvable problem for Habermas. This means that within his normative and interpretative framework, communicative action does not in any sense mean communicative power. Communicative action can influence the political system, but it cannot challenge the logic of sovereign authority. Habermas's concessions to Weber's theory of rationalisation and Niklas Luhmann's theory of autonomous systems induce him to repeat what has by now become a left-liberal litany: post-traditional societies have become far too complex for any ideal of democratic self-government to exist in practice, and recognition struggles and their consequences must be confined to a safely protected sphere of spontaneous, non-instrumental communication.[22]

[21] Habermas, *Faktizität und Geltung*, pp. 83, 363.

[22] Habermas, *Faktizität und Geltung*, p. 364. Thus after the student protests of the 1960s and the middle period featuring the works on legitimation crises and communicative action, Habermas comes practically full circle back to Kant's very pristine conception of the public sphere! Even though he does in fact criticise systems theory (p. 16) and agrees that under certain conditions civil disobedience can be considered, the argument as a whole rings astonishingly true to the Kantian caveat that we can argue as long as we like, but there is one person who must be listened to when he says, 'obey!' (political authority in the person of the sovereign in Kant's *What is Enlightenment?*). It is clear that there is a tension in Habermas's work between the tendencies operative in systems and the ways in which conflicts are presently mediated in favour of power and money (*Faktizität*), on the one hand, and the norms of ethical, legal and communicative rationality and what potentially might exist in the future (*Geltung*), on the other. What is curious is how Habermas throughout the book plays these two off against each other without ever really taking a firm position. For a more positive but also critical position, see Chris Thornhill, *Political Theory in Modern Germany: an Introduction*, Cambridge: Polity, 1999, chapter 5.

The question is: What remains of the concept of recognition once it has been restricted to these criteria of application, that is, once communicative action is strictly qualified as a form of action co-existing with instrumental and administrative forms of behaviour, limited to a functional sphere which can exert influence against but not decisively challenge the other two? It becomes, in Habermas's own words, a 'channel',[23] which like the other channels, leads either to an indivisible *centre* or to a vertically structured *pinnacle*. The struggle for recognition is thus denied its transformational potential, since all recognition struggles in civil society must eventually culminate at a sovereign centre or at the top of a pinnacle from which it will be virtually impossible to recognise legislation in terms of the joint authorship of individual citizens. From neither vantage point is the space of socio-political visibility enlarged, and the problems linked to a concept of recognition which ultimately culminates in a return journey to the self posed by Hegel are not overcome; unsurprisingly, individuals are thrown back on their own identities which they must then seek to defend.[24]

At first sight the demand in thinkers like Honneth and Habermas for a transition from practical to communicative reason seems to provide politics with an intersubjective dimension. In theory this dimension would incorporate yet also move beyond liberal versions of neutrality and respect without lapsing into communitarian dogmas. But clearly this would be impossible in practice within the frameworks they offer. This is because the state, or, in Habermas's terms the political system, transforms a given recognition struggle in civil society into a struggle for power or money by channelling it into a steering or integration mechanism such as political parties or government ministries. As long as parties and bureaucracies govern, there can be no value or perspectival pluralism, since these institutions function on the basis of technical competence; competence signifies efficiency in strategic

---

[23] Habermas, *Faktizität und Geltung*, p. 364.

[24] Kant's *Critique of Judgement* convincingly suggests that the possibility of a moment of inner wordly transcendence and genuine neutrality requires not only that we respect the autonomy of other people, but that we are actually capable of putting ourselves in their position. This has important political implications which I attempt to elaborate later on in this chapter. See Kant, *Kritik der Urteilskraft* (*Critique of Judgement*, 1878), Stuttgart: Reclam, 1963, pp. 215–16.

terms, rather than plurality in value terms.[25] Put more simply, communication and recognition struggles cannot compete with struggles for power and money within a framework where arriving at a centre or on top of a chain of command is the basis of political legitimacy. The politics of recognition require a space where individuals can see issues from another perspective, rather than either standing above other individuals or getting to the political 'centre' before they do.

In the absence of such a political space where different perspectives can simultaneously attain mutual visibility, freedom is restricted to successful access to the most coveted status positions in the state and civil society, i.e., access to a competition in which zero-sum logics are almost inevitably operative. Under these conditions, political recognition struggles come back to citizens in an unrecognisable form as the defence of individual and group identities. The latter have more to do with social struggles for economic and other forms of equality than politics in terms of a public sphere or the collective action of communities. Since access to status positions is normally secured in terms of the equal rights that individuals and groups attain to be successfully competitive, the pluralist, non zero-sum dimension of political liberty is obscured. Competitive success entails strategic recognition of the position of potential opponents, while the communicative and intersubjective dimension of recognition dims. To the extent that other perspectives and values become barely visible, I become politically blind and need, by extension, to find the sense of what I am doing in myself and my identity alone. This will prompt me to attempt to valorise the identities of those like me against potentially hostile competitors: the strong state becomes inevitably necessary the more individual actors in civil society are atomised. In modified Tocquevillian terms, the tyranny of the majority is really the atomisation of the majority and its utter dependence on the state for the recognition of individual and group lifestyles. However, what unites both me and my opponents in our blindness is the inevitable conclusion that both status and safety can only be

[25] Hence Habermas actually helps confirm the validity of Weber's and Schmitt's suspicion that liberalism's universal normative dimension is undermined by the actual workings of parliamentary institutions within the terms set by capitalist economies. See Schmitt, *Die geistesgeschichtliche Lage des heutigen Parlamentarismus*, pp. 12–13.

gained through access, via representation, to the top or centre – the state – where by geometric definition a plurality of positions cannot be occupied. By the time the successful negotiation of interest representation has been concluded, political conflict has indeed been mediated insofar as its political, i.e., communicative and perspectival charge, has been defused. The current 'political' system's transformation of political differences into social ones is a transformation of clashes between different energies, perspectives and values into status, identity and security struggles. It then appears that we are all seeking something identical, and the outcome of the struggle merely registers the more and less successful strategies. Here law functions not as a hermeneutic map locating different political perspectives in civil society, but is in large measure restricted to its coercive dimension. The immediate consequence is that (1) if I make myself visible and recognised, someone or other group cannot and (2) in our isolation from one another we are all dependent on the state for protection. The resulting institutionalisation of fear and mutual suspicion offers a wide margin of electoral and cultural manoeuvre for populism and plebiscitary manipulation of the kind discerned by Weber.

There are thus major difficulties with theories of recognition in civil society based on the idea of legal recognition. Honneth and Habermas's ideas indicate the obstacles to mediating different starting positions through recognition struggles when existing forms of economy, law and state remain in vigour. Although powerfully suggestive, the ideas of the young Hegel do not offer definitive solutions within a Hegelian framework, which is borne out by Hegel's own evolution towards a statist theory of the political in his mature writings. Moreover, law cannot assume the universal significance ascribed to it by theorists like Honneth and Habermas within a framework where arriving at a centre or at the top of a chain of command is the basis of recognition and political legitimacy. One possible response might be to give up, that is, to concede that there are no possible forms of action which suggest alternative ways of enacting freedom in political terms beyond behaviour rooted in power, strategic interest, status and security concerns (politics disappears due to the tyranny of the social). Alternatively, one could argue instead that there are universals such as care, anxiety and *Dasein* which outweigh perspectival as well as class, racial, religious and other divides (politics is regarded

as secondary to more fundamental, ontological categories). Another possible response, which will be the focus of the next section of this chapter, is that there is neither any such thing as an autonomous individual *subject* in and for itself, as idealist philosophy posits in varying ways, nor any possible neutral supra-individual *being* in and for itself, as ontologists assert in varying ways. From the standpoint of the view to be considered below, there is a mediating term between categories like subject/object, being/nothingness, individual/state. This third term strives to mediate between standpoints without absorbing one standpoint into the other or establishing a hierarchy between different standpoints. In theoretical terms, this occurs as a deliber-
• ate rejection of the idea that recognition results as the outcome of a struggle after which both struggling actors are forced to modify their starting points, and which law then registers at the level of institutions. Radical ethical theorists argue in modified Kantian terms, that if individuals from different standpoints are to be able to recognise the values of democracy and equality in existing institutions, then these institutions must enable them to treat each other like ends in themselves and never as means only. This approach would seemingly offer an alternative framework for analysing contemporary civil societies, where there are obviously a plethora of forms of political action beyond violence and contract, but which within existing institutions are insufficiently recognised as such.

Recognition, ethics and alterity

It is clear to the theorists of radical ethics that the possibility of treating all other individuals as ends in themselves is linked with the ability to recognise them in their alterity and separateness. In this way it might be possible to resist both seeking isolation and protection from them, on the one hand, or trying to fuse them into a single body politic, on the other. This possibility is established in the face-to-face relation that each of us has with the *other*, where our relation to the other takes the form of a meeting or encounter that in some ways preserves the mystery and ultimately unfathomable position of the interlocutor. Many writers argue that in this space opened up by the meeting or encounter between two or more individuals, it is neither necessary to seek protection from them nor absorb them into a higher unity. The third term between I/you, or master/slave, is the space which makes their encounter a reality and points beyond the rigid dichotimisation that once governed their interaction as a master–slave/friend–enemy relation.

In order to reconstruct the radical ethical position before moving on to the concluding section of this chapter which posits an alternative to both the modified Hegelian and radical ethical standpoints, it will be necessary to return very briefly to Feuerbach (chapter 1). Feuerbach effectively shows that the price that Hegel pays for absolute knowledge is the positing of an identity between thought and being. The movement of the Hegelian dialectic leads to the ultimate dissolution of the difference between the individual knowing subject and the known object in the identity of being and thought. The identity of thinking with itself means that the distance between the subject and the world of objects is abolished in Hegel's notion of the concept. Whereas Kant posits a noumenal world beyond the scope of human cognition, Hegel reclaims the unity of subject and object in what one might call the praxis of thought. Feuerbach is alive to the predatory aspect of this conception of thinking. For Feuerbach, the Hegelian subject is constantly involved in a process of reclaiming all exteriority back into the limits of the subject, and mistranslating this exteriority into a mode of subjective experience. In practice this justifies a kind of knowing which refuses to acknowledge exteriority and difference, and thereby assimilates the latter to the modes of subjective experience. Thus the Hegelian mind is a conquering mind which, when confronted with other minds, tends to initiate a process culminating either in the integration or abolition of all that is foreign to it.[26]

Feuerbach noted that for the Hegelian mind it is extremely difficult not to regard other minds as either identically-thinking minds or wrong-thinking minds. Consequently, any form of recognition likely to issue from such an encounter is going to be narcissistic – the recognition of the self in the other. The other is not recognised in their particularity; they are, rather, apprehended as an object of perception, and hence remain a mean rather than an end in itself. Feuerbach's critique of Hegel has had a major impact on Martin Buber and other thinkers seeking to explore the social and political consequences of radical ethics. Buber argues that there is a fundamental difference between the 'I–it' relation of the kind the

[26] Feuerbach, 'Grundsätze der Philosophie der Zukunft' ('Fundamental Principles of the Philosophy of the Future'), p. 205.

Hegelian or Satrean subject would have with others, and the 'I–you' relation that might approach the Kantian ideal. The I–you does not represent a subject knowing an object by epistemologically or institutionally making that object one with subject. The person who says 'you' is in a relationship which has its own life independently of either subject. This formulation resembles the Kantian one in that it is not based on experience, as Buber explicitly states. But it is also distinct from Kant in that it is not based on a conception of reason conceived of independently of experience. Buber thus holds out the possibility for an inner-worldly moment of transcendence not based on law in its anthropological significance as intersubjective rationality, as Honneth and Habermas do in different ways. In Buber's writings it is based instead on the notion that the idea of there being such a thing as 'now' or 'the present' depends on their being a dialogue between two or more people in which 'presence' becomes a worldly reality, and time becomes absolute rather than merely relative. That is, in the moment of dialogue there is presence which is created as an *absolutely singular* encounter with no past antecedents or necessary future development, such that it defies the logic of representation and law. Thus for Buber the I–it world is the world of time and space as normally experienced, while the I–you time is much closer to a moment of illumination which discloses what was previously opaque or buried.[27]

Buber employs a number of metaphors to explain how he thinks the I–you relation potentially represents an absolute now amidst the relative nows operating in the state and economy. One is the idea that if we are going our way and experience various things during the course of our particular journey, we may well meet another person whose unique path is absolutely unknown to us. The meeting of our two 'I's' is potentially akin to the miracle of human and divine creation, in that it brings to life something

---

[27] Feuerbach, 'Grundsätze der Philosophie der Zukunft', pp. 271–2; Buber, *Ich und Du*, pp. 19–20, 42. Here Buber seems to be thinking of something similar to Benjamin's notions of 'nowtime' (*Jetztzeit*, see chapter 2) and profane illumination. Both the idea of nowtime and the profane illumination are in part utopian responses to Schmitt's notion that a so-called normal situation can suddenly turn into a friend–enemy relation. Both Benjamin and Buber argue that a change in our relations with others and, by extension, between ethics and politics, may be more likely to ensue on the basis of an illuminating experience than on the basis of enlightened self-interest or a successful bid for state power.

which did not previously exist – what Buber calls 'you'. 'You' is thus a relation which cannot be seized or manipulated or simply used in the way we might use a tool or instrument. He casts our ability to create an I–you situation in existential terms; it depends on our willingness to choose to know and have knowledge in a non-manipulative and non-colonising manner. We do not seize or invent the truth by ourselves; our journey to the you encounter is not a return of the subject to itself after the various stages of the knowing process have been accomplished, for this would result in an I–it positivist epistemology. In marked contrast to the state and economy, where ephemeral struggles for power and money are played out, recognition occurs in our encounter with the concrete other through 'the word', where for Buber the word is the eternal call to responsibility, humility and gratitude. Through the word, the other person emerges and separates him or herself from the tools and instruments of the 'it world'. In dialogue, the word illuminates 'the eternal now' which is normally clouded over by the routines of social, political and economic life structuring our experience of past and present. Drawing on Feuerbach, Buber argues that in this space created by two or more interlocutors, a universal standpoint emerges which is neither a compromise nor the product of an individual consciousness.[28]

These ideas are anticipated by Feuerbach, who in the 'Fundamental Principles of the Philosophy of the Future' (1843), remarks that Greek philosophy is in some senses a more humanist philosophy than modern philosophy.[29] This is because Greek philosophers are anthropologists, while modern idealist and romantic philosophers tend to be epistemologically closer to theologians. By this he means that modern idealist philosophy either assimilates all reality to mind, or juxtaposes a world known to the mind to an unknowable noumenal world: in both cases, sensual experience is excluded from the realm of valid knowledge. By contrast, Greek philosophy neither attempts to assimilate all of reality to mind nor to assimilate being to thought; the clas-

[28] Feuerbach, 'Grundsätze der Philosophie der Zukunft', p. 249; Buber, *Ich und Du*, pp. 56–60.

[29] Buber, *Ich und Du*, pp. 56–60; Martin Rotenstreich, 'Dialog und Dialektik', in Werner Licharz and Heiner Schmitt (eds), *Martin Buber (1878–1965): Internationales Symposium zum Zwanzigsten Todestag*, Volume I, Frankfurt: Haag and Herchen, 1989, pp. 267–72.

sical world was able to creatively experience the world of external forms as a sensual world in which reason runs up against its external boundaries. Rather than abolishing this boundary in the concept, or relegating the unknowable to the realm of faith, in the Greek world there remained an inner-worldly mystery of otherness, of exteriority, which coexisted in an unthreatening way with the different forms of human inquiry.[30] For Feuerbach the pain caused by this distance between thought and reality, between subject and extenal world, is not only a source of poetry and creativity: this boundary also offers a field of resistance against coercive attempts to know by abolishing the distance between subject and object.[31]

Philosophical abstraction attempts to portray thought as something clear, distinct and separate from the sensual individual thinking subject. This process reaches its pinnacle in Hegel's speculative idealism, which for Feuerbach is a form of rationalised theology of absolute knowledge. Feuerbach argues that what Hegel ignores, however, is that prior to philosophising, the child experiences other individuals and even objects as another 'I', as another subject, such that the object first becomes an object as a you, which at this stage is another 'I become object'. This means not only that for the child the object is another I, but that the child is also aware of a not I within itself, i.e., that which becomes object for another I. Thus objectivity is mediated by the you, such that I am I and you at the same time; the you is that part of me which becomes externalised in the form of another person. As the child matures, he or she realises that they are both an I for themselves and a you for others. The relation of the I to any future you will thus be a matter of education and culture rather than ontology. This is Emmanuel Lévinas's point of departure in his discussion of the various

[30] By the time of the painter Giorgio De Chirico (1888–1978), this sense of otherness of the external world of objects and forms assumes a much more menacing form. See Paolo Baldacci, *De Chirico, 1888–1919: la metafisica*, Milan: Leonardo Arte, 1997, p. 8.

[31] Thus he suggests that suffering (*Leiden*) is not simply something individual. The experience of suffering has a collective dimension as *Mit* (with) (*Leid*): *Mitleid*: compassion. Without equating one person's suffering with another's, compassion comes from the shared experience of life that makes the suffering of another equal to but not identical with our own. That this sharing can also be positive is suggested by Feuerbach's use of the word *Leidenschaft* (passion). Because I am passionate I can perhaps recognise your passion without seeking to understand it in the terms of my own experience.

aspects of recognition in *Totalité et infini (Infinity and Totality)* (1971).[32]

Lévinas argues that our relation to the other is prior to any ontology assumed as an overarching neutral background or horizon of all-encompassing being. Whereas Buber, following Feuerbach, posits the primacy of the I–you in dialogue, Lévinas maintains that the face-to-face interaction, or simply 'the face' (*le visage*) of the other, commands our immediate response. He makes a categorical distinction between types of thinking tending towards a totalisation of what is multiple and incommensurable, on the one hand, and his notion of infinity, on the other: totality and infinity are thus starkly opposed conceptions in his work. Where idealist, historicist and ontological thinking are characteristically totallising in their approach, only a radical ethics is capable of even posing the question of radical otherness in all of its ramifications. Lévinas argues that our point of departure in relations with others is wholly different than the model suggested in *Phenomenology*. First of all, the presence of the other is not a shocking moment of confrontation which sets in motion the master–slave dialectic. As in Feuerbach, the I is always an I–you, insofar as we are both subjects and at the same time a you for somebody else, and indeed it is this situation that makes a basic level of communication possible. But Lévinas gives Feuerbach and Buber's I–you a more radical dimension, which he attempts to outline in his notion of the face of the other. For Lévinas the face of the other in its phenomenological immediacy represents an appeal or a call, which if properly understood and experienced subverts the logic of self-interest and power in any of its guises. The presence of the other transcends both the individual ego and any hypothetical supra-ego ontological horizon outside human experience like being. Lévinas attempts to think of recognition in opposition to what he regards as the Hegelian attempt to assimilate alterity, on the one hand, and the Heideggerian attempt to give being the status of a Kantian noumenon with a terrestial presence, i.e., something akin to Hölderlin's ether, on the other.[33]

Lévinas's version of the other is implicitly contained in his belief that true pedagogy must proceed on the assumption that

[32] Feuerbach, 'Grundsätze der Philosophie der Zukunft', pp. 247–50.

[33] Lévinas, *Totalité et infini*, pp. 38–9; *De l'existence à l'existant (From Existence to the Existing)*, Paris: Vrin, 1963, pp. 63–4; Wildt, *Autonomie und Anerkennung*, p. 192.

the pupil educates the teacher, in the sense that truth resides in every individual's experience of the world, rather than what any one pedagogue can impart to the members of a classroom. While the master–slave dialectic presupposes an initial unity that is rediscovered, the teacher–pupil relation assumes a hierarchy of command that presupposes that 'pupil' is merely a less advanced stage on the same journey to 'teacher'.[34] For Lévinas the asymmetry of the pupil–teacher relation is the potential basis of a non-hierachical relation between people in which reciprocal dependence is recognised as the foundation of pluralism. In order for this to be so in practice, however, the teacher must experience the appearance of the face of the pupil as more than their mere presence. He or she must be prepared to fully assume the consequences of the fact that it is actually the student who is the source of their knowledge. To the extent that the teacher recognises this in the face of the pupil and is fully prepared to accept the pedagogical primacy of the student, a truly ethical relationship between them is possible, and the Kantian categorical imperative can assume a living form.[35]

Whether referring to a conventionally practised teacher–pupil relation as discipline, or love between two people as fusion, in institutional terms they spell different versions of the master–slave, that is, a totallising rather than infinite relation. Earlier in this chapter it was argued that the possibility of a politics of recognition in practice requires moving beyond the reified thinking suggested by friend/enemy or political system/civil society. According to Lévinas, this means breaking with the concept of totality, insofar as totality is a concept which fundamentally rests on the notion of the ultimate identity of merely temporarily estranged parts which seek fusion as the result of an immanent *telos* which guides them – even if they are not aware of this. Against the notions of immanence and totality, Lévinas deploys the idea of what he refers to as the *surplus*. The surplus which will not be squeezed into the totality exceeds

[34] In *Le temps et l'autre* (*Time and the Other*), Lévinas suggests that the erroneousness of the master–slave dialectic and a conventional understanding of the teacher–pupil relation is reproduced once again in the notion of love as the fusion of two beings. In his terminology this is to confuse totality (fusion) with infinity (the unknowability of the other which is an infinite source of power incapable of being translated into political or any form of worldly power). *Le temps et l'autre*, Paris: PUF, 1979, pp. 68–80; *De l'existence à l'existant*, p. 63.

[35] Lévinas, *Totalité et infini*, pp. 43, 224.

the totality.[36] He describes this surplus as a modality of desire, as an energy which precedes any and all forms of ontology or interest. The face is thus different than simply 'the other' or 'the you'. The face transforms the relative horizontal distance between two people into the absolute vertical distance of infinity. Lévinas maintains that the distance between two people cannot be bridged through any technical medium which might bring them closer in geographical/physical terms – it remains absolute. He argues further that there is no longer more or less time, but the transcendent time of the other which cannot be recuperated within the totality of their aggregation as a pair (as distinct from their existence as two separate individuals).[37]

But Lévinas mistakenly insists that recognition in political terms obscures the face of the other and re-institutes a relation of reciprocal interest. Thus he thinks that genuine recognition is not political but religious or ethical, that is, that there can be no political form of recognition which does not tend to cast the I–you relation as a *struggle* for recognition. For Lévinas political struggles are zero-sum enterprises which in legal terms require reciprocity as a compromise rather than understanding: the asymmetry of absolutely unique individuals is channelled into the coercive symmetrical logic of interest mediation in which my loss is your gain. Thus Lévinas argues that the transcendence of interest is also the transcendence of politics, which for him must be replaced by and unconditional humility and sacrifice. In effect, however, Lévinas deprives recognition of its worldly, political dimension by exalting unconditional sacrifice and what he calls 'the time of the other' over pluralism, perspective and action. Framed in these terms, Lévinas denies the epistemological nature of politics discussed towards the end of chapter 4, and strangely seems to put us back in a solipsistic relation with the other. His radical ethical critique of Hegelian imperiousness finishes in mutual incomprehension, and politically one is stuck once again with the strong state protecting individuals from one another. There is little to prevent those individuals and groups who do not share Lévinas's ethical relation of desire with the other to simply say, why do I

---

[36] The idea of surplus is also employed in a totally different context by Georges Bataille in his critique of bourgeois political economy. See *La part maudite* (1949), Paris: Éditions de minuit, 1967, pp. 50–1.

[37] Lévinas, *Totalité et infini*, pp. 323–7.

need recognition from whites, straights, non-disabled, etc., and why do they need recognition from me? If I do not and cannot know the other, is it not equally plausible that I might find shock and fear rather than mystery and wonder in their presence?[38]

Seen comparatively, both the defence of law as a moment of this worldly transcendence analysed in the first section of this chapter, and the standpoint of radical ethics as a moment of unconditional acceptance of the other looked at in section 2, offer divergent perspectives on the concept of recognition. Both attempt to formulate the bases of possible forms of non-contractual communicative action and rationality which theorise how humans can co-inhabit a world in which they regard each other as ends, rather than instrumentally as the means to private ends. In the first section, it was seen how and why legality cannot fulfil the claims made for it by its defenders; within a framework separating civil society from the economy and the political-administrative system, the defence of legal normativity is a concession to existing economic and state structures. Under these structural constraints, the law does not represent a moment of inner-worldly transcendence, but becomes instead the means by which the economy and the state are able to justify their systemic autonomy – and indemnity from normative critique. In the second section, it was seen how the radical ethical critique of Hegel and contractual thinking finishes in the abandoning of any attempt to construe freedom in non-coercive terms; the state is implicitly postulated as a necessary evil in a world where politics must mean interest, violence and power. The recognition of otherness and difference assumes the form of an unconditional acceptance of the other which leaves no political spaces of freedom, but rather insists on the primacy of ethics above any conceivable kind of politics. It could be argued that Lévinas is not really interested in freedom or ethics, but rather in the unconditional surrender of all forms of subjectivity, which for him seem to be tainted with ambition and self-interest. Thus he either misreads or simply ignores the non-coercive forms of recognition in contemporary civil societies, and fails to discern the important political dimension of ethics and freedom that they illustrate. As will be argued below, they suggest new forms of subjectivity and a new practice of the political.

---

[38] Feuerbach, 'Grundsätze der Philosophie der Zukunft', pp. 240–1.

Political democracy and recognition

The preceding discussion has attempted to show that although recognition is indeed an important concept for an understanding of non-strategic and non-instrumental political action in civil society, it fails in both its legal-communicative and radical ethical versions. On the one hand, the first version strips the practice of recognition of its political character. What begins as the demand to see the world from a different perspective in civil society becomes the aggregation of interests at the level of state, since markedly different recognition struggles are channelled to the same systemic centre or legislative summit in an essentially technical process more appropriate to consumption than politics. From this vantage point it is virtually impossible to recognise legislation in terms of the joint authorship of the individual members of a political community. As such, legality assumes the codification of a vertical aggregation of inputs (contractual) rather than a mapping out of different standpoints (understanding through recognition). If the ideal of legislative joint authorship is to be retained as a fundamental component of democracy understood as self-government, politics cannot be reduced to the technical process of 'channelling' information upwards to the monopoly on the legitimate use of political action: civil society must enjoy this monopoly. On the other hand, it is impossible to see the political consequences of an ethics of sensual responsibility which at the same time claims to be either beyond experience (Buber) or beyond instinct and yet not rooted in reason, i.e., a powerful but ultimately pious appeal to goodness and the disposition to welcome (Lévinas) which the young Hegel quite rightly questions.[39]

In addition to the formation and re-formation of public spheres and the sustaining of diverse forms of community, contemporary civil societies manifest a variety of inchoate forms of recognition. Their theoretical significance as well as the distinctness of the

---

[39] Buber, *Ich und Du*, p. 16, p. 39; Lévinas, *Totalité et infini*, p. 146. Although not fully developed, Feuerbach presents a more convincing and political account of recognition than Buber and Lévinas. He manages to retain what is critical and important in Hegel, and, in contrast to the theological rejection of politics suggested to some extent by Buber and especially by Lévinas, suggests how recognition struggles might be institutionalised in the form of a self-governing civil society. The critique of Hegel's epistemological premises and the Hegelian state in conjunction with the notion of democracy as self-government constitute the obvious link between Feuerbach and Marx.

struggle for recognition will be discussed below in the last section of this chapter. To begin, one might say that as in the instances of the public sphere and community, these are forms of political action which elude the logic of interest representation and instrumental reason which currently structure political representation. This chapter has thus far sought to demonstrate that neither legal nor radical ethical standpoints fully grasp how non-instrumental action can at the same time be political yet non-strategic. In the case of the application of law by the modern state, the notion of the state as possessing the monopoly on the use of legitimate force within a given territory is extended, such that legality constitues the monopoly on the recognition of legitimate instances of the political. This is to arrest, interpolate and categorise forms of action in legal terms, and to consign them to the parties as the legitimate voice of civil society in the state. The parties re-present these voices in the legislature, though by this time these voices have been transformed into mute interests that more or less resemble each other, rather than divergent perspectives which mutually require each other to stand out as unique. To anticipate the argument below, recognition as politics indicates ways of seeing what is going on in the relations between individuals and groups in civil society – it is a form of epistemological praxis, i.e., a form of knowledge which can only be attained through political action which is carried on for its own sake. Thus it is equally mistaken to construe non-strategic action in ethical as opposed to political terms. This would be in effect to make ethics a private matter, and to reduce the political to simple obedience or to contractual or other forms of utilitarian behaviour.[40] On the contrary, in its manifestations in the public sphere and community, politics opens spaces for non-violent and non-contractual action which becomes visible through various forms of recognition. The potentially revolutionary content of the issue of recognition is suggested by the question, just how big might these spaces become?

A careful examination of political projects in contemporary civil societies points towards the conclusion that for the most part they do not aim to seize power or replace one political class with another. Thus they will remain powerless as long as the only institutionally recognised forms of political action are those seeking to use politics as

[40] As we saw in chapter 1, this is why Hegel is not satisfied with Kant's defence of the public sphere as it stands in Kant's formulation.

a means to the end of power. An important dimension of their organ-isation and aims reveals instead a desire to enlarge the space for political judgement and perspective. In many cases, the sustained effort to create and enlarge this space assumes the form of a struggle for the recognition of various forms of action as *political* action, as forms of praxis in which humans are free in a specifically political sense which will now be elaborated. In chapter 3 on the public sphere it was seen that on the one hand *life* and the life-cycle are to a large extent governed by processes which require human beings to use technology in order to control and manipulate nature. In that chapter it was suggested that these are processes that do not necessarily require other people for their successful completion. Agriculture, house construction, etc. are activities that at least in principle can be performed by humans working by themselves on nature and external objects. *The world*, on the other hand, requires the presence of other human beings who speak, remember and perhaps above all else act in a space or forum that they open up, or *give*. Thus with reference to the hypothetical case of Robinson Crusoe, one might say that alone on his island he had to cope with life, but he never had direct experience of the world and the plurality standpoints which become visible when humans undertake individual and collective projects. In Kantian terms he would probably have little occasion to sharpen his own appreciation of the differences between interest, understanding, reason and judgement. The latter would be particularly difficult to develop alone, since our ability to judge the beauty of a painting depends not only on where we stand in relation to it. It depends also on our ability to look at it with no pecuniary or other interest which might distort our ability to appreciate the work in its own terms. Our appreciation of the work will also be influenced by the various ways in which others see it and speak about it, for our own judgement stands out and takes shape in relation to the differing opinions that others have. If our faculty of judgement is sharp enough, it will be possible for us to recognise the fact that neither our or their judge-ments are either completely arbitrary or objectively valid in the sense of scientific knowledge. Thus for Kant, the faculty of judgement is closely bound up with our ability to place ourselves in the position of others without thereby losing our own perspective.[41]

The political significance of accepting the validity of different

---

[41] Kant, *Kritik der Urteilskraft*, p. 215.

perspectives in a way which is neither arbitrary nor objective is obvious. Where such a relationship between individuals exists, it becomes possible to avoid the problems of a relativism which tolerates the most unacceptable positions, on the one hand, without being bound to the 'objectivity' of the decisions of states and bureaucracies, on the other. Both relativism and the potential authoritarian structure of positive law are interrelated and hardly avoidable problems when the space for political judgement is eclipsed by the technical exigencies of aggregating preferences in the manner of a competition or as a modified form of consumption. The space of the political in civil society is a space for the articulation of values which are neither relative or arbitrary, nor absolute in any conceivably objective sense. This space cannot be opened up or achieve sufficient visibility by the electoral competition of parties vying for control of the state. In practice, this usually turns out to be an institutional form for regulating the competition of different organised wills to power, or adjudicating between competing claims for material security. A casual glance at such struggles for influence on the state would indeed suggest that there is little in the way of non-strategic yet political action in civil society today – but this would be looking at the wrong phenomena. The key to understanding how this space in civil society can and does open is to be found by observing how in different ways citizens have returned to the original Hegelian question arising in connection with the significance of recognition, i.e., 'Under what conditions will I see others not as a limit to my freedom, but rather as the very condition of that freedom?'. The provisional answer seems to be the following: enacting situation-specific forms of recognition in the ongoing project of giving democracy a political as opposed to merely social character.

    Fundamental to the ideology of technology is the assertion that technology reduces the distance between individuals (through phones, faxes, computers, etc.), as if they were objects that can be placed closer to each other. By contrast, the truth of politics is a worldly truth of the absolute (rather than the merely relative) distance between people. The struggle for recognition is enacted politically when citizens starting from different standpoints undertake to preserve this distance in the form of individual freedoms protected by law. This distance must be preserved if there is to be perspective and plurality, without which citizens are reified into legitimation fodder or simply the welfare clients of parties, bureau-cracies and states. But whereas the law is a necessary condition for preserving individual rights, only the actual action of citizens can preserve the political space in which different standpoints can distinguish themselves. The mutual recognition of their difference and distinctness is an essential component of democracy under-stood politically as the praxis of clashing but nonetheless collectively self-governing citizens, rather than democracy in the social sense as welfare and equality. The collapsing of these two very different senses of democracy in practice signifies the domina-tion of the social which can, under the conditions dictated by the modern state, become total. Thus both the theoretical distinction between social and political democracy, and the practice of the latter, indicate the contours of spaces of free, undetermined praxis and self-creation in individual action in the public sphere and collective projects like communities. Yet in order for these projects to take shape and to be *recognised* as political projects rather than merely hobbies, private concerns or simply wasted energy, and in order for law to be able to mediate between individual liberty and political democracy in a way that might allow law to function in reality as Habermas says it does now, democracy in the social sense must be secured together with the practice of politics. The mainte-nance of a socio-economic system that continues to deny the overwhelming majority of people democracy in a social sense ensures the predominance of 'the risk society', and the concomitant suppression of the political content of civil society. This form of social tyranny requires citizens to consecrate a vast proportion of their time to the concerns of reproducing the material necessities of life. This, in turn, suppresses political freedom, and denies virtu-ally everyone recognition in the explicitly political sense used here in contrast to the legal and ethical positions sketched in the first two sections of this chapter.[42] There is little possibility for people who live as competitors for what are held out to be scarce resources to be citizens; they instead become competing clients. As a direct consequence, people cannot see in each other the condition for their mutual freedom – only politics and political democracy can make this possible.

[42] The term 'risk society' is taken from Ulrich Beck, *Risikogesellschaft: Auf dem Weg in eine andere Moderne*, Frankfurt: Suhrkamp, 1986.

Everyone refers to that part of each individual that is not subsumable under one of the sociological categories that generally guide the study of NSMs, such as gender, race, etc., but which is currently excluded from the world of political visibility. Rather than romanticising individuals and groups that are currently marginalised – which is to patronise them – the politics of recognition is a political project to open spaces for that at-present excluded voice of each citizen *qua individual citizen*. In taking the baton from the working-class struggle for socialism, NSMs attempt to go beyond a class perspective in political terms. This is both a forward and a backward step as far as political democracy is concerned, since (a) there will never be a democratic polity as long as there is systematic class exploitation and (b) NSMs all too often limit their contestation to forms of identity politics which exist in an ambivalent relation of dependence on the state. Since the space of political action stands in tension with the time of clientelistic representation, NSMs are at present caught between the possibilities of enlarging the space of the political, on the one hand, and the systemic logic of material representation of identities, on the other. The freedom of politics in terms of the constant possibility of new beginnings and unforeseeable outcomes is at odds with the necessity of re-presenting an identical relation of sameness (i.e., the identity of workers, women, blacks, etc.), i.e., with the strategic nature of vertically-channelled interest. The political space of recognition between citizens is thus not the same space as the vertical chain of representation of identities and interests. There is thus at present an asymmetry between the horizontal, pluralist and perspectival nature of politics in civil society, on the one hand, and the vertical and functionalist representation of *all* forms of activity and action as strategic interest in the state, on the other.[43] This asymmetry is a

---

[43] Thus the functionalist moment in Habermas's thinking does indeed accurately reflect political struggles today to a certain degree. The argument in the present book is that (a) the functionalist separation of system/*Lebenswelt* or civil society/political society/state/economy, etc. nonetheless misses the extent to which current attempts to enact politics in civil society (the public sphere, community and recognition) try to articulate a new language of politics and new forms of praxis which resist *the functional transformation of the political world*, and (b) it is this functional mispresentation/transformation of practically all struggles into interest and identity struggles which in contemporary states undermines the potential capacity of law to play the role it is supposed to in the work of Honneth, Habermas and other theorists.

source of conflict between political and social democracy. Public sphere and community-sustaining action attempt to resist the institutional pressure to collapse these two distinct dimensions of democracy together. This resistance is in its turn sustained in the attempt to formulate a series of specifically political responses to the question of how individual citizens might see in each other the condition of their mutual freedom, i.e., in the attempt to create and enlarge the space for political forms of recognition beyond the logic and practice of interest, violence and contract. Rather than being centrally about changing life or seizing power, the struggle for recognition is an attempt to make the world larger.

Conclusion

Civil society is the creation of the modern world.

Hegel, *The Philosophy of Right*

This book attempts to demonstrate that the 'rebirth of civil society' in Eastern and Western Europe as well as in other parts of the globe offers the bases for a theory of the political based on perspectival pluralism and a conception of action rooted in the public sphere, community and recognition. What emerges is a theory of freedom drawn from two main sources: (1) the writings of Kant, Hegel, Feuerbach, Marx and, more recently, Weber, Schmitt, Benjamin, Adorno and Arendt and (2) an analysis of actual attempts to sustain a public sphere, political forms of community and new forms of recognition in contemporary civil societies. The theory of freedom developed from these two sources places politics at its centre, and distinguishes the political from religion, economics, technology, administraton, ethics, aesthetics, the social, intimacy and violence. The crystallisation of the conceptual, epistemological and normative specificity of politics in the preceding pages proceeds in the first instance as a critique of the existing paradigm political institution – the state. This critique is followed by arguments demonstrating that a close look at civil society suggests that the public sphere, community and struggles for recognition are best interpreted as projects in which citizens attempt to enact their freedom in ways which point beyond the discourses of interest, identity and power.[1] Two main objections are likely to be formu-

[1] It has been the explicit aim of this book to provide a theoretical and philosophical analysis of civil society on the basis of actual civil societies. In order to make the argument in the detail required, I have had to by and large omit

lated in opposition to the central theses in this book. The first might be: why continue to read Hegel, Marx, Benjamin, Arendt, etc. in order to understand the relation between state and civil society today? The second is likely to be, why civil society and the political? Why do these terms have greater explanatory and normative cogency in interpreting contemporary social and political struggles than liberalism, or better still, some version of critical theory drawing on elements of both liberalism and Marxism, such as Habermas's theory of law and communicative action? In concluding I will attempt to answer these two questions and to summarise, beginning with a brief recapitulation of the relevance of Kant *et al.* for an understanding of the relationship between civil society and the state today.

I

It is argued in chapter 1 and than at various points throughout the book that the attempt to enact freedom in contemporary civil societies beyond struggles of interest, identity and power continues to be largely frustrated for reasons that are first illustrated in Marx's early writings, such as 'Zur Judenfrage' ('On the Jewish Question') and the *Ökonomisch-philosophische Manuskripte vom Jahre 1844* (*Economic and Philosophical Manuscripts of 1844*). These are reasons which have to do with the problems inherent in attempting to mediate civil freedoms of contract, property and the regulation of exchange with political freedoms of assembly, expression, suffrage and equality before the law. In seeking to play down and even deny these problems, liberals and followers of the mature Hegel argue that the modern world cannot hope to replicate the conditions of classical Greek or republican politics.

---

empirical refernces to actual contexts in the text itself. Nonetheless, references to existing civil societies past and present around the globe have been made at various points throughout in the footnotes. In addition to those already cited, see the excellent contributions in Chris Hann and Elizabeth Dunn (eds), *Civil Society: Challenging Western Models*, London: Routledge, 1996. Chapters 6 (on Albania), 7 (on Turkey), 8 (on Jordan and Syria) and 10 (on community and civil society in contemporary China) are particularly good. Jeffrey Alexander has recently edited a collection of essays on civil society with articles on Los Angeles, Australia and post-communist Eastern Europe, and elsewhere. See Jeffrey Alexander (ed.), *Real Civil Societies: Dilemmas of Institutionalization*, London: Sage, 1998, chapters 3, 8, 10 and 11.

Thus freedom for us is not the same as it was for the ancients or even the citizens of the Italian city-states during the Renaissance. The important assumption in this argument is that because we supposedly value material comfort, economic growth, individual freedom and privacy much more than they did, freedom for us means reconciling individual freedoms with largely formal and strictly limited forms of political participation and legitimation of state power. This is precisely where the status of civil society becomes extremely ambiguous in liberal theory and practice: should civil society, for analytical purposes, be considered synonymous with civil law, i.e., *droit civile* or *bourgeois society*, as it is sometimes called?[2] Or does civil society still carry remnants of republican values which imply far more than the rules of contract, the regulation of exchange and property, etc., to include elements of *Publizität* in the Kantian sense and some of the praticipatory characteristics Hegel ascribes to corporation, which in theory should legitimate sovereign power beyond mere interest? Kant's insistence that the public sphere plays a decisive role in the legitimation of political power is echoed in even more forceful terms in Hegel's (and later in Schmitt, Kirchheimer and Habermas's) insistence that no substantive agreement on values and no legitimation of political authority can be achieved on the simple basis of either majority decisions or contractually formulated compromises between material interests.[3] If this is true, some principle and functioning institution beyond the rules governing property, contract and exchange must exist in order for both civil law and the state to have more than mere ideological

[2] It is not a pedantic point or a small point of translation to bear in mind that in *The Philosophy of Right* Hegel explicitly uses the term bourgeois society (*die bürgerliche Gesellschaft*) rather than the term civil society (*die Zivilgesellschaft*). The latter term has far more inclusive, participatory and associative connotations than bourgeois society.

[3] Habermas's argument and why it fails, which is analysed in chapter 5, will be briefly recapitulated below. Otto Kirchheimer gives a convincing account as to why any substantive agreement on values and questions of political liberty will only be possible as a consequence of collective social control of the economy. See Otto Kirchheimer, 'Verfassungsreaktion' (1932), in *Funktionen des Staats und der Verfassung: 10 Analysen* (1932), Frankfurt: Suhrkamp, 1972, pp. 76–7, and 'Bemerkungen zu Carl Schmitts Legalität' (1933), in *Von der Weimarer Republik zum Faschismus: Die Auflösung der demokratischen Rechtsordnung*, edited by Wolfgang Luthardt, Frankfurt: Suhrkamp, 1976, pp. 113–51.

status as justifying inequalities in wealth, power and property. Otherwise, the Marxist critique of parliamentary democracy will be proved correct: the political freedoms of equality, assembly, expression, etc. will be shown to be closer to modified forms of contract and exchange (which are pre-formed by the logic of the capitalist economy) than any substantive political principles valid for all of the citizens in a democracy. Weber's appeal to charismatic leadership and Schmitt's appeal to political theology indicate that no such principles or institutions are possible within the terms established by a capitalist economy, which is to concede that capitalism and parliamentary democracy suppress politics in civil society in favour of the particular interests codified in civil law. In chapter 4 this is analysed as the suppression of the political and the simultaneous politicisation of the social in civil society.

Hegel's theory of ethical life presupposes the prior moments of abstract right and morality as part of the total movement of objective spirit, which enables him to claim that we now have both the contractual freedoms appropriate to modern forms of economy and more substantive freedoms which are located in the state. With his theory of objective spirit Hegel skirts the issue of the legitimacy of state power by arguing that the contractual moment of freedom is reconciled with the more substantive moment of freedom in the movement of spirit in its totality, which preserves what is true in the moment of particularity, calculation of individual interest and contract, and harmonises it with the more substantial unity of political agreement in the state. As seen in chapter 2, Weber, Schmitt and Benjamin offer good grounds for rejecting liberal and Hegelian claims for the legitimacy of the state. Weber and Schmitt show that Marx is correct: liberal democracy's claim to mediate between civil and political law fails. The admission of this failure is a concession that the modern state is not legitimate in its claim to represent all citizens, beyond class and other forms of material interest, through formal-legal equality and the political freedoms of press, assembly and expression. To admit that the state is not legitimate in this sense is to grant that to a considerable degree political authority is based on the play of competing strategic interests and the extra-parliamentary alliances necessary to secure their success – power, in the last analysis – and therefore does not oblige the obedience that a general will or some other form of sovereign authority would do, had it been able to prove its emanation from more universal political principles.[4] This conclusion is consonant both with Weber's theory of rationalisation and the young Schmitt's appeal to theological bases of sovereignty.

The pathos of Weber's theory of rationalisation consists in the political implications of the seeming inescapability of reified forms of consciousness and the irrepressible spread of distinctly instrumental forms of reason. As the categories with which citizens might make sense of their political experience increasingly resemble those borrowed from capitalist forms of economy, the possbilities for non-contractual mediation between civil and political liberty become more tenuous, and political equality is quietly transformed into a process of exchange and accumulation between unequal exchange partners. As a form of economic behaviour based on hierarchically-organised and technical processes with inegalitarian outcomes and correspondingly bureaucratic remedies, it is clear that modern capitalism cannot 'produce' democratic or pluralist politics. On the contrary, the economy must be subordinate to the latter in order for there to be democracy rather than varying degrees of 'political' efficiency or inefficiency. The implications of Weber's analyses are that in order for people to truly recognise each other as non-identical equals in a political community, they must also be able to do this to the greatest possible extent in the economic and social processes in civil society. As long as this is not the case, the manifest inegalitarian outcomes of strategic behaviour rooted in contract, exchange and interest will continue to transform citizenship into a modified version of economic behaviour as clientelism, i.e., as the politicisation of the social. In return for votes, politicians promise as many different groups as possible what they can in terms of goods, services and better life-

---

[4] In the context of the Weimar Republic, this was more or less to predict that state power was available for the taking for the most ruthless and best-organised party. Thus the closing pages of Schmitt's *Legalität und Legitimät (Legality and Legitimacy)* (1932) anticipate the catatrophe which was about to come. But Schmitt is also correct to argue that the exception proves the rule, and that by extension Weimar is not an aberration. In a contemporary context, this suggests that if non-statist socialism is the key to social equality, self-government in civil society is the answer to the riddle of non-statist politics. Since universal rules like those governing the buying and selling of property do not provide the bases for principles of democratic self-government, self-government is best understood as political action in the sense discussed in chapters 3 to 5.

Conclusion   181

chances in the competition for material prestige and enhanced status. The entire process is characterised by the bureaucratic adjustment of the claims of the best-organised clients, punctuated by the largely symbolic exercises in the popular choice and control of professional politicians which are offered by elections. But despairing of alternatives to this system of clientelistic populism with its plebiscites and demagogues, Weber sees no other way of stemming the tide of bureaucratisation and the divorce of reason from rationalisation than the charismatic leadership of strong personalities. Schmitt comes to similar conclusions after observing the steady widening of the franchise and the transformation of the legislature, as the last possible school of political values and perspectives, into an executive committee for managing the entire affairs of society's best-organised interests.[5]

Just as Weber's analysis of the transformation of state and civil society under modern capitalism stands in tension with the curious hope he places in charismatic élites, Schmitt's theology, however mediated by functionalist considerations in his later writings, is also flawed. In both cases, the brilliance of the analysis is offset by the defence of the state and sovereignty on the part of two theorists committed to the grandeur of the nation and national power interests. It is clear from Schmitt's work that legal, theological and functionalist versions of decisionism are incorrect answers to important questions such as: what is the relationship, beyond contractually mediated forms of interest, between politics, freedom and truth? If democracy cannot be produced by the economy or result from the interventions of charismatic leaders or sovereign authority in a state of exception, can it be conceived in terms of the political action of citizens in civil society? In order for there to be such a thing as a secular notion of truth such as Havel's notion of 'living in truth', power must be to the greatest possible extent decoupled from interest – this is Kant's great insight. Otherwise, rationality is reduced to strategy, politics becomes little more than an index of force, and law and the state become institutions largely consecrated to the protection of particular interests. If this happens, there is no reason why anyone should adhere to the law or abide by election outcomes. The idea of the rule of law and free elections

[5] Carl Schmitt, *Der Hüter der Verfassung* (1931), Berlin: Duncker & Humblot, 1996, pp. 60–70, 91–4.

is that law is not the same thing as force, and the state is a neutral arbiter between the advocates of conflicting values and practices. As distinct from former and current state socialist regimes, where state power is simply legitimised through rigged elections and other spurious institutions of popular control, free elections can potentially function in ways which are de-stabilising to powerful interests. From the perspective of powerful interests within a capitalist framework, there must be a network of institutions and a series of fall-back measures which ensure continuity, calculability and propitious conditions for investment both before and after elections. This continuity is achieved to some extent through the institutions of law and contract, which span the moment of political decision and to the largest possible degree deaden its impact if unfavourable to the best-organised factions of capital. If these factions are still unhappy they can usually invest abroad. This often results in job losses and currency problems which tend to force the elected government to either change its policies or relinquish power – hence the plausibility of the idea that people do not vote because it will not change anything much, nor bring them any closer to the institutions of government.

This is likely to remain to be true as long as politics revolves around questions of security and control of the economy; since private property and civil law starkly limit the political possibility of change, elections reveal themselves to be largely symbolic exercises in popular sovereignty. This is most flagrantly true in state socialist regimes, where the possibility of political change is impeded by party rule rather than the interests of capital and private law. But this also happens in a less obvious way in parliamentary democracies where political parties are able to offer themselves as representatives of popular sovereignty guaranteeing security. Weber and Schmitt show that despite the rule of law, parties operating within a parliamentary framework under capitalism reduce democracy to its plebiscitary dimension. The political visibility of the individual is obscured by state and private-funded election campaigns, while the collective voice is reduced to a yes/no, more/less to respective party promises to best manage the economy. More generally, party rule in yes/no, more/less terms confuses politics with a technical aggregation of preferences on the model of passive consumption. On this model, consumers do not choose what is produced but can only accept what is offered or leave the shop: their experience of the political is that they are forced to be passive or they are simply manipulated. Under these circumstances it is unsurprising that many people look for control of their lives where they can most reasonably expect to find it: in entertainment, sport and private life. One might argue that it must be so because of increasing complexity, globalisation, the end of history and ideology, etc. On the contrary, the argument in this book is that a very different theory and practice of politics to that understood and practised in populist and plebiscitary terms is possible, and is actually being enacted in ways which are perhaps not obvious at present.

II

The theorisation of the specificity of politics in civil society in this book provides the conceptual framework for analysing the failure of liberal democracy in its most basic aspiration – to reconcile civil and political liberty. In the preceding chapters this failure is explained in terms of: (1) the manifest distortion of equality of citizenship into economic behaviour as different forms of clientelism, (2) the politicisation of the social as an attempt to substitute bureaucratic and technical forms of administration for authentic politics, which, as Arendt shows, are always unpredictable and often revolutionary, and (3) the conflation of liberal with bourgeois democracy in the actual practice of existing liberal democracies. Depending on the specific context, this third dimension is implemented to a greater or lesser extent through a rational-legal structuration of the relation between the citizens of civil society and the state on the model of a vertical contract borrowed from the horizontal model of exchange in the capitalist economy. Whether undertaken as clientelism, the politicisation of the social, the transformation of contractual exchange into 'political exchange' or some combination of these, the attempt to suppress politics is an attempt to forestall the possibility of new beginnings and prevent the emergence of an altogether different kind of time and rationality than those operative in the processes of capital accumulation. Institutions like states, parties and parliamentary elections which transform the categories of political experience such as those explored in chapters 3 to 5 into the categories of interest, strategy, accumulation, profit, loss, and success or failure are institutions which force citizens to equate civil freedoms with political liberty, and to accept that there is no distinct political experience of equality or real political liberty as such. Insofar as it then becomes almost impossible to articulate the difference between socio-economic exploitation or social discrimination, on the one hand, and lack of political liberty, on the other, nearly all struggles for political change and distinctly political forms of recognition are recast as social struggles to make the terms of the life-chances and status competition fairer. This is a subtle but extremely important ideological victory for a socio-economic system which champions competition above liberty by equating them. Liberalism fails to mediate civil with political liberty in theory and conflates them in practice at the almost complete expense of the latter, with the result that technocratic and plutocratic interests marginalise democratic political values.

The argument in this book is nonetheless more centrally concerned with the relationship between politics and liberty than a defence of democracy, which, especially in its most banal formulations as the greatest good for the greatest number or majority rule, generally translates into the demagogic and bureaucratic manipulation of passive electorates. Thus neither liberalism nor unqualified conceptions of democracy provide the key to understanding and enacting political liberty, and in this regard Habermas's work is very important. Habermas is correct to emphasise both the lack of a theory of the political in liberalism, as well as the lack of an explicit and theoretically developed normative political content in most versions of Marxism. He is also right to point out that the lack of a theory and practice of the political contributes to our inability to fully realise a vision of freedom consonant with the utopian moment in modern art, civil society and revolutionary politics.[6] This critical dimension to Habermas's thinking appears in

---

[6] *Der philosophische Diskurs der Moderne* (*The Philosophical Discourse of Modernity*), Frankfurt: Suhrkamp, 1985, chapters 5–12. For the utopian dimension in the theory of communicative action, see Rolf Eickelpasch, 'Bodenlose Vernunft. Zum utopischen Gehalt des Konzepts kommunikativer Rationalität bei Habermas', and Gerd Nollman, 'Dreistrahlige Vernunft? Zum utopischen Potential des Aesthetischen in Habermas' Kommunikationstheorie', both in Eickelpasch and Nassehi (eds), *Utopie und Moderne*. Weber once remarked that the intellectual world of his time was largely shaped by Nietzsche and Marx, and one could understand Weber's work in part as an attempt to set himself up against the latter. In terms of range and depth of analysis, Habermas's work

the *Strukturwandel der Öffentlichkeit* (*Structural Transformation of the Public Sphere*), and reappears in his *Theorie des kommunikativen Handelns* (*Theory of Communicative Action*) and then again in *Faktizität und Geltung* (*Between Facts and Norms*). In this latter work (1992), Habermas asserts that the indispensable condition of democratic politics is that the law must to the greatest possible extent be transparent to structures of communication in civil society and the lifeworld not directly linked to the articulation and defence of specific interests. His emphasis on communicative action in the middle period is a concession to the idea that formal codification alone does not confer validity to legal norms. He logically turns to speech and communication as possible sources of legitimating legal norms outside the structures of exploitation (capitalism-money) and domination (administrative-bureaucratic) which, he argues, nonetheless do have a major impact on the systems of administration of justice. He thus never abandons the Kantian dimension of his argument that positive law is not legitimate unless it is underpinned by the universal claims of morality discursively redeemed in the public sphere.

In order for Habermas to maintain that both (a) capital and market forces are the only means of organising the bases of economic life, and that at the same time (b) this does not prevent legal norms based on speech and communication having a universal significance (and therefore providing compelling grounds of legitimation for social, economic and administrative-bureaucratic power structures), he must have recourse to the idea that (c): this is so because the institutions of economic life, political-administrative power and civil society are insulated enough from each other in functionalist fashion to ensure economic growth, bureaucratic-administrative efficiency, as well as normative and ethical pressure on the political system. It is true that in important respects *Between Facts and Norms* marks a turn from previously held quasi-functionalist positions. In this latter work Habermas admits that legal norms, constitutions and systems of justice will not by themselves guarantee democratic politics, because there must be enough citizen participation in public affairs so that they are able to

---

clearly surpasses liberal, communitarian and new social movement theory. Hence anyone who attempts to formulate a radical theoretical and practical political alternative to present institutions must at some level convincingly refute Habermas.

recognise themselves as authors of the laws. One might describe
this position as the last outpost within liberalism this side of
Marxism, but it is still inadequate for reasons brought forth in
chapter 5. One cannot defend the need for citizen participation and
also maintain that all inputs must be channelled up to the political
system as the sole source of sovereign authority. It is also incoher-
ent to insist on the universal legitimating significance of legal
norms, and to simultaneously maintain that capitalism does
nothing to undermine these, as if 'On the Jewish Question' had
never been written. To make this argument one has to demonstrate
that the legal systems can decisively check the power of capital and
other blatantly non-universal interest structures, and redeem the
political moment of action as decisive in human interaction.
Whereas this may have been remotely plausible with the help of
objective spirit in *The Philosophy of Right*, it is a hopeless argument
in *Between Facts and Norms*.[7]

The recasting of political projects as social struggles to make the
terms of socio-economic competition for money, status and bourgeois forms of recognition fairer consolidates the hegemony of
instrumental over other possible forms of practical reason. By
contrast, contemporary political projects in civil society are not
taking shape primarily in terms of demands for economic justice or
race and gender neutrality in the labour market. Without denying
the immediate importance of such struggles, a very different sensi-
bility is emerging amongst citizens in relation to questions of
perspective, political judgement and political time, existing boundaries between state and civil society, the possible conditions of
genuine pluralism, and the sense of human action. They are articulated in connection with the public sphere, community and
recognition, though not as the means through which class, gender,
race, identity, etc. struggles receive their due from a state which
can absorb virtually all difference and particularity within
exchange-based forms of politicisation. The forms of action studied
in chapters 3 to 5 are oriented by the experience that if the state can
absorb these struggles and cancel them as modified forms of
exchange, liberty must be enacted in ways which completely break
with exchange and social and economic forms of behaviour based

---

[7] This was already clear to legal theorists of the Weimar period in Germany,
especially Schmitt and Otto Kirchheimer.

on strategically negotiated interest. This entails breaking with the time of the commodity, the implicit extortion in supposedly neutral forms of contractual obligation, the closing down of plurality and perspective yielded by zero-sum transactions, and also breaking with the notion of equality in narrowly redistributive or spuriously meritocratic terms. It entails a different set of possible responses to liberal democracy's failure to mediate civil with political liberty.

In the work of Jürgen Habermas the most brillant attempt to theorise this mediation within the framework of regulated capitalism and parliamentary democracy fails. This is because at present, civil liberty is not a form of liberty, but a set of legal codes for regulating competing private interests. Crucially, however, it is argued in chapter 2 and at various points throughout the book, that alongside the current practice of civil liberty, political liberty is not a form of liberty either, but also by and large a set of legal codes for regulating competing private interests. Thus the conclusion of this book is that a form of political liberty not mired in exchange categories and subordinate to the logic and practices of capital accumulation requires a non-statist socialist economy, which, in its turn, will fully emerge when political liberty is enacted in the public sphere, community and recognition. In a free, democratic association of citizens there can be no rigid distinction between civil and political liberty, or before and after the revolution, but rather permanent revolution as a response to a permanent state of exception: political emancipation *is* human emancipation.

Select bibliography

Abensour, Miguel, and Buci-Glucksmann, Christine (eds). *Ontologie et Politique: Actes de Colloque Hannah Arendt*, Paris: Éditions Tierce, 1989.

Adorno, Theodor W. *Minima Moralia: Reflexionen aus dem beschädigten Leben* (1951), Frankfurt: Suhrkamp, 1997.

Adorno, Theodor W. *Negative Dialektik* (1966), Frankfurt: Suhrkamp, 1992.

Adorno, Theodor W. *Stichworte: Kritische Modelle, 2*, Frankfurt: Suhrkamp, 1969.

Adorno, Theodor W. *Soziologische Schriften, I*, Frankfurt: Suhrkamp, 1979.

Adorno, Theodor W. *Philosophie und Gesellschaft: Fünf Essays*, edited by Rolf Tiedemann, Stuttgart: Reclam, 1984.

Agamben, Giorgio. *La comunità che viene*, Turin Einaudi, 1990.

Aguiton, Christophe and Bensaïd, Daniel. *Le retour de la question sociale: le renouveau des mouvements sociaux en France*, Lausanne: Éditions Page deux, 1997.

Alexander, Jeffrey C. (ed.). *Real Civil Societies: Dilemmas of Democratization*, London: Sage, 1998.

Anderson, Benedict. *Imagined Communities: Reflections on the Origins and Spread of Nationalism*, London: Verso, 1993.

Arendt, Hannah. *Love and St. Augustine* (1929), edited by Joanna Vecchiarelli Scott and Judith Chelius Stark, Chicago: University of Chicago Press, 1996.

Arendt, Hannah. *Elemente und Ursprünge totaler Herrschaft* (1951), Munich: Piper, 1986.

Arendt, Hannah. *Between Past and Future: Eight Exercises in Political Thought*, New York: Penguin: 1954.

Arendt, Hannah. *The Human Condition*, Chicago: University of Chicago Press, 1958.

Arendt, Hannah. *On Revolution*, New York: Penguin, 1963.
Arendt, Hannah. *Crises of the Republic*, New York: Harvester, 1972.
Arendt, Hannah, and Blücher, Heinrich. *Briefe, 1936–1968*, Munich: Piper, 1996.
Baldacci, Paolo. *De Chirico, 1888–1919: la metafisica*, Milan: Leonardo Arte, 1997.
Balibar, Etienne. 'Marx, le joker', in Delorme (ed.), *Rejouer le politique*.
Bataille, Georges. *La part maudite* (1949), Paris: Éditions de minuit, 1967.
Beccalli, Bianca. 'The Modern Women's Movement in Italy', *New Left Review*, No. 204 (1994).
Beck, Ulrich. *Die Risikogesellschaft: Auf dem Weg in eine andere Moderne*, Frankfurt: Suhrkamp, 1986.
Beck, Ulrich, and Beck-Gernshein, Elizabeth. *The Normal Chaos of Love*, Cambridge: Polity, 1995.
Benhabib, Seyla. 'Demokratie und Differenz', in Brumlik and Brunkhorst (eds), *Gemeinschaft und Gerechtigkeit*.
Benhabib, Seyla (ed.). *Democracy and Difference: Contesting the Boundaries of the Political*, Princeton: Princeton University Press, 1996.
Benjamin, Walter. *Ursprung des deutschen Trauerspiels* (1925), Frankfurt: Suhrkamp, 1978.
Benjamin, Walter. *Illuminationen*, Frankfurt: Suhrkamp, 1977.
Benjamin, Walter. *Das Passagen-Werk*, 2 vols (1927–40), edited by Rolf Tiedemann, Frankfurt: Suhrkamp, 1983.
Benjamin, Walter. *Angelus Novus*, Frankfurt: Suhrkamp, 1988.
Benjamin, Walter. *Ein Lesebuch*, edited by Michael Opitz, Frankfurt: Suhrkamp, 1996.
Black, Antony. *Guilds and Civil Society in European Political Thought from the Twelfth Century to the Present*, London: Methuen, 1984.
Blanchot, Maurice. *L'éspace littéraire*, Paris: Gallimard, 1955.
Blanchot, Maurice. *La communauté inavouable*, Paris: Éditions de Minuit, 1983.
Blobel, Martin. 'Polis und Kosmopolis: Naturrecht in der Zeit der nachrevolutionären Verzerrungen der Mimesis. Über Benjamin's Passagenwerk', doctoral dissertation at the Freie Universität, Berlin, 1994.
Bloch, Ernst. *Naturrecht und menschliche Würde* (1961), Frankfurt: Suhrkamp, 1980.
Bobbio, Norberto. 'Gramsci and the Concept of Civil Society', in Keane (ed.), *Civil Society and the State*.
Bove, Arianna. 'Gramsci and Foucault', forthcoming D.Phil at the University of Sussex.

Brumlik, Micha and Brunkhorst, Hauke (eds). *Gemeinschaft und Gerechtigkeit*, Frankfurt: Fischer, 1995.

Buber, Martin. *Paths in Utopia*, New York: Macmillan, 1949.

Buber, Martin. *Ich und Du*, Cologne: Jacob Hegner, 1962.

Cassin, Barbara. 'Grecs et Romains: les paradigmes de l'antiquité chez Arendt et Heidegger', in Abensour and Buci-Glucksmann (eds), *Ontologie et Politique*.

Castoriadis, Cornelius. *L'institution imaginaire de la société*, Paris: Seuil, 1975.

Cohen, A.P. *The Symbolic Construction of Community*, London: Routledge, 1985.

Cohen, Jean L. *Class and Civil Society: the Limits of Marxian Class Theory*, Amherst: MIT Press, 1982.

Cohen, Jean L. and Arato, Andrew, *Civil Society and Political Theory*, Cambridge, Mass.: MIT Press, 1992.

Cole, G.D.H. *Social Theory* (1920), London: Methuen, 1970.

Debord, Guy. *La société du spectacle* (1967), Paris: Gallimard, 1992.

Deleuze, Gilles and Guattari, Félix. *Capitalisme et schizophrénie: l'anti-Oedipe*, Paris: Éditions de Minuit, 1973.

Delorme, Michel (ed.). *Rejouer le politique*, Paris: Éditions Galilée, 1981.

Demirovic, Alex. *Demokratie und Herrschaft: Aspekte kritischer Gesellschaftstheorie*, Münster: Westfälisches Dampfboot, 1997.

Derrida, Jacques. *Politics of Friendship*, London: Verso, 1997.

Donati, Pierpaolo (ed.). *La società civile in Italia*, Milan: Mondadori, 1997.

Downs, Anthony. *An Economic Theory of Democracy*, New York: Harper & Row, 1957.

Ebeling, Hans. *Das Subjekt in der Moderne: Rekonstruktion der Philosophie im Zeitalter der Zerstörung*, Hamburg: Rowohlt, 1993.

Eickelpasch, Rolf, and Nassehi, Armin (eds). *Utopie und Moderne*, Frankfurt: Suhrkamp, 1996.

Eickelpasch, Rolf. 'Bodenlose Vernunft. Zum utopischen Gehalt des Konzepts kommunikativer Rationalität bei Habermas', in Eickelpasch and Nassehi (eds), *Utopie und Moderne*.

Engels, Friedrich. *Ludwig Feuerbach und der Ausgang der klassischen deutschen Philosophie* (1888), Frankfurt: Verlag Marxistische Blätter, 1971.

Esposito, Roberto. *Communitas: Origine e destino della comunità*, Turin: Einaudi, 1998.

Fetscher, Iring (ed.). *Karl Marx und Friedrich Engels: Studienausgabe, Vol. I*, Frankfurt: Fischer, 1990.

Feuerbach, Ludwig. *Das Wesen des Christentums* (1841), Berlin: Akademie Verlag, 1984.

Feuerbach, Ludwig. *Philosophische Kritiken und Grundsätze, 1839–1846*, Leipzig, Reclam, 1966.

Fichte, Johann Gottlieb. *Ausgewählte politische Schriften*, edited by Zwi Batscha and Richard Saage, Frankfurt: Suhrkamp, 1977.

Flego, Gvozden. 'Gemeinschaften ohne Gesellschaft? Zur Problematik des "Postsozialismus"', in Brumlik and Brunkhorst (eds), *Gemeinschaft und Gerechtigkeit*.

Forst, Rainer. *Kontexte der Gerechtigkeit: Politische Philosophie jenseits von Liberalismus und Kommunitarismus*, Frankfurt: Suhrkamp, 1996.

Foucault, Michel. *Il faut défendre la société*, Paris: Gallimard/Seuil, 1997.

Frankenberg, Günter. *Die Verfassung der Republik: Autorität und Solidarität in der Zivilgesellschaft*, Frankfurt: Suhrkamp, 1997.

Gautier, Claude. *L'invention de la société civile*, Paris: PUF, 1993.

Gellner, Ernest. *Conditions of Liberty: Civil Society and its Rivals*, London: Hamish Hamilton, 1994.

Giegel, Hans-Joachim (ed.). *Konflikt in modernen Gesellschaften*, Frankfurt: Suhrkamp, 1998.

Graf von Krockow, Christian. *Die Entscheidung: Eine Untersuchung über Ernst Jünger, Carl Schmitt, Martin Heidegger*, Frankfurt: Campus, 1990.

Gramsci, Antonio. *Il materialismo storico*, Rome: Editori Riunti, 1979.

Gramsci, Antonio. *Note sul Machiavelli e sullo stato moderno*, Rome: Editori Riunti, 1979.

Gugenberger, Berndt, and Offe, Claus (eds). *An den Grenzen der Mehrheitsdemokratie: Politik und Soziologie der Merheitsregel*, Opladen: Westdeutscher Verlag, 1984.

Habermas, Jürgen. *Strukturwandel der Öffentlichkeit* (1962), Frankfurt: Suhrkamp, 1990.

Habermas, Jürgen. *Erkenntnis und Interesse*, Frankfurt: Suhrkamp, 1968.

Habermas, Jürgen. *Technik und Wissenschaft als Ideologie*, Frankfurt: Suhrkamp, 1968.

Habermas, Jürgen. *Legitimationsprobleme im Spätkapitalismus*, Frankfurt: Suhrkamp, 1973.

Habermas, Jürgen. *Theorie des kommunikativen Handelns*, 2 vols, Frankfurt: Suhrkamp, 1981.

Habermas, Jürgen. *Der philosophische Diskurs der Moderne*, Frankfurt: Suhrkamp, 1985.

Habermas, Jürgen. *Faktizität und Geltung: Beiträge zur Diskurstheorie des Rechts und des demokratischen Rechtstaats* (1992), Frankfurt: Suhrkamp, 5th edn, 1997.

Hall, John A. (ed.). *Civil Society: Theory, History, Comparison*, Cambridge: Polity, 1995.

Haltern, Utz. *Bürgerliche Gesellschaft: sozialtheoretische und sozial-*

historische Aspekte, Darmstadt: Wissenschaftliche Buchgesellschaft, 1985.

Hann, Chris and Dunn, Elizabeth (eds). *Civil Society: Challenging Western Models*, London: Routledge, 1996.

Hegel, G.W.F. *Frühe Schriften*, Frankfurt: Suhrkamp, 1994 (3rd edn).

Hegel, G.W.F. *Die Phänomenologie des Geistes* (1807), Stuttgart: Reclam, 1987.

Hegel, G.W.F. *Grundlinien der Philosophie des Rechts* (1821), Frankfurt: Suhrkamp, 1989.

Heidegger, Martin. *Sein und Zeit* (1927), Tübingen: Max Niemeyer, 17th edn, 1993.

Henning, Eike, Hirsch, Joachim, Reichelt, Helmut, and Schäfer, Gert (eds). *Karl Marx, Friedrich Engels: Staatstheorie*, Frankfurt: Ullstein, 1974.

Herberg, Will (ed.). *Four Existentialist Philosophers*, New York: Doubleday, 1958.

Hering, Christoph. *Die Rekonstruktion der Revolution: Walter Benjamins messianischer Materialismus in den Thesen 'Über den Begriff der Geschichte'*, Frankfurt: Peter Lang, 1983.

Höffe, Otfried. *Immanuel Kant*, Munich: C. Beck, 1992.

Höffe, Otfried. 'Politische Ethik im Gespräch mit Hannah Arendt', in Kemper (ed.), *Zur Zukunft des Politischen*.

Höffe, Otfried. *Vernunft und Recht: Bausteine zu einem interkulturellen Rechtsdiskurs*, Frankfurt: Suhrkamp, 1996.

Honneth, Axel. *Kritik der Macht: Reflexionsstufen einer kritischen Gesellschaftstheorie*, Frankfurt: Suhrkamp, 1989.

Honneth, Axel. *Kampf um Anerkennung: Zur moralischen Grammatik sozialer Konflikte*, Frankfurt: Suhrkamp, 1992.

Honneth, Axel. 'Die soziale Dynamik von Mißachtung: Zur Ortbestimmung einer kritischen Gesellschafstheorie', *Leviathan*, 1, (1994).

Horkheimer, Max. 'Traditionelle und kritische Theorie' (1937), in Horkheimer, *Traditionelle und kritische Theorie*, Frankfurt: Fischer Verlag, 1970.

Horowitz, Ascher, and Maley, Terry (eds). *The Barbarism of Reason: Max Weber and the Twilight of Enlightenment*, Toronto: University of Toronto Press, 1994.

Horster, Detlef. *Niklas Luhmann*, Munich: C.H. Beck, 1997.

Jameson, Frederic. 'On Negt and Kluge', *October*, 46 (1988).

Kafka, Franz. *Der Prozeß*, Berlin: Schocken Verlag, 1935.

Kant, Immanuel. *Kritik der praktischen Vernunft* (1878), Stuttgart: Reklam, 1961.

Kant, Immanuel. *Kritik der Urteilskraft* (1878), Stuttgart: Reklam, 1963.

Kant, Immanuel. *Schriften zur Anthropologie, Geschichtsphilosophie, Politik and Pädagogik, I*, Frankfurt: Suhrkamp, 1993.

Keane, John (ed.). *Civil Society and the State: New European Perspectives*, London: Verso, 1988.

Keane, John. *Democracy and Civil Society*, London, Verso, 1988.

Kemper, Peter (ed.). *Zur Zukunft des Politischen*, Frankfurt: Fischer, 1993.

Kirchheimer, Otto. *Funktionen des Staats und der Verfassung: 10 Analysen* (1932), Frankfurt: Suhrkamp, 1972.

Kirchheimer, Otto. *Von der Weimarer Republik Zum Faschismus: Auflösung der demokratischen Rechtsordnung*, edited by Wolfgang Luthardt, Frankfurt: Suhrkamp, 1976.

Koselleck, Reinhart. *Kritik und Krise: Eine Studie zur Pathogenese der bürgerlichen Welt* (1959), Frankfurt: Suhrkamp, 1992.

Koselleck, Reinhart. *Preußen zwischen Reform und Revolution: allgemeines Landrecht, Verwaltung und soziale Bewegung von 1791 bis 1848*, Stuttgart: Ernst Klett, 1967.

Kößler, Reinhart, and Melber, Henning. *Chancen internationaler Zivilgesellschaft*, Frankfurt: Suhrkamp, 1993.

Krippendorf, Ekkehart. *Staat und Krieg: Die historische Logik politischer Unvernunft*. Frankfurt: Suhrkamp, 1985.

Kumar, Krishan. 'Civil Society: an Inquiry into the Usefulness of an Historical Term', *The British Journal of Sociology*, 44 (1993).

Lefebvre, Henri. *La vie quotidienne dans le monde moderne*, Paris: Gallimard, 1968.

Lemke, Harald. *Die Praxis politischer Freiheit: Zur Bedeutung Hannah Arendts Philosophie des politischen Handelns für eine kritische Gesellschaftstheorie*, Maastricht: Jan Van Eyck Academy for Fine Arts, Design and Theory, 1996.

Lévinas, Emmanuel. *De l'existence à l'existant*, Paris: Vrin, 1963.

Lévinas, Emmanuel. *Totalité et infini: essai sur l'extériorité*, Paris: Martinus Nijhoff, 1971.

Lévinas, Emmanuel. *Le temps et l'autre*, Paris: PUF, 1979.

Lévinas, Emmanuel. *Hors sujet*, Paris: Fata Morgana, 1987.

Licharz, Werner and Schmitt, Helmut (eds). *Martin Buber (1878–1965): Internationales Symposium zum zwanzigsten Todestag, Volume I*, Frankfurt: Haag und Herchen, 1989.

Lipietz, Alain. *Towards a New Economic Order*, Cambridge: Polity, 1992.

Löwith, Karl. *Von Hegel zu Nietzsche*, Zurich: Europa Verlag, 1941.

Luhmann, Niklas. *Soziale Systeme* (1984), Frankfurt: Suhrkamp, 1987 (2nd edn).

Luhmann, Niklas. *Macht* (1975), Stuttgart: Ferdinand Enke, 1988.

Lukács, Georg. *Geschichte und Klassenbewusstsein* (1923), Cambridge, Mass: MIT Press, 1971.

Maritain, Jacques. 'Natural Law and Moral Law', in Herberg (ed.), *Four Existentialist Philosophers*.

Marx, Karl. *Ökonomisch-philosophische Manuskripte vom Jahre 1844*, Leipzig: Reclam, 1988.

Marx, Karl. *Das Kapital*, Vol. I (1867), Berlin: Akademische Verlag, 1955.

McCormick, John P. *Carl Schmitt's Critique of Liberalism: against Politics as Technology*, Cambridge: CUP, 1997.

Meier, Heinrich. *Die Lehre Carl Schmitts: Vier Kapitel zur Unterscheidung politischer Theologie und politischer Philosophie*, Stuttgart: J.B. Metzler, 1994.

Melucci, Alberto. *L'invenzione del presente: movimenti sociali nelle società complesse*, Bologna: Il Mulino, 1991.

Mennighaus, Winfried. *Walter Benjamins Theorie der Sprachmagie*, Frankfurt: Suhrkamp, 1995.

Miller, Max. 'Bürgerarenen und demokratischer Prozeß', in Giegel (ed.), *Konflikt in modernen Gesellschaften*.

Morrow, Raymond. 'Mannheim and the Early Frankfurt School', in Ascher Horowitz and Terry Maley (eds), *The Barbarism of Reason*, Toronto: University of Toronto Press, 1994.

Mouzelis, Nicos. 'Modernity, Late Development and Civil Society', in Hall (ed.), *Civil Society*.

Nancy, Jean-Luc (*et al.*, ed.). *Le retrait du politique*, Paris: Éditions Galilée, 1983.

Nancy, Jean-Luc. *La communauté désoeuvrée* (1986), Paris: Christian Bourgeois, 1990.

Nancy, Jean-Luc. *Le sens du monde*, Paris: Éditions Galilée, 1993.

Nancy, Jean-Luc. *Etre singulier pluriel*, Paris: Éditions Galilée, 1996.

Negt, Oscar, and Kluge, Alexander. *Öffentlichkeit und Erfahrung: Zur Organisationsanalyse von bürgerlicher und proletarischer Öffentlichkeit*, Frankfurt: Suhrkamp, 1977.

Negt, Oscar, and Kluge, Alexander. *Geschichte und Eigensinn*, 3 vols, Frankfurt: Suhrkamp, 1993.

Neocleous, Mark. *Administering Civil Society: Towards a Theory of State Power*, London: Macmillan, 1996.

Neumann, Franz. 'Zum Begriff der politischen Freiheit' (1953), in Herbert Marcuse (ed.), *Demokratischer und autoritärer Staat: Studien zur politischen Theorie*, Munich: Fischer Verlag, 1970.

Neumann, Franz. *Die Herrschaft des Gesetzes*, Frankfurt: Suhrkamp, 1980.

Newcomb, Steven T. 'The Evidence of Christian Nationalism in Federal Indian Law: the Doctrine of Discovery, Johnson v. McIntosh, and

Plenary Power', *New York University Review of Law and Social Change*, 20 (1993).

Nietzsche, Friedrich. *Jenseits von Gut und Böse* (1886), Stuttgart: Reclam, 1988.

Nietzsche, Friedrich. *Zur Genealogie der Moral* (1887), Munich: Goldmann, 1983.

Nollman, Gerd. 'Dreistrahlige Vernunft? Zum utopischen Potential des Aesthetischen in Habermas' Kommunikationstheorie', in Eickelpasch and Nassehi (eds), *Utopie und Moderne*.

O'Neill, John. *The Market: Ethics, Knowledge and Politics*, London: Routledge, 1998.

Pelcynski, Z.A. 'Solidarity and the Rebirth of Civil Society', in Keane (ed.), *Civil Society and the State*.

Perez-Diaz, Victor. *The Return of Civil Society: the Emergence of Democratic Spain*, Cambridge, Mass.: Harvard University Press, 1993.

Plant, Sadie. *The Most Radical Gesture: the Situationist International in a Postmodern Age*, London: Routlege, 1992.

Plessner, Helmut. *Die verspätete Nation: Über die Verführbarkeit des bürgerlichen Geistes* (1959), Stuttgart: W. Kohlhammer, 1969.

Polanyi, Karl. *The Great Transformation: the Political and Economic Foundations of our Time* (1944), Boston: Beacon Press, 1957.

Raulet, Gerard. 'Die Modernität der Gemeinschaft', in Brumlick and Brunkhorst (eds), *Gemeinschaft und Gerechtigkeit*.

Reiss, Hans (ed.). *Kant: Political Writings*, Cambridge: CUP, 1970.

Remoti, Francesco. *Contro l'identità*, Bari: Laterza, 1996.

Richter, Dirk. 'Zivilgesellschaft – Probleme einer Utopie in der Moderne', in Eickelpasch and Nassehi (eds), *Utopie und Moderne*.

Riedel, Manfred. 'Transcendental Politics? Political Legitimacy and the Concept of Civil Society in Kant', in Schnurmann (ed.), *The Public Realm*.

Rosenberg, Justin. *The Empire of Civil Society: a Critique of the Realist Theory of International Relations*, London: Verso, 1994.

Roth, Klaus. 'Neue Entwicklungen der kritischen Theorie', *Leviathan*, 3, (1994).

Rotenstreich, Martin. 'Dialog und Dialektik', in Licharz and Schmitt (eds), *Martin Buber*.

Rousseau, Jean-Jacques. *Du contrat social* (1762), Paris: Éditions Garnier frères, 1960.

Sartre, Jean-Paul. *L'être et le néant: essai d'ontologie phénoménologique*, Paris: Gallimard, 1943.

Schecter, Darrow. *Radical Theories: Paths beyond Marxism and Social Democracy*, Manchester: MUP, 1994.

Schmitt, Carl. *Politische Theologie* (1922), Berlin: Duncker & Humblot, 1996.

Schmitt, Carl. *Die geistesgeschichtliche Lage des heutigen Parlamentarismus* (1923), (8th edn), Berlin: Duncker & Humblot, 1996.

Schmitt, Carl. *Römischer Katholizismus und politische Form* (1923), Stuttgart: Klett-Cotta, 1984.

Schmitt, Carl. *Der Hüter der Verfassung* (1931), Berlin: Duncker & Humblot, 1993.

Schmitt, Carl. *Der Begriff des Politischen* (1932), Berlin: Duncker & Humblot, 1996.

Schmitt, Carl. *Legalität und Legitimität* (1932), Berlin: Duncker & Humblot, 1993.

Schmitt, Carl. *Über die drei Arten des rechtswissenschaftlichen Denkens* (1934), Berlin: Duncker & Humblot, 1993.

Schmitt, Carl. *Verfassungsrechtliche Aufsätze aus den Jahren 1924–54: Materialien zu einer Verfassungslehre*, Berlin: Duncker & Humblot, 1954.

Schnurmann, Reiner (ed.). *The Public Realm: Essays on Discursive Types in Political Philosophy*, New York: State University at Albany, 1989.

Schutz, Alfred, and Luckmann, Thomas. *Strukturen der Lebenswelt*, Frankfurt: Suhrkamp, 1979.

Scott, Alan. *Ideology and the New Social Movements*, London: Routledge, 1990.

Seitz, Brian. *The Trace of the Political*, Albany: State University of New York at Albany Press, 1995.

Seligman, Adam. *The Idea of Civil Society*, New York: The Free Press, 1992.

Shaw, Martin. *Civil Society and the Media in Global Crises: Representing Distant Violence*, London: Pinter, 1996.

Shaw, Martin, (ed.). *Understanding Politics in Globalisation: Knowledge, Ethics, and Agency*, London: Routledge, 1999.

Siep, Ludwig. *Hegels Fichtekritik und die Wissenschaftslehre von 1804*, Freiburg and Munich: Karl Albert Verlag, 1970.

Siep, Ludwig. 'Der Kampf um Anerkennung: Zu Hegels Auseinandersetzung mit Hobbes in den Jenaer Schriften', *Hegel-Studien*, 9 (1974).

Siep, Ludwig. *Anerkennung als Prinzip der praktischen Philosophie: Untersuchungen zu Hegels Jenaer Philosophie des Geistes*, Munich: Verlag Alber, 1979.

Simmel, Georg. *Die Philosophie des Geldes* (1900), Frankfurt: Suhrkamp, 1989.

Skinner, Quentin. *The Foundations of Modern Political Thought*, Volume II, Cambridge: CUP, 1978.

Sommier, Isabelle. *La violence politique et son deuil: l'après '68 en France et en Italie*. Rennes: Presses Universitaires de Rennes, 1998.

Spencer, Jonathan. 'State and Civil Society in Prussia: Thoughts on a New Edition of Reinhart Koselleck's *Preußen zwischen Reform und Revolution'*, *Journal of Modern History*, March-December (1985).

Splichal, Slavko. 'From Civil Society to Information Society?', in Slavko Splichal (ed.), *Information Society and Civil Society: Contemporary Perspectives on the Changing World Order*, Indiana: Purdue University Press, 1994.

Stammers, Neil. 'Human Rights and Power', *Political Studies*, XLI, 1, (1993).

Stammers, Neil. 'A Critique of Social Approaches to Human Rights', *Human Rights Quarterly*, 17 (1995).

Stammers, Neil. 'Social Movements and the Challenge to Power', in Shaw (ed.), *Understanding Politics in Globalisation*.

Tarrow, Sidney. *Power in Movement: Social Movements, Collective Action and Politics*, Cambridge: CUP, 1994.

Tester, Keith. *Civil Society*, London: Routledge, 1992.

Thornhill, Chris. *Political Theory in Modern Germany: an Introduction*, Cambridge: Polity, 1999.

Tönnies, Ferdinand. *Gemeinschaft und Gesellschaft: Grundbegriffe der reinen Soziologie* (1887), Berlin: Karl Kurtius, 1921.

Touraine, Alain. *La production de la société*, Paris: Seuil, 1973.

Touraine, Alain. *Le voix et le regard: Sociologie des mouvements sociaux*, Paris: Seuil, 1978.

Vaneigem, Raoul. *Traité de savoir-vivre à l'usage des jeunes générations* (1967), Paris: Gallimard, 1992.

Villa, Dana. *Arendt and Heidegger: the Fate of the Political*, Princeton: Princeton University Press, 1996.

Vogl, Joseph (ed.). *Gemeinschaften: Positionen zu einer Philosophie des Politischen*, Frankfurt: Suhrkamp, 1994.

Von Gierke, Otto. 'Über die Geschichte des Majoritätsprinzips', in Guggenberger and Offe (eds), *An den Grenzen des Mehrheitsprinzips*.

Walzer, Michael (ed.). *Toward a Global Civil Society*, Oxford: Berghann Books, 1995.

Weber, Max. *Soziologische Grundbegriffe*, Tübingen: J.C.B. Mohr, 1960.

Weber, Max. *Staatssoziologie*, Berlin: Duncker & Humblot, 1966.

Weber, Max. *Gesammelte politische Schriften*, edited by Johannes Winkelmann, Tübingen: J.C.B. Mohr, 1988.

Weber, Max. *Schriften zur Soziologie*, Stuttgart: Reclam, 1995.

Weber, Max. *Schriften zur Sozialgeschichte und Politik*, Stuttgart: Reclam, 1997.

Wildt, Andreas. *Autonomie und Anerkennung: Hegels Moralitätskritik im Lichte seiner Fichte-Rezeption*, Stuttgart: Klett-Cotta, 1982.

Williams, Robert R. *Recognition: Fichte and Hegel on the Other*, Albany: State University of New York at Albany Press, 1994.

Zizek, Slavoj. 'Geniesse Deine Nation wie Dich selbst! Der Andere und das Böse – vom Begehren des ethnischen "Dings"', in Vogl (ed.), *Gemeinschaften*.

Index

Please note that page numbers with an 'n' denote references to footnotes.

absolutism 27–31, 54
Adorno, T.W. 12, 71, 129n, 133n
allgemeines Leben (universal life) 38
alterity 160–8
Althusius, J. 28
American Revolution 14, 98
Arato, A. 5–6, 9–10
Arendt, H.
  action 94
  Christianity 101
  economy, control of 95
  equality 103–4
  freedom 49, 86
  Human Condition 78, 90n, 97n, 100n
  labour process 94
  life and world, on 95
  love 4n
  On Revolution 92
  pluralism 103–4
  politics 23
  public sphere 78, 90n, 92, 94, 95
  revolution 96
  social, rise of 84
  utopia 23
  work 94
Aristotle 4n, 27
Ausnahmezustand (state of exception) 64–5, 66, 73, 119
authoritarianism 9, 22, 50, 52, 58, 80

autonomy 32–6, 55, 56, 61, 85

Balibar, E. 80n
Bauer, B. 43
Benjamin, W.
  commodities 70–1, 94
  justice 69, 74
  legality 69–70
  Nietzsche, and 69, 71
  'nowtime' 70, 162n
  politics 69
  Schmitt, and 69, 71
  time considerations 69–73
  violence 69
  Weber, and 69, 71
Black, A. 28
Blanchot, M. 4n
Bobbio, N. 7n, 33n
Bodin, J. 27, 28
boundaries 75–6, 105, 137–9
Buber, M. 144, 161–3, 165, 169

Caesarism 57, 58
capitalism
  attempts to abolish 20
  community 134
  democracy 20
  globalisation 18
  Marxism 44–6, 52, 54, 94
  money 140
  NSMs 109
  private interests, integration

into state 13
Weber 55
see also socialism
Castoriadis, C. 51n
citizen participation, public
    affairs 9, 11, 50, 140, 182
    see also voting behaviour
civil society
    Benjamin 69–73
    boundaries 75–6, 105
    bourgeois society 178
    communication 156
    contract law 67–8
    defined 2–3, 80–1
    economy *see* economy and civil
      society
    educational institutions 3
    elitist theory 7–8
    family 37
    friendship 3
    functionalism 4, 81
    Gellner, E. 3
    globalisation 14–18
    Hegel *see* Hegel, G.W.F.
    historical background 5, 26–36
    interest groups 3, 113–20
    leisure time activities 3
    liberalism-communitarianism
      debate 10–13
    lifeworld 3, 81, 185
    love 3, 4n, 67
    Marx *see* Marx, K.
    mass media 3
    origins of political theory 25–48
    politics 3–4, 7, 25–48, 66–77
    public sphere *see* public sphere
    recognition 141–75
    rediscovery 1–2, 101
    religious groups 3
    self-government, possible
      sphere of 18
    state authority, challenging
      82
    state, separation of
      Hegel 37, 38

    historical background 6,
      37, 38, 42, 43, 45, 48
    Marx 42, 43, 45
    totalitarianism 10
    status, ambiguous 178
    theatre of human history, as
      46
    see also state
Cohen, J. 5–6, 9–10
Cole, G.D.H. 64, 124n
collective behaviour
    common interests 113–20
    unity and identity 120–30
    will, collective 32
communism 108
    see also Marx, K.; socialism
communitarianism 10–13
community
    action, as 118, 134
    association, as 134
    boundaries 137–9
    capitalism 134
    collective behaviour 113–30
    common interests 113–20
    equivalents, exchange of 132
    pluralism 133
    as politics 130–40
    public sphere, and 112, 139
    purposes 139
    rule, and 118
    syndicalists 114, 115
    trade unions 113, 114
    unity and identity 120–30
    utopian nature 112
    vanguards 113–15
conflict settlement
    community 132
    mediation, supra-national
      institutions for 17
    recognition 147, 149
    Schmitt, on 64–8
consciousness 146, 152
corps intermédiaires 8
councils, revolutionary 102, 104,
    108

democracy
  capitalism 20
  community, common interests 114
  Feuerbach 41
  Marx 43
  morality and politics, unity 31
  Nietzsche 54
  plebiscitary nature 8, 54–5, 63, 127
  populism 8
  public sphere 89
  recognition, and 169–75
  sovereignty and 50
  trade unions 114
'democracy of unfreedom' 43, 62, 76
domination, state 53–6, 58, 68, 76, 79
Downs, A. 72n

Eastern Europe
  capitalism, and 20
  dissident movements 1, 13
  Leninism 20
  public sphere 13
  rediscovery of civil society 2
  revolutions 2
  Soviet Union, bureaucracy in 115, 116
  state and civil society, tension between 125
economy and civil society
  Arendt 95
  definitions 3–4, 80–1
  Hegel 37, 38
  planning 106
  Schmitt 71–2
  separation 117
  'system of needs' 37, 87, 121
  see also capitalism; socialism
elections 7, 60, 61, 127, 172, 182
élite theory 7
Engels, F. 25, 46, 124
Enlightenment 30, 36, 55

equality
  administration, and 104
  non-identical equals 88–9, 112, 113, 142
  pluralism 103–4
  public sphere 88–9, 102, 103–4, 112
Essay Concerning Human Understanding (Locke) 29–30
ethics
  Kant on 31–6, 38
  recognition and 144, 160–8
  state, and 38–9
  see also morality
existentialism 150n, 153

Feuerbach, L.
  Essence of Christianity 39
  ethics 161, 165
  Greek philosophy 163–4
  Hegel, critique of 39, 40–1, 161
  morality 39–40
  philosophy 39, 163–4
  Publizität 40
  religion 39, 41
  state, on 39
Fichte, J.G. 146
Flego, G. 125
Foucault, M. 55, 135n
France, sovereignty in 28
France, A. 75
free will 85, 86
freedom
  Arendt 49, 86
  boundaries, and 75–6, 105
  democracy of unfreedom 43, 62, 76
  Fichte 146
  Hegel 38, 77, 121, 130
  Kant 32–3
  politics 176
  public sphere 61, 89, 90, 117
  recognition, and 158
  theory, development of 176–8

French Revolution 14, 28, 48, 54, 97
friend/enemy model 4–5, 63, 73, 75, 79, 142
functionalism 4, 5, 81, 174n

GATT (General Agreement on Tariffs and Trade) 18
Geist (objective spirit) 36
Gellner, E. 3, 8–9
general will
  élite theory 7
  Rousseau 31, 85, 119
  Schmitt 82–3, 120
  Tocqueville 9
  Weber 120
Genossenschaftsrecht (co-operative law, Germany) 29
German Ideology (Marx) 25, 46
Germany, self-government, demand for 28–9
globalisation, civil society 14–18
Goethe, J.W. 40
Gramsci, A. 6, 13, 134n
Greece, ancient 26–7, 148, 163–4, 177
guilds 28, 29

Habermas, J.
  citizen participation, public affairs 11
  civil society, rediscovery of 1, 5
  Der philosophische Diskurs der Moderne (*The Philosophical Discourse of Modernity*) 184
  Faktizität und Geltung (*Between Facts and Norms*) 152, 155, 156n, 185, 186
  freedom 117
  Honneth, and 155
  'legitimation crisis' 92
  liberalism 156, 184–5
  lifeworld 81
  public sphere 78, 91, 92, 117
  recognition 155, 156, 157, 174n
  Strukturwandel der Öffentlichkeit

  (*Structural Transformation of the Public Sphere*) 1, 91n, 155, 185
  Technik und Wissenschaft als Ideologie (*Science as Ideology*) 155
Hegel, G.W.F.
  ancient Greece 27, 148, 177
  Christianity 148
  civil society, origins 36–48
  communitarianism 11, 12
  destiny 147, 148
  Die Phänomonologie des Geistes (*Phenomenology of Spirit*) 87, 143, 145, 150, 151
  Feuerbach, critique by 39, 40–1, 161
  freedom 38, 77, 121, 130
  Jena writings 145, 147, 151
  Kant, on 12, 36–40, 147
  liberty 12
  Marx, critique by 41–3, 121n
  Philosophy of Right 36, 38, 42, 43, 47, 144, 178
  Publizität 36, 38, 42, 43
  recognition 143–53
  state, theory of 87
  struggle 149
  will, the 86–7
Heidegger, M. 64n
Herrschaftssoziologie (sociology of domination) 52, 83n
Hobbes, T. 27, 32, 35, 49, 149–50
Holland, Dutch Revolt in 28
Honneth, A. 143n, 145n, 152, 153, 154, 159
Horkheimer, M. 24n, 71

International Monetary Fund (IMF) 15

Jetztzeit ('nowtime') 70, 162n

Kafka, F. 90n, 103n, 151n
Kant, I.

absolutism 31
Critique of Practical Reason 31–2
fact, norm distinguished 83n
freedom 32–3
Hegel, critique by 12, 36–40, 147
judgement 171
Kritik der Urteilskraft (*Critique of Judgement*) 157n, 171n
legality 33, 34, 35
morality 30–6, 38, 147
needs and interests 85
Nietzsche, and 53, 55
Publizität 32, 33, 34, 35
rationality and reason 32–6, 40
recognition 161, 162, 171
violence 35
Weber, and 55
Keane, J. 7n
Kierkegaard, S. 87, 88
Kirchheimer, O. 178
Koselleck, R. 29n, 30
Kumar, K. 7n

labour contract 67–8
see also capitalism; Marx, K.
Laski, H. 64
law and legality,
authority as source 32, 35
Benjamin 69–70
Kant 33, 34, 35
legitimacy, and 119
morality, and 33, 34, 35
recognition as 146–60
Schmitt 180n
sovereignty, and 64
Leninism 20, 22
Levinas, E.
Buber, and 165
ethics and recognition 144
Feuerbach, and 165
Le temps et l'autre (*Time and the Other*) 166n
master-slave 166
pupil-teacher relationship 165–6

Totalité et infini (*Infinity and Totality*) 141, 164–5
lexis (speech) 26, 27
liberalism 10–13, 156, 184
lifeworld 3, 81, 185
Locke, J. 29–30, 33n
Luhmann, N. 156
Luther, M. 27

Machiavelli, N. 29, 30
Maritain, J. 144
Marx, K.
capitalism 44–6, 52, 54, 94
civil society, origins 41–8
Communist Manifesto 124
democracy 21–2, 43
Economic and Philosophical Manuscripts of 1844, 45-46, 177
emancipation, political 43–5
'German Ideology' 25, 46
Hegel, critique of 41–3, 121n
planning 95
public sphere 95
religion, on 41, 43–4, 63, 128–9
see also socialism
Montesquieu, C.L. 8, 28, 134n
morality
ethical life 152
Feuerbach 39–40
Kant 30–6, 38, 147
legality 33, 34, 35
Marx 44
Nietzsche 53–4
recognition 152, 160–8
Rousseau 30, 31
Weber 61–2

National Front 93
National Socialism 64
natural world 71–2
Neocleous, M. 7n
Neumann, F. 8n, 9, 11, 80n
neutrality 13–14, 118
New Social Movements

Arato on 6
capitalism 109
civil society, rediscovery 2
Cohen on 6
community 129–30, 131, 135–6
public sphere 2, 108–11
recognition 153, 174
Western Europe 6
NGOs (Non-Governmental
Organisations) 17
Nietzsche, F.
Benjamin, and 69, 71
Beyond Good and Evil 53
Christianity 87
commodities 71, 94
Genealogy of Morals 53
human spirit 69
morality 53–4
power and struggle 55
Schmitt, and 79
Weber, influence on 53–4, 55
will 79, 87
'nowtime' 70, 162n
NSMs *see* New Social Movements
(NSMs)

objective spirit, movement of 36
Öffentlichkeit 88n, 96
see also public sphere

Paris Commune 52
parliamentary regimes 116
Pelcynski, Z.A. 1n
plebiscites 8, 54–5, 63, 127
plurality
community 133
equality, political 103–4
recognition 145
Schmitt 64, 73
sovereignty 83
Polanyi, K. 26
political parties
common interests 113
community 113, 126
division of 104

parliamentary regimes 116
public sphere 82, 84, 100
voting, and 7, 50, 60, 84, 127,
140
politics
citizen participation 9, 11, 50,
140
civil society 66–77
community as 130–40
defined 141–2
democracy *see* democracy
elections 7, 60, 61, 127, 182
freedom 176
morality *see* morality
origins of modern theory
25–48, 119
'political', defined 4
public sphere and 105–11
Schmitt 4, 50, 63–6, 79
state distinguished 52–3
theology 51–66
populism 8, 50, 57
pouvoirs intermédiaires 28
praxis (action) 26, 27, 82, 131, 142
public sphere
action 93–6
authority 35–6
autonomy 61
civil society, network within
81, 156
community, and 112, 139
democracy 89
Eastern Europe 13
equality 88–9, 102, 103–4, 112
exclusions from 32–3
experience 93–6
freedom 61, 89, 90, 117
Habermas 78, 91, 92, 117
Hegel 36–7
longevity, and 101
neutrality 13–14
NSMs 2, 108–11
politics, world of 84–5, 105–11,
170
psychology 88

Publizität see *Publizität*
rule 97–9
social, rise of 84–93
time, aspects of 93–4
voting 60
Weber 60, 79
will, the 85–7, 99–100
Publizität
Feuerbach, critique by 40
Hegel, critique by 36, 38, 42, 43,
78
Kant on 32, 33, 34, 35

QUANGOs (Quasi-Governmental
Organisations) 17
quasi-functionalism 5, 81

*Radical Theories: Paths Beyond
Marxism and Social
Democracy* (Schecter) 20, 21
rationalisation 52, 55, 59, 156, 180
rationality and reason
Kant 32–6, 40, 86
Weber 55–6, 59, 61, 74
Rechtslehre (theory of law) 34
Rechtstaat (state of law) 31, 74
recognition
alterity 160–8
Buber 144, 161–3, 165, 169
civil society 141–75
consciousness 146, 152
democracy, political 169–75
ethics 144, 160–8
Habermas 155, 156, 157, 174n
Hegel 143–53, 159
Honneth 143n, 145n, 152, 153,
154, 159
'I–it' relation 161–2
'I–you' relation 160, 162, 163
law as 146–60
master-slave relation 161, 166
pluralism 145
political democracy 169–75
pupil-teacher relationship
165–6

self-consciousness 146, 150
state 157, 168, 172
religion
Christianity 27, 28, 39, 87, 101
Feuerbach 39, 41
life and world 96
Luther 27
Marx 43–4, 128–9
Weber 52
revolutions
American 14, 98
Arendt on 96
councils 102, 104, 108
Eastern Europe 2, 97
French 14, 28, 48, 54, 97
public sphere 96–105
syndicalist perspective 114
Velvet 82, 102
Ricardo, D. 36
Riedel, M. 83n
'risk society' 173
Rousseau, J. 82, 86, 119
general will 31, 85
majority rule 56–7
morality 30, 31
self-analysis 86
rule
majority 56–7
public sphere 97–9
totalitarian 102–3

Say, J.B. 36
Schmitt, C.
Benjamin, and 69, 71
conflict, settlement of 64–6
Der Begriff des Politischen
(*Concept of the Political*) 15,
63, 64, 79
Der Hüter der Verfassung 181
*Die geistesgeschichtliche Lage des
Heutigen Parlamentarismus*
(*Crisis of Parliamentary
Democracy*) 119
friend / enemy dichotomy 4–5,
63, 73, 75, 79, 142

globalisation 15
justice, on 74
Legalität und Legitimät (Legality and Legitimacy) 119–20, 180n
pluralism 64, 73
political theology 4, 63–6, 79, 119–20, 179, 181
public sphere 81, 105
states of exception 64–5, 66, 73, 119
Über die drei Arten des rechtswissenschaftlichen Denkens (On the three forms of Legal Thought) 73n
Weber, and 62, 66, 120
self-consciousness 146, 150, 153
self-government 18, 28–9, 50, 63, 64, 114
Seligman, A. 7n
Simmel, G. 55
single market 15n
Sittlichkeit (ethical life) 38, 151
social contract 8, 31, 86, 105, 152
socialism
    community 114, 116
    Eastern Europe, transition to capitalism 125
    legitimation of state 108
    non-statist 20–2
    NSMs 129–30
    parliamentary regimes distinguished 116
    public sphere 91, 107
sovereignty
    authoritarianism 50
    Caesarism 57, 58
    community 135
    democracy 50
    France, in 28
    law, and 64
    mutual dependence 31
    non-political character 82
    pluralism 83
    political community, founding
        of 57
    populism 50
    Schmitt 82
Stalinism 22
Stammers, N. 19n
state
    authoritarianism 9, 22, 50, 52, 58, 80
    basis of 38–9
    Benjamin, rejection by 69
    capitalism *see* capitalism
    domination 53–6, 58, 68, 76, 79
    ethical idea 38–9
    Feuerbach, L. 39
    globalisation 18
    Hegel 36–48, 121
    law and 68
    legitimation 179, 182
        community concepts 123, 124
        domination, Weber on 56, 57, 62
        freedom, political 89
        general will 120
        globalisation, and 14
        Habermas 92
        Hegel 179
        legality, and 119, 122, 170
        property relations 68
        public sphere 79, 84, 92
        Schmitt 62–3, 65
        social contract tradition 8
        socialism 108
        Weber 79, 84, 119
    Marx *see* Marx, K.
    morality *see* morality
    Nietzsche *see* Nietzsche, F.
    NSMs 136
    politics distinguished 52–3
    recognition 157, 168, 172
    Schmitt 63–6
    self-government 18, 28–9, 50, 63, 64, 114
    sovereignty *see* sovereignty
    violence and 49–77

Weber 52–63
see also civil society
'state of nature' 8, 31, 33, 34, 36, 57
states of exception 64–5, 66, 73, 119
syndicalists 113–15
'system of needs' (economy) 37, 87, 121

theology, political 51–66, 179
time issues 16, 71–3, 93–4
'nowtime' 70, 162n
Tocqueville, A. 6, 8, 9
totalitarian rule 102–3
trade unions 113, 114
Treaty of Westphalia (1648) 27–8
Tugendlehre (theory of virtue) 34

unity and identity 120–30
universal suffrage 15n

vanguards 113–15
'Velvet Revolutions' 82, 102
violence
    Balkans 16
    Benjamin 69
    civil society, politics of 66–77
    conflict mediation, need for 17
        see also conflict settlement
    Gulf War 16, 17
    Kant 35
    political theology 51–66
    revolutions 98
    rule, and 98
    state, and 49–77
    UN 17
    Weber 52
voting behaviour 7, 50, 60, 84, 127, 140

Weber, M.

authoritarianism 52
autonomy 61
Benjamin, and 69, 71
bureaucracy, critique on 63
Caesarism 57–8
capitalism 52, 55
civil society, history 5
domination, forms of 53–6, 58, 179
electoral behaviour 60
ethics 61–2
Habermas on 156
Kant, and 55
leadership, charismatic 53–6, 179
Nietzsche, influence on 53–4, 55
politics 52–3, 119
Politik als Beruf (Politics as a Vocation) 52, 119
public sphere 60, 79
rationalisation theory 52, 55, 59, 156, 180
rationality 55–6, 59, 61, 74
Schmitt, and 62, 66, 120
state 51–2, 54–63
violence 52
Weimar Republic 180n
will
    of all 85, 119
    collective 32
    free 85, 86
    general see general will
    Hegel 86–7
    Kant 85
    needs and interests 85
    Nietzsche, and 79, 87
    public sphere 85–7, 99–100
World Bank 15–16
world, life distinguished 72, 95, 171

Zizek, S. 125

Lightning Source UK Ltd.
Milton Keynes UK
UKOW040640040512

191986UK00002B/15/P